TECHNOLOGY AND THE
POLITICS OF INSTRUCTION

TECHNOLOGY AND THE POLITICS OF INSTRUCTION

Jan Nespor
Virginia Polytechnic Institute and State University

Lawrence Erlbaum Associates, Publishers
2006   Mahwah, New Jersey   London

Copyright © 2006 by Lawrence Erlbaum Associates, Inc.

Lawrence Erlbaum Associates, Inc., Publishers
10 Industrial Avenue
Mahwah, New Jersey 07430
www.erlbaum.com

Cover design by Tomai Maridou

CIP information for this book can be obtained by contacting the Library of Congress

ISBN 0-8058-5817-2 (cloth : alk. paper)
ISBN 0-8058-5818-0 (pbk. : alk. paper)

Books published by Lawrence Erlbaum Associates are printed on acid-free paper, and their bindings are chosen for strength and durability.

Printed in the United States of America
10   9   8   7   6   5   4   3   2   1

Table of Contents

Preface

This book is the odd-shaped product of my efforts to make sense of changes going on in one of the things I do, teach, in the place I work, the public research university. The spur, in the late 1990s, was the increasing importance of computers and technology in my own teaching and that of my colleagues, and the heated language in the press about impending technology-driven changes in university instruction. These predictions, promises, and warnings seemed to gain credibility from the fact that so much was unquestionably being transformed in university life as a result of budget cuts and successive reorganizations. In addition, people like Michael Milken, the junk-bond criminal turned instructional technology advocate and philanthropist, were being quoted telling the president of Teachers College, Columbia, "You guys are in trouble and we're going to eat your lunch" (cited in Taylor, 2001, p. 235). More academic writers were offering specific recipes:

> State-of-the-art courses employing multimedia components can be designed by expert teams of knowledge specialists and instructional technologists and then sold to individual campuses. Similarly, the information dissemination function of lecturing can be done by authorities captured technologically, thus eliminating the repetitive aspects of course instruction and freeing professors for more creative aspects of college teaching. (Baldwin, 1998, p. 10)

The problem was that it was hard to see how this was supposed to happen and what was driving it along particular paths. How had my work ended up as meat on somebody's lunch line? Most of what I could find to read focused on technologies, usually in particular courses and programs, and not on the larger milieu and politics that were pushing the technologies along. The devices and software *are* indisputably important, but far from the whole story. Thus I depart here from the mainstream of research on instructional technology partly by focusing on mundane and widespread forms of computer-mediated instruction (CMI)—PowerPoint slides, CD-ROMS, self-paced labs, and the like—but more so by looking at these things from multiple standpoints: what they mean not just for professors, but also for administrators and students.

The book thus complements research on "virtual universities" (e.g, Pollock & Cornford, 2003) and cutting-edge, high-resource artifacts and systems: If you imagine that kind of research as analogous to studies of experimental, high-speed levitating trains, the work before you is more like research on the slow, uneven transformation of an urban bus system, with less attention to the buses than to the managers, drivers, and passengers. It departs as well from the main emphases of higher education research (Fry, Ketteridge, & Marshall, 2003; Rudestam & Schoenholtz-Read, 2002; Tight, 2004) in that the focus is not really on administrative policies and practices (admissions, tenure, budgeting formulas, etc.) or the experiences of faculty, students, or staff subgroups. Instead, my aim is to trace the varying material and organizational entanglements of a constantly reconfiguring network of people, things, categories, and ideas that are sometimes loosely, sometimes tightly, entangled in forms of CMI.

The first part of the book examines where CMI came from. What were the professional backgrounds of early innovators and what logics did they import into the new technologies? How did the state get involved? Absent evidence it worked or saved money, why did CMI bloom during a period of budget cuts? To answer such questions I show how specific assumptions about teaching and learning got embedded in early CMI demonstration projects, and how such projects were used to produce networks of trust within the organization, aligned developers with national innovation networks, and were eventually transformed into stable funding lines and administrative commitments. I show how these efforts were then hooked up to state policies and the administrative and finance discourses that came to shape those policies in the 1990s.

The second part of the book contains three cases that show how these policies and discourses were refracted through departmental and curricular structures and organizational pressures on differently situated faculty members. The results were varying uses of CMI that made visible different facets of the instructional process: practice-related professional knowledge in one case, students' errors in another, the professor's lectures in a third. The cases show that professors' uses of CMI were influenced by the university's administrative agendas, but that at least as important were curricular organization (the connections across courses within the program), disciplinary strength, assumptions about the nature of the subject matter, and the professors' "practical logics" of teaching.

Finally, the third section examines the role of CMI in students' academic work. Instead of focusing exclusively on aspects of the students' practices that involve instructional technology—a common practice in CMI research—I look at how coursework employing CMI fits into the larger temporal rhythms and routines of students' lives and study. Not intended as definitive statements about students' experiences with CMI, the chapters in this section unpack a few key claims about the uses and implications of CMI for students, in particular, claims that it loosens the constraints of time and space and makes study possible anytime, anywhere.

The book thus ties together a range of issues usually separated in discussions of instructional technology and examines often slighted topics, such as the articulations of local and national practices. It questions our common vocabulary for making sense of CMI (e.g., *synchronous, vs. asynchronous*) and contributes to educational change theory by showing how CMI has unfolded both top down and bottom up.

That said, many people, especially those deeply invested in the technical side of the issue may find the work lacking. Others, especially those in universities, may be discomfited to see aspects of university politics unpacked. Qualitative studies are known for dissatisfying the people about whom they're written, especially when those people are professionals and researchers in their own right. Becker (1964), for example, suggested that "the socio-logical view of the world–abstract, relativistic, generalizing–necessarily deflates people's view of themselves and their organizations.... A good study...will make somebody angry" (pp. 273, 275–276; cf. Hess, 1999, p. 31). This may be one reason, as Morrill (1995) noted, that the number of qualitative studies in a setting "varies inversely with the social status of its incumbents" (p. 9). Then again, others find the idea of rousing emotion optimistic. Forsythe (1999), an anthropologist doing ethnographic fieldwork inside technoscience firms, remarked that the people she worked with "are largely positivists; they tend to believe that a point of view is either right or wrong, and that the difference is a matter of evidence. Anthropological evidence, however, is often dismissed as 'anecdotal'" (p. 8).

So be it. I don't, in fact, try to make any grand judgments about CMI. Like many people I think it can be used for good or ill—indeed, that's precisely the reason for focusing on the politics that shape uses rather than trying to imagine what might be possible if technologists ruled the world. And although calling it anecdotal would be unfair, the book does not try to provide a total description of CMI (impossible in principle for such a fast-moving object) or even a comprehensive history of its development at Virginia Tech. Rather, the idea is to take everyday, familiar university practices and give you a different sense of how they fit with other familiar practices by looking at the ways they play out at different scales, showing their antecedents, excavating the conditions that made them possible, tracing the ongoing circuits in which they're constituted, describing how they work in space and time, and contrasting the standpoints of their different participants (administrators, professors, and students). In one sense this is a modest agenda—making no claims, for example, that the specific events described here are characteristic of CMI at other universities. But it is also ambitious in this way: At its most basic level the book is meant to provide a set of images, embedded in plausible stories, that map out some of the variability, complexity, and spatial and temporal extensiveness of CMI in universities. These images and maps differ from those that university administrators and many faculty members rely on. They are offered up here as tools (though not as the only ones needed) for navigating the complexities of teaching and learning in higher education. Whether you'll find them superior to older, more familiar ones, or to the ones administrators favor, depends entirely on where you want to go.

Some of the people who have tried to help me find my way in this over the years by talking with me or reading earlier versions include Pat Bevan and Zeke Erskine, both of whom helped me interview students, Sandi Schneider, Susan Groenke, Rebecca Scheckler, Liz Barber, and David Hicks. My apologies for anyone I've left out. I also want to thank the reviewers from Lawrence Erlbaum Associates—Michele Knobel and Christian Schunn, and of course all the people named in the book who took time to talk to me. None of these people are likely to like everything here, and clearly none are to blame for my mistakes and misunderstandings.

Introduction

Nespor: What if it doesn't work?

AM: It doesn't work.

Nespor: So you back off entirely, you think?

AM: No. No. It's here to stay.

Nespor: Why is it here to stay? You've built an infrastructure and you can't take it apart?

AM: No, no. Um [pause]. You remember last summer when that satellite pointed away for about 3 days and nobody could do anything? I turned to my colleagues and said, if that satellite was pointed away for about 3 months, everybody would understand the extent to which these technologies are just embedded in everything that we do.

—Interview with AM, Director of Virginia Tech's
Center for Innovations in Learning (1999)

During the 1990s a cluster of practices I'll call computer-mediated instruction (CMI)[1] became a standard prescription at American universities for everything from saving space and reducing costs to developing new student markets and improving teaching. Administrators encouraged faculty to create distance education programs and put courses online. Funds were reallocated to purchase equipment and "wire" classrooms. By the turn of the century upwards of 90% of colleges and universities in the country were offering online programs and about 1.5 million students were taking online courses (Allen & Seaman, 2003; Carnevale, 2001; Hawkins, Rudy, & Madsen, 2003). To use Nardi and O'Day's (1999) phrase, a general "rhetoric of inevitability" had come to hold sway in

---

[1]Terms vary. Some speak of CAI (computer-aided instruction), CBL (computer-based learning), or online learning—all of which seem to me overly optimistic—whereas others use ICT (information and communication technologies), CCT (computing and communicating technologies), or IT (for either information or instructional technology)—this latter group seeming too vague (telephones and blackboards are IT in this sense).

1

discussions of information technologies, with CMI "presented as an inevitable adjunct of educational progress" (Strathern, 1997, p. 317).

Why should you care? Mostly because the rise of CMI suggests that changes are taking place in one of the core functions of a central institution of modern society. Undergraduate education is a key mechanism for connecting people to careers and jobs; an arena in which friendships, social networks, tastes, and identities are forged; a shaping ground for elites; and a big public and private expense. It can be a place where young people experience diversity, encounter a range of viewpoints on the world, engage with basic cultural controversies, and make contact with great intellectual traditions. It even shapes elementary and secondary schooling insofar as instructional assumptions cultivated at the university—of teaching as content delivery and content as knowledge defined by university-based disciplines—push their way down the grades. Big changes in undergraduate instruction, then, have broad implications.

Just what the changes will look like, however, remains uncertain and contested. How one teaches is shaped by complex relations linking subject matters to training, experience, organizational agendas, disciplinary jurisdictions, technical artifacts, political fields, economic networks, and discursive regimes. CMI has spread unevenly across the university as the emergent product of contentious processes (Tilly, 2001) in which actors ranging from legislators and university administrators to professors and students try to configure these relations to protect or extend their autonomy and influence. Both the cutting-edge, technology-intensive versions of CMI that attract most attention ('virtual universities,' real-time computer-supported cooperative work, etc.; see, e.g., Barab, Kling, & Gray, 2004; Watson & Andersen, 2002) and the more banal versions of CMI examined in this book percolate out of such processes. All of them are heated up and organized through a politics of visibility that shapes the categories and conventions of educational decision-making and debate (e.g., Scott, 1998).

Instruction is the product of multiple streams of activity organized at different spatial and temporal scales, and to count elsewhere and later, work, ideas, events, and people have to be made visible in forms that can move across these scales. Faculty members, for example, have to make their teaching visible not only to students but in different ways to administrators within the university and to bureaucrats operating at the scale of the state. Administrators and bureaucrats need teaching to be visible in ways that allow them to weigh its costs and value against other state and organizational functions. Students need to translate lectures, presentations, and labs into visible forms that can be moved around and studied. Professors have to turn that study (e.g., through tests) into forms (e.g., grades) visible in the university's system of instructional accounting. Finally, the grades have to get wrapped up in degrees that make students visible to employers or other schools. CMI seems to have the potential to change all this by changing how teaching (and student work) is mobilized, translated, and made visible for different audiences in and across these scales.

It follows that works like this one, which try to make CMI visible to various book-reading audiences, have tricky relationships to the processes they describe. Different ways of making teaching visible in research—whether the focus is on, say, machines, politics, administrators, teachers, or students—either align with or grind against the ways in which organizational actors want themselves and their work to be visible. Alignment usually means adopting the categories and concerns of the organization: asking, for example, if some kind of CMI increases students' test scores, raises instructors' ratings, or saves someone time or money. These are all good questions, but the problem is that one can end up only registering and making visible the things that matter to the organization—and organizations are strategically blind. As Scott (1998) observed, bureaucracies make things visible by simplifying them into forms that are:

> rather like abridged maps. [These forms] did not successfully represent the actual activity of the society they depicted, nor were they intended to; they represented only that slice of it that interested the official observer. They were, moreover, not just maps. Rather, they were maps that, when allied with state power, would enable much of the reality they depicted to be remade. (p. 3)

To be out of alignment, then, questioning categories or histories, and looking for the paths leading in and out of events, is the better tactic for a study of an emergent phenomenon like CMI. The strategy here is to try to shift the angle of vision by bringing back into the frame some of the key tensions and complexities of teaching typically deleted in administrative abridgments of CMI. In particular, I try to situate CMI in the organizational politics and activity systems of the university. Instruments like computers are tools only "in practice, for someone, when connected to some particular activity" (Star & Ruhleder, 1996, p. 112). If these activities are ignored, electronic technologies turn into fetishes (Hornborg, 2001), supposedly with "the power to communicate and convey information stripped of the encumbrances of social relations, and physical limitation on travel" (Strathern, 2000a, pp. 1–2). The computer is reified into a repository of predetermined instructional potentials—the supposedly inevitable or intrinsic implications of CMI—not only by state politicians who want to capitalize teaching through CMI investments, but also by researchers who foreground the imagined potentials of machines instead of situating them in specific historical, economic, and political conjunctions. As Slater (2001) suggested, "The new media have been studied less as media that are used within existing social relations and practices, and more as a new social space which constitutes relations and practices of its own" (p. 534).

In CMI research this neglect of social milieu and history encourages a style of inquiry in which teaching is treated as the work of an individuated actor, the teacher, and made visible as a local and segmentable process involving this bounded actor delivering stable bodies of decontextualized content that supposedly means the same thing across situations and uses. The function of CMI in such a view is to allow instructional events to be temporally and spatially detached from the teacher so that students can become flexible academic workers, learning what they need for their jobs whenever and wherever they can.

Like a lot of research on university teaching (e.g., Chickering & Ehrmann, 1996; Chickering & Gamson, 1991; Fry et al., 2003; Magolda, 2000; McKeachie, 1999; Pescosolido & Aminzade, 1999), work that proceeds from such assumptions ends up being about the sectioned-out experiences of students and professors—tasks or courses abstracted from everyday activities and the constellations of tasks and courses taught or taken before, after, or simultaneously. Findings are either generic—small classes are better, on the whole, than extremely big ones, faculty-student contact is good, and so are interaction, feedback, emphasizing time on task, communicating high expectations, letting students lead discussions, and establishing presence—or specific to efforts that depend on unusual or unusually high levels of technological resources (e.g., Bates & Poole, 2003; Bonk & Cummings, 1998; Dutton & Loader, 2002; Institute for Higher Education Policy, 2000; Mehrotra, Hollister, & McGahey, 2001; Naidu, 2003; Pelz, 2004; Rudestam & Schoenholtz-Read, 2002; University of Illinois Faculty Seminar, 1999).

The problem is that this kind of work slices out of the picture things like the political contexts that drive (or inhibit) particular pedagogical agendas, the assumptions about knowledge and teaching that shape course materials and guide how technical artifacts are glued into instructional configurations, the logics that organize courses into sequences (or don't), the kinds of work futures or everyday activities to which faculty are trying to connect instruction, the processes through which decisions are made about the equipment provided to faculty, the scheduling and assignment of courses, the allocation of graduate assistants, and so on.

These are the kinds of issues examined here. The focus is one setting, Virginia Tech, or "Tech" as it's known locally, a 25,000-student land grant university nestled in its own "Electronic Village" (Schorger, 1997)—at one time "the most wired town in the nation" (Stepanek, 1999). Tech is clearly not a typical institution. In addition to an unusually robust information technology infrastructure, the university's CMI efforts have garnered national attention, its IT administrators have been nationally prominent,[2] and it's played a notable role in shaping Virginia higher education policy regarding CMI. At the same time, the basic problems faced at Tech in creating and using CMI are far from unique. How, for example, do the efforts of individual developers get coordinated with centralized university agendas? What role does the state play? How do departmental structures and disciplinary strength influence the forms CMI takes? How are its uses aligned with national agendas? What kinds of economic and political forces are relevant? Answering questions like these, even partially and for one setting, is a necessary step in any effort to understand the implications of CMI for university teaching.

OVERVIEW OF THE BOOK

The book is divided into three parts. The first examines how CMI developed as an organizational agenda and became intertwined with state and institutional policies. The second looks at some of ways pressures to use CMI were negotiated, appropriated, and reshaped by differently positioned faculty members. The third examines what some common forms and uses of CMI might mean for different kinds of students.

The four chapters that make up part I of the book trace, in rough chronology, how CMI was translated from something on the periphery of the university to a central place in its instructional policy. The key to this transformation, I argue, wasn't the development of particular artifacts or softwares but the creation of a context in which their development could flourish. If "the uptake and use of the new technologies depend crucially on local social context" (Woolgar, 2002, p. 14), we have to begin by asking how local contexts are shaped to be receptive to technologies. This is basically the story of the first four chapters. Chapter 1 describes how innovators at Tech built an organizational base and generated trust and participation among professors interested in developing CMI, by making not-yet-worked-out technologies visible to them in demonstrations.

---

[2]For example, the vice president for Information Systems at the beginning of the period discussed here retired to become president of the influential national technology advocacy group EDUCOM (e.g., Heterick, 1998). EDUCOM was a consortium of approximately 600 colleges, universities, and businesses involved in using and promoting CMI. It played an influential role in lobbying at the federal level (e.g., DeLoughry, 1993a, 1993b) and in shaping CMI discourse in higher education. It merged with a similar group, CAUSE, in 1998 to form EDUCAUSE (see Slaughter & Rhoades, 2004, pp. 24, 318–319).

The second chapter describes how these local efforts got connected to state and national policies. Key here were the categories and accounting practices invoked in policy documents by various task forces, commissions, and administrators. These categories made CMI and traditional university teaching visible to state officials as competing policy options. The third chapter continues this story by showing how larger political and economic developments contributed to the growing prominence of financial discourses in higher education and how this favored CMI development. The fourth and final chapter in part I describes how CMI was made to appear as an investment that could increase teaching productivity without detracting from the university's research mission: an argument that depended on making CMI visible as a relatively inexpensive innovation for delivering instruction to very large classes of students.

The reason for spending even a little time on this history, most of it forgotten even at Tech, is that how things work at a given time can depend on the particular sequences of events through which they've unfolded (David, 2000; Pierson, 2003; Thelen, 2003; Tilly, 2002, p. 76). Assumptions current when policies and practices are developed can get embedded in standard operating procedures and persist after their origins are forgotten. Decisions made in the face of historically specific pressures and opportunities congeal into organizational and institutional forms that eventually make them look natural and inevitable.

The four chapters of part II show how differently positioned faculty responded to the politics of CMI described in part I (Allen & Seaman, 2003, p. 6; University of Illinois Faculty Seminar, 1999, section 2). Chapter 5 examines some of the implications of CMI for faculty work by comparing the experiences of three professors, each of whom received a university grant for CMI development. The case studies in chapters 6, 7, and 8 examine these courses in more depth. In chapter 6 the focus is on a course where CMI was used to make elements of professional practice visible in the form of a digital adjunct—a CD-ROM of visual images. Chapter 7 examines an effort to use CMI to make the difficulties of students at computer work stations visible to distant professors who could help them. Finally, chapter 8 examines how a professor working with instructional designers crafted objectives and developed PowerPoint slides and online materials to make lectures and coursework visible to students in a blended or hybrid course—the most common use of CMI at Tech.

These cases are not typical, but they illustrate the variation in political-administrative climate, field-specific construction of subject matter, organizational location of courses, dynamics of instructor status, and practical logics of teaching that shape how professors use CMI.

Part III of the book shifts perspective to examine student uses of CMI. Chapter 9 describes how students in the hybrid course discussed in chapter 8 strategically used PowerPoint lecture slides and web notes to do their academic work, and how these uses depended on such things as the students' fields of study, year in school, and the relation of the web-based materials to the classroom-based instruction.

In chapter 10 the emphasis shifts to CMI's role in the ways students fit the nutrition course into their larger temporal routines. One key claim for things like web notes is that they allow students to reorder instruction spatially and temporally. CMI supposedly makes instruction asynchronous and provides instructional materials to students anytime, anywhere. Drawing on interviews and student time logs, the chapter shows how CMI allowed academic work to be fitted into broader streams of practice, including other coursework, paid employment, and various social activities.

Each of these 10 chapters deals with ways of making facets of teaching visible for specific audiences and purposes. Chapter 11 distills some of the mechanisms at work in these strategies and considers their practical implications. Finally, an appendix describes data sources and the logic used in assembling them into the account that follows.

Here, perhaps, it would be appropriate to offer a word about how the book is meant to be read. This is not a comprehensive review of everything that's happened with CMI at Virginia Tech, let alone all of higher education. Rather, it sketches what I came to understand as key episodes in the process of weaving CMI into the instructional infrastructure of the university. The cases presented in part II do not reveal the entire range of CMI work at universities, but point to some of the mechanisms involved in creating that variation. Part III does not summarize everything we would want to know about students, but does suggest some of the dimensions along which different forms of CMI begin to influence their academic efforts.

In the main, I depict CMI development as a set of problems likely to recur in a wide range of settings. Some of these problems—for example, how one mobilizes resources to introduce CMI—may seem obvious, others less so, for example, how one links technology work done at the local scale (say, on a particular project) to state policy networks. In describing how such problems were dealt with at Tech the assumption is that the responses, though unique in their particulars, belong to more widely shared repertoires of educational change strategies. There's no claim that every university has or will develop CMI agendas in the ways described here, that all departments fit into one of the three patterns described in part II, or that all students do the kinds of things done by the students described in part III. Even if some of the problems and mechanisms identified are common across universities, the ways they combine and concatenate will differ across settings to produce different outcomes (Tilly, 2001).

The idea, in short, is not to try to show what will happen but to show how different agendas can combine in complex, sometimes unintended ways.

The aim is not to provide teachers, students, and researchers a set of specific directions for getting somewhere with CMI, but to partially map the landscape they'll have to travel through, and give them a few conceptual tools—ways of analyzing and talking about CMI practice and mapping the processes and ideologies through which it's woven—that might help them negotiate the terrain.

I

SCENES FROM THE CONSTRUCTION OF INSTITUTIONAL INVESTMENT

Making CMI Visible Within the University

Seeing comes before words.

—Berger (1972, p. 7)

Instructional innovators, at least those who start outside or on the margins of an organization, encounter a paradox. They're usually trying to promote changes that require investments by the organization, but organizations don't commit money, time, or energy to something they can't see in some sense. Sometimes innovators get around the problem by pointing to examples or analogies elsewhere, but when the thing in question just doesn't exist, they're faced with the problem of making it visible before they can get the support to actually make it. This was the problem CMI developers faced in the early 1980s. The instructional uses of computers weren't yet widespread and there weren't readily accessible exemplars of the technical and social infrastructure they required. There were mainframe systems, of course, but no networks of desktop computers (cf. Suter, 2001, p. 30), no:

> digital information resources, course management systems, high-end display devices, high-speed connections in residential and learning spaces, not to mention faculty who use the technology-rich learning environment and information technology (IT) staff to provide twenty-four-hour support to students and faculty. (Ingerman, 2001, p. 79)

As JM,[1] a pioneer of CMI at Virginia Tech explained:

---

[1]The faculty members and administrators interviewed gave permission for their names to be used (with one exception: Professor "DS" is a pseudonym), but I am following the strategy developed by Born (1995), who similarly studied an unavoidably named organization (the famous IRCAM music center in Paris), of referring to participants by acronyms. As the reader will see, it would have been impossible to write this work without naming Virginia Tech (see also Nespor, 2000), and once that step is taken a dedicated investigator can determine which professors or administrators (though not, I'm confident, students) I'm talking about. Using the acronyms makes this a bit harder.

There were essentially no classrooms equipped to show any computer display.... Very few faculty had connections in their offices at that time. There were a considerable number of computer labs, and faculty would assign problems which you would typically do on the mainframes. And these would be mostly statistical, and in a few cases simulation work, typically written in Fortran. We had no support staff whatsoever to deal with this.

The first question, then, is how, lacking appropriate infrastructure, established models, or proof it can work, you develop CMI and get administrators and policymakers to put money into it. How do you get them to see CMI and its supposed potentials when it doesn't exist in a readily available and standardized form? And how do you persuade faculty members to invest time in it?

PROFESSIONAL MIGRATION

One part of the answer is that you anchor the new stuff in old stuff: You draw on ideas, resources, and ways of doing things developed for earlier instructional technologies, and tether the new approaches and actors to these already established ones.

The people doing the early work on CMI didn't come out of nowhere. They migrated from and brought along the organizational and conceptual resources of other fields, in particular instructional television (ITV). A key distance education medium from the 1950s to the 1970s, nowadays likely to be neglected in the CMI literature or treated as a past disappointment (e.g., Weller, 2002, pp. 8–9), ITV was not just a communications and instructional medium but also a network of people, professional associations, and journals. When funding priorities shifted and the creation of the public broadcasting system took some of the wind out of ITV's sails, the people who'd built careers around ITV didn't disappear, they broadened the scope of their work and redefined it as IT (Reiser, 2001a). The major ITV professional organization changed its name from the Department of Audiovisual Instruction to the Association for Educational Communications and Technology (AECT), and the journals *Audiovisual Communication Review* and *Audiovisual Instruction* became *Educational Communication and Technology Journal* and *Instructional Innovator*, respectively:

> By the early 1970s, the terms educational technology and instructional technology began to replace audiovisual instruction to describe the application of media for instructional purposes.... The advent of [microcomputers], many professionals in the instructional design field turned their attention to producing computer-based instruction. (Reiser, pp. 59, 62)

Along with this organizational infrastructure, ITV bequeathed a conceptual infrastructure to the IT field. Assumptions and techniques from programmed instruction, for example, an approach popularized in military and vocational training and widely used in ITV, were transformed into instructional design principles (see Goldfarb, 2002, pp. 51–55)[2] and served as key premises for early (and many later) developers.

At Virginia Tech, the migration from ITV to IT provided an important plot point in the story of the university's move into CMI. Now Director of Tech's Educational Technologies unit, which oversees course management software and faculty development efforts in CMI, JM arrived at the university in 1971 not as a computer specialist but as a "television producer-director." His initial job was to "help set up the Instructional Television" in the university's Learning Resources Center (LRC), but like others in the ITV field his interests shifted and broadened over time. Earning a doctorate from Tech's Instructional Systems Development program in 1982, his job title at the LRC changed from "producer-director" to "instructional developer." As he recalled:

> In the role of instructional design person, in 1981–82, the first thing I did of any substance was go back and produce 20 half-hour video tapes aimed at inserving K-12 teachers about using media, technology, in their teaching. One of the half hours was about computers. And at that time those were Apple II computers. We had internally moved towards using the mainframe computer at that time for script production. I treated that series as—it was, in fact, an independent study, distance learning project. We produced study guides—our students were all over the state, we delivered on PBS. So it was my first venture into creating a package that was self-sufficient. We used study guides, we had a graduate student in Richmond who wrote the study guides based on the scripts. Homework was sent back here. There were audio teleconference calls on Saturday with teachers. We did everything that there was to do that seemed appropriate at the time.

Elements of later CMI efforts were already present in this effort—the self-sufficient or modular organization of content packets, the distribution of instructional responsibilities across multiple participants, the effort to mine nontraditional student markets—but here computers were the topic of instruction, not its medium. This changed as JM's interests moved away from linear instructional systems like ITV toward the possibilities offered by combining video with computers.

At this point in time, the mid-1980s, computers were impractical channels for distance education. Unlike televisions, they were not ubiquitous technologies, and even students who had them had nothing like Internet access. This lack of an everyday infrastructure meant that JM had to shift

---

[2]Programmed Instruction underwent an evolution paralleling the field as a whole: The National Society for Programmed Instruction became the National Society for Performance and Instruction and later the International Society for Performance Improvement.

focus from the creation of distance education for new student markets to the transformation of already established campus-based courses. As an instructional designer he didn't have his own courses so JM had to collaborate with regular faculty members. As he recounted in a 1999 interview: "[My] first significant [CMI] project was with MS.... And that project was kind of a way for me to get into the notion of interactive and the video.... We experimented and did several projects in which we had a VCR driven by this Apple computer." MS recalled that JM:

> sent out a memo, around campus ... that "If anybody wants to do interactive video, we've got the resources to make it happen." ... And ... ever since I took this job in 1980, I'd been reading non-stop in trade publications ... sort of computer nerd stuff.... So, you know, I think I'd probably read about interactive video before I had JM's note. I thought, "That's probably out of my reach, but it'd be a real interesting thing to do in my instruction if it were within my reach." And then one day JM's note showed up and I thought, "Well, what the heck?"

As these comments suggest, the project wasn't undertaken because of concerns that students weren't learning well or because evidence suggested that interactive video would improve instruction. Rather, this work was what I'll call an aesthetically driven change effort. The focus was on the form of the object or practice being developed—the elegance of its design or procedures, its fit with some theory or image of good practice—rather than its immediate utility and what it actually might do in the everyday world (Bauman, 1984, p. 7; Bourdieu, 1984). These kinds of change efforts focus on what's inside the aesthetic frame—in this case the technical problems of interactive video[3]—and may or may not imply changes in anything left outside that frame. In this instance, a focus on the technology of delivery—from classroom lecture to interactive video—meant the developers could hold constant the instructional assumptions of the practices being remediated: the role of the course itself, for example, and the fundamental design of instruction. The instructional logic of the interactive video, as JM explained, was "classic programmed instruction, but with video and a computer." In MS's description:

> The gist of it was to videotape some instructional stuff, and create to run parallel to that a program that ran on the Apple IIE which essentially got the student up and running through the instructional videotape. And at various

---

[3]In a contemporary account of the project featured on the front page of *InCider* (the Apple IIE magazine), MS (1985) described the software he used (and listed other commercially available software) and noted other options that might have been pursued in designing responses to student error. The article dealt with technical aspects of the project and was written for a technologically knowledgeable audience.

points throughout that instruction it would stop and ask a question. For example, if the student got the question right, they would proceed forward according to the software code that I created, and if they got it wrong it would perhaps route them back to some remedial instruction.

Programmed instruction (discussed further in chap. 8) is basically a logic for organizing instruction around behavioral objectives. Student learning is represented in terms of paths consisting of hierarchically arranged content elements leading to these objectives. Instruction involves creating mechanisms (quick feedback, contingencies of reinforcement, etc.) to get students on the path and help them stay on it.[4] An instructional logic of this kind, widespread in training and school settings for decades, would have looked familiar to administrators and professors watching the interactive video. If the interactive video was a material manifestation of CMI making it visible to a wider audience, it was this familiar picture of learning as an individual student's encounter with supplied course material across a relatively short time frame that made CMI legible. The event in which this seeing and reading took place was the demonstration.

DEMONSTRATIONS

It's easy to think of cases in which organizational changes move across space and time through media like reports or plans, policies or laws, carried by innovators or their followers, or administered through some bureaucracy. But change also can be initiated through artifacts or, more accurately, through demonstrations of them.

Produced during 1983 and 1984 and actually used in MS's course in 1984, the interactive video amounted to only about half an hour of a single lesson in a single course. That might seem like a small innovation, but the brevity suited other uses, in particular presentations and demonstrations. As JM recounted, "We actually used this maybe three or four semesters. Got a whole lot of conference presentations, a couple of articles. Our whole thrust was, 'Here's how faculty can get involved in this new kind of way to teach, give students some control over how they learn.'"

These conference presentations of the computer-plus-television-and-courseware artifact did not demonstrate CMI: There were no students, after all, no teaching, no learning, no course. But then a demonstration is never a veridical manifestation of the thing demonstrated. Rather, it works

---

[4]The basic ideas of programmed instruction are deeply embedded in the instructional design practices (about which more in chap. 8) that guide current CMI development in higher education. As Reiser (2001b) noted, "The processes for developing programmed materials involved many of the steps found in current instructional design models" (p. 59).

as a window to imagined situations elsewhere at other times. It makes visible things that aren't actually present in the demonstration setting—or perhaps anywhere else. Demonstrations focus attention on an in-principle repeatable short-term presentation or operation—a highly stylized set of movements, a scripted speech or action, a device that runs through some legible cycle, or, as in the case of the interactive video, an artifact that couples content with on-screen tasks and remediation scripts.

Demonstrations of technology are commonly used to market new versions of already widely available artifacts (e.g., a new word-processing system introduced into a world full of them; cf. Suchman, Trigg, & Blomberg, 2002), or in a closer parallel to the situation considered here, to secure support for the development of a specific product (cf. Latour, 1996, pp. 51–83). Indeed, as Hakken (2003) complained, demonstrations of the latter variety "are the kinds of activities that pass for 'research' in engineering and technology fields like informatics (Forsythe, 2001). Success at showing that a system can be deployed is erroneously treated as evidence that it should be" (p. 295).

But the problem for JM and MS was a bit different. Instead of trying to get someone to adopt or invest in their interactive video courseware, they were demonstrating it to show that CMI could work—and in JM's case that he and his colleagues were people who could work it.

ASSEMBLING INTERESTED PARTICIPANTS

Demonstrations are useful tools of change in part because their brevity and mobility allow them to be taken around to different audiences and distant meeting places.[5] And because hardware, software, and courseware can't speak for themselves, there's a need for a presenter or demonstrator to travel with them. This travel provides occasions for innovators to construct public identities and enlist new allies. MS recalled:

> Whether it was physically on this campus, or whether it was at a national conference or a regional conference, when people hear about "oh, interactive video, oh, wow, that sounds pretty neat. Could you do that at our conference?" In those days I was younger and more naive, and I would say, "Sure!" And then I would pack up 28,000 lbs. of equipment and tool on off, either in car or on plane with way more stuff that I ever wanted to haul anywhere....

---

[5]Traditional forms of university pedagogy—in particular, written lectures read aloud—can also be transported outside the instructional frame. However, lectures remain too closely attached to their authors to work as effective demonstrations of scalable instruction (even if, as is likely the case, trained actors could present the lecture as well or better). Also, in the absence of students, someone reading a lecture would appear to be doing something other than teaching. Demonstrations of computer-mediated instruction don't have the same problem. They can represent instructional possibilities as content events, without students present.

> In the interactive videotape days what it literally meant was hauling an APPLE IIE and an APPLE IIE monitor, and a VCR, and a big, hopefully a big TV, or maybe they had a big TV, and then hooking that all up, and literally demoing the ... courseware ... and explaining the how and why and answering questions after it. That's what that dog and pony show looked like.

As Bechky (2003) suggested, artifacts have social as well as technical functions, they "mediate" social relations, and "by symbolizing the work of occupational groups, the objects can also represent and strengthen beliefs about the legitimacy of the work the groups perform" (p. 725). These effects are important because early networks of innovation are organized as much around trust as technical expertise. Before investing time, money, or reputation, people make judgments about the people attached to whatever it is they're thinking about investing in (Reed, 2001; cf. Shapiro, 1987). Demonstrations are one mechanism for building this trust: They make innovators visible as competent practitioners. They demonstrate the demonstrators as well as the focal artifacts.

A corollary is that trust can be buttressed by demonstrations of artifacts developed at more prestigious institutions—in CMI, for example, this might be places like the Massachusetts Institute of Technology (MIT). JM recounted that at one point he:

> rented a videodisc player in Roanoke, I bought the videodisc that I could find, from MIT media lab, that had, again, examples. And people flocked to these sessions. We had to double and triple schedule these. There was a quite considerable interest among 30, maybe 40 faculty, in trying to figure out how they could apply technology differently.

Such demonstrations could reinforce the legitimacy of CMI efforts by pointing to networks of use and development stretching beyond the local setting, to the existence of broader professional communities (Bechky, 2003, p. 724). And when faculty members took up the invitation to develop CMI of their own, their participation provided opportunities for new demonstration projects that could ultimately become vehicles for accumulating organizational resources. As JM explained, after the interactive video project with MS, he:

> worked with several different faculty to write and get grants for interactive videodisc projects. We used that to buy a lot of equipment. We built up our internal development base in this department. We used it to hire and train a number of people on salary, wage and salary. Again, building up a resource base. Ultimately most of those were converted into positions. We stepped up from really being kind of backwater and really peripheral, really marginal, to having a resource base at least that some people could use. We went through at least three federal grants in different areas to get to that point.

The result was that by the early 1990s Educational Technologies had become the key node in a growing network of CMI activity at Tech. JM explained:

> This group [Educational Technologies] was the group that had a long-standing working relationship with faculty on instruction. Not many faculty, but we were well perceived as the people—if you had an issue with technology or media or teaching, we were the group you would talk to.

Finally, the brevity and modularity of demonstrations allowed them to be collected and anthologized with efforts elsewhere, making Tech visible nationally (at least to other CMI developers) as an institution on the forefront of CMI development. JM recounted that through the effort that began with the interactive video he:

> hooked up with several other people doing similar projects. In a span of three years ... I collected demonstrations of what they were doing and produced several compilations, anthologies really, of people's work at other universities, for AECT, and they sold these tapes.

Becoming "the group you would talk to" on campus while "hooking up" with others around the country made CMI visible both within the university and nationally. And again, all this took place before any proof of the effectiveness or viability of CMI could be provided.

CROSSING SCALES

I suggested earlier that much of the literature on CMI underplays the role of extended social relations in shaping teaching and learning. Even among the works that take up this topic, there's a tendency to ignore the kinds of organizational trajectories described earlier. The politics of shifting professional jurisdictions (Abbott, 1988) are often left out of accounts that suggest computers will be domesticated in educational organizations, and older approaches to instruction and curriculum will persevere because of continuities in organizational forms and teacher training (Cuban, 1993) or because of the persistence of industrial-era ideas (Bigum, 2002). In fact, these older ideas about instruction have not persisted in spite of the introduction of CMI, but were the media of its introduction. As Bowker and Star (1999, p. 35) pointed out, new infrastructures develop on top of old ones and inherit many of their characteristics. Although some aspects of computer-mediated instruction are unquestionably new, others have been fitted to a preexisting infrastructure of organizational forms and pedagogical logics. Organizational change and reform agendas selectively preserve, even harden, older practices.

I've made it look simple, then. You begin from some professional base (like ITV), make a claim on some new domain (like CMI), get allies and collaborators interested in some "boundary object" (Star & Greisemer, 1999) like the computer, build a demonstration artifact, put on some dog and pony shows, get other people involved in doing demonstrations, construct a public profile for your work group, accumulate organizational resources, and off you go. Change is less about dissemination than moving around and building organizational bases.

And of course, this is much too simple. Tracing how CMI emerged from the work of individual innovators can help us see how certain assumptions about instruction became associated with CMI, and how CMI efforts developed within the organization, but that's far from the whole story. CMI spread rapidly through U.S. higher education in the 1980s and 1990s, hurried along not only by instructional designers and technology enthusiasts, but by state governments (e.g., Barrow, 1995, p. 169) and advocacy groups. In chapters 2 and 3 I try to show how the organizational efforts I've described so far became articulated with these state and national agendas. I'll begin at a key juncture in the development of CMI at Tech, as described by JM:

> There was an annual program that SCHEV [State Council of Higher Education in Virginia] ran called "Funds for Excellence" that was open to faculty across the state. In 1989 or '90, one of their program focuses, they wanted RFPs [Requests for Proposals] on, was "demonstrations of use of technology in teaching."

Being old hands at demonstrations by this point, JM and his colleagues wrote a proposal that would allow them to continue building the organizational infrastructure of the Educational Technologies unit:

> I had that proposal set up as a demonstration that would work over a two year period. We would do two internal RFPs and have faculty propose projects. We ultimately worked with I think 5 faculty.... We used the money to buy summer salaries for them, we bought them out of courses during the year.... Like 90% of the money went to staff, personnel costs. We hired some programmers, an artist. It was a CAI [Computer-Assisted Instruction] development lab that was essentially put together.

When professors used the services of this lab, their projects could become parts of demonstration efforts as well. As JM recalled:

> That went very well. Those projects, plus the earlier work with the federal projects, produced some local content that we could trot out on stage to visitors, or to the board, or to the people in the Provost's office, or to Deans.

I remember making a lot of demonstrations, little demos. Once we got the faculty on board with courses we started doing that kind of demonstration.

Local content helped make local CMI more visible within the university, and began to make the university visible to state and national organizations:

There was some end-of-the-year money left on the second year with SCHEV, and they asked for mini proposals to do dissemination conferences. At literally the same time, we were asked by AECT to host a summer technology conference, for high tech.... They came here to do one that had a technology focus, a high tech focus. I got the two things to be at the same time, the same weekend. So we used state money and invited faculty from all over the state to come free to this thing, and we also pulled in like 100 people from all around the country for three or four days at the Marriott. I had several people within the university presenting, as well as some external people. That was a very significant conference, because we were wrapping up the SCHEV Funds for Excellence project, and there was this gap in front of us, that we had a lot of local faculty come to this kind of excited. We had a couple of top administrators talk to these people, and I think it was extremely useful for them to see that there was this fairly large room full of people that they recognized.

But why would SCHEV have earmarked money for CMI development in 1989 or 1990? Why would there have been "top administrators" at a meeting like this? How did something like a CMI demonstration—absent evidence that what was being demonstrated could save money (cf. Carr, 2001) or improve teaching—attract favorable attention?

Making CMI Visible as Policy: Instructional Accounting

> *To move beyond demonstrations to the reality of fundamentally changed practice, one needs very high levels of careful, long-term, coordinated pressure on institutions.*
> —Hakken (2003, p. 294)

> *Work is not ever organized instrumentally, as some would have it and as it is treated in many management textbooks. It is organized to be "read" by other members, including oneself. Accountability is about making the invisible visible.*
> —Munro (1996, p. 5; see also Hopwood, 1987, 1990, p. 8)

It helps to rephrase the last question: How, we should ask, are demonstrated artifacts transmuted into forms that administrators can work with, invest in, and justify to legislators and constituents who never see the demonstrations? In Tech's case the solution involved turning the artifacts into words and phrases that could fit into policy documents and then circulate across levels of government and administration.

A key moment in this alchemy occurred in 1989, when JM's boss, Robert Heterick, then Tech's Vice President of Information Systems (and later president of Educom),[1] created a University Task Force on the Impact of Digital Technologies on the Classroom Environment (hereafter University Task Force). JM recalled this as:

A very significant event.... This was a committee of perhaps a dozen to 15 well-established, respected faculty, basically from all over the university. TH [later Director of Instructional Services] and I were staff to that committee,

---

[1]Apparently this is the same person Noble (2001) referred to as "Heterich" in his critique of "digital diploma mills" (p. 33).

consequently gave a number of demonstrations to them about what was coming on the horizon.

Perhaps the most significant part of the University Task Force's final report (1989) was the language it provided for contrasting CMI to supposedly conventional forms of university teaching. In a characteristic passage the 1989 report asserted that:

> The overwhelmingly dominant model of instruction in American university education, especially at the undergraduate level, is credit-for-contact. In this model, the student's progress and the faculty member's instructional contribution are measured by hours of contact in lecture hall, seminar room, or laboratory. Consequently, genuinely independent study is effectively discouraged, and true tutorial systems like those of Oxford and Cambridge are virtually absent in undergraduate education. However, the new digital technologies may make it possible to break this mold, thereby permitting the decoupling of contact from credit. (p. 1)

As JM recalled, this language and much of the argument of the University Task Force's (1989) report were quickly appropriated by the state:

> There were a whole series of ideas that came out of [Tech's] report that were quoted substantially in the chapter of a report that SCHEV [State Council of Higher Education in Virginia] wrote called The University of the 21st Century—something like that. The technology chapter liberally quoted that [Virginia Tech] report.

"Quoted liberally" is right: The portions of the SCHEV report (Commonwealth of Virginia Commission on the University of the 21st Century, 1989) dealing with instructional technology are basically glosses of the University Task Force's (1989) report (the paragraph cited earlier, e.g., was quoted directly in SCHEV publications as late as 1993; see SCHEV, 1993). The staff director of the state commission that produced the report, AM, recounted how it ended up relying so heavily on the University Task Force's document:

> Well, we were doing a lot of environmental scanning. We had 10 commissioners, and two of them were from outside Virginia.... One of the commissioners at the time happened to be president of the MLA, and was vice-provost for research at a major Northeastern university, and then one of the other members had been president of a university in the Northeast and had just gone on to be the president of a huge foundation in New York City.... We even talked to newspaper reporters. We had somebody from the ... editorial page from *The New York Times, Washington Post* ... from the education sections, come in and tell us what they were seeing.... And

technology was figuring really large in all of their conversations, even though, that was before the days when anything was easy. The only people who were doing anything were basically the engineers and the number crunchers. It wasn't happening anywhere else, except a little bit of word processing. And even then, there was still the argument over whether you could write as well when you left your yellow pad. So when these national people said we have to be able to speak to technology, then we went to the colleges and universities in Virginia and we said, "Who's looking at this"?—and it was a fluke. I mean, it was one of these seridipitous things, Virginia Tech had just pulled together this task force on the impact of digital technology.... They had just done this report. And when the group read it ... they thought it was visionary. And they also thought it felt right, that it was right on the money. And it had a resonance with everything that we were hearing from all these other people that we were talking to. So we wrote a chapter on technology that pretty much used that [Virginia Tech] report as a basis for the chapter.

Two particular phrases from the University Task Force's (1989) report— "credit-for-contact" and "breaking the mold"—bubbled out of the state commission chapter as critical tropes that were to reappear for years in state and university policy documents and pronouncements on CMI. How is this significant? Policies, as Ball (1994) pointed out, are not just rules and directives: They consist also of rhetorical or discursive strategies that shape how issues can be understood. A policy discourse "changes the possibilities we have for thinking 'otherwise'" and "limits our responses to change" (Ball, 1994, p. 23). One way it does this is by propogating phrases like *credit for contact* that operate like trapdoors that shift the geographical scale of public reference. In the case here, they helped transform formerly local issues—for example, how big should a course be? Should it use CMI?—into state issues that had to be argued and justified in the terms of the official policy language. To understand what this detour entailed we need to step back from the narrative for a moment and examine the media of deflection: the slogans themselves. *Breaking the mold* was by this time a hackneyed phrase used by countless boosters and change entrepreneurs (the U.S. federal Department of Education even gave out a Breaking the Mold award during the first Bush presidency). Credit for contact, by contrast, had more complex resonances. To understand its role as a mantra for officials and administrators we have to briefly unpack its history and logic.

UNPACKING CREDIT FOR CONTACT

Credit for contact describes higher education's version of one of the basic organizing mechanisms of public schooling in the United States: the Carnegie unit, set up early in the 20th century under the aegis of the

Carnegie Foundation "to raise standards in American secondary and higher education through unifying and centralizing academic practice" (Tyack & Cuban, 1995, p. 91). Defined as "a quarter of the total high school instructional time for a student in a given year" (Labaree, 2000), the Carnegie unit allowed universities to structure their relations with secondary schools by requiring that students complete a certain number of units to gain college admission:

> [This] set the standard for much of what became distinctive about the American education system ... a system that stresses attendance over performance, that encourages students to pursue the tokens of academic success rather than to demonstrate mastery of academic content. The Carnegie unit quickly evolved into the credit-hour system that is so fundamental to our form of education today. (Labaree, 2000, p. 31)

Not surprisingly, the University Task Force (1989) report's criticisms of credit for contact closely resembled earlier critiques of the Carnegie unit, for example, that it "measures ... education (and diploma) in terms of time served and credits earned by the pupil" (Tompkins & Gaumnitz, 1954, p. 19; see also Tyack & Cuban, 1995, p. 93). In neither context, however, were the basic terms of the argument interrogated: How exactly are time and credit supposedly linked in conventional teaching, and how is CMI supposed to change their relationship?

CONTACT AND CREDIT FOR WHAT?

Sitting with 300 other students in a vast lecture hall is one kind of contact with a professor. But so are giving a presentation in a small seminar, posting remarks on a class listserv, or turning in a paper. As the authors of the University Task Force's (1989) report recognized, digital technologies actually increase the possibilities for contact:

> A variety of formats should be able to coexist: fairly traditional lecture and laboratory courses, extensive independent study improved by remote access to resources and the ability to submit papers and reports electronically, group and individual tutorials supplemented by self-paced materials available in an assortment of media, and a wide variety of seminars. We hope not simply to replace one mold with another but to find ways to increase freedom without compromising quality. (pp. 2–3)

The critique of credit for contact, then, wasn't about contact per se but about the reputed practice of giving credit for physical copresence. But how common was such a practice? Students, after all, can attend classes regularly and still fail a course, or get good grades without showing up for anything but tests (Moore, 2003; St. Clair, 1999). One professor heavily involved in CMI at Virginia Tech recalled that for one of his large, conventionally taught lecture courses he had:

> asked someone from statistics to do an analysis for us on the relationship between attendance and their grades. And there was a slight correlation. That is, and I don't remember all of the proper terms, but when certain types of tests were done it looked like there was a little, a slight correlation, between being there at a high attendance rate and getting a good grade. But in my—looking at it as a nonstatistician—it didn't convince me that students [who] came to class did any better than [laughs].... There are students that just ... "get it" and students that don't. And sometimes it's rather depressing when I realize that maybe I'm not making any difference at all for those people.

In fact, of course, rather than getting credit for showing up at the appointed time, students get credit for turning in things like tests, papers, and problem sets, many of which they prepare (asynchronously) outside scheduled contact times. Courses are basically administrative fictions for summarizing a set of spatially dispersed tasks of variable duration. Credit is negotiated payment for products supposedly arising from the performance of these tasks. As Becker, Geer, and Hughes (1968) explained:

> Students define their relationship with professors as one in which professors contract to reward performance in predictable ways. They devote much effort to discovering the terms of the contract and to trying to hold up their end of it, as they understand it, by appropriate academic performance. Students decide what the terms of the contract are by observing and interpreting the words and actions of the teacher as the semester goes on. A class, for them, is not a series of isolated encounters, but rather a connected sequence of events extending over four and a half months. During that period, they engage in two simultaneous enterprises. They search for cues that, properly interpreted, will yield an understanding of what the teacher will demand in return for a given grade. At the same time, they attempt to do things they have decided are important to get the grade they want. (p. 64)

This is notably a contract between unequal participants. Professors need not explain it with any precision, which means that students' understandings of it are functions of evolving calculations based on their search for cues and past experiences with similar courses and tasks. As grades are usually important to students, and the highest grades are usually rationed, students try to get instructors to make performance requirements predictable in ways that allow shortcuts (cramming, getting tips or old tests through social networks, cheating) to the needed grade (e.g., Norton,

Tilley, Newstead, & Franklyn-Stokes, 2004). The needed grade is defined by the student's program of study and career ambitions, both of which can change within or across semesters, or take on different meanings as graduation draws near.

Credit for contact, then, does not describe a form of instruction but a method for making teaching and learning administratively visible. Like the Carnegie unit, it names a kind of instructional accounting system.

ACCOUNTING FOR INSTRUCTION

Organizations use accounting systems to make their operations visible to critical audiences, in particular, other organizations on whom they depend or with whom they have to coordinate their work. Double-entry bookkeeping and business accounting, for example, were developed in Europe in the Middle Ages to provide public, defensible, trust-inducing representations of the relationships of costs or effort to profits or outcome:

> Accounting makes it possible for capitalists to evaluate rationally the consequences of their past decisions. They can calculate exactly the resources currently available to them and those that will be forthcoming in the future. Capitalists can use the information provided by an account to assess and compare various alternatives for investment. (Carruthers & Espeland, 1991, p. 32)

The instructional bookkeeping of educational institutions serves analogous functions. Credit for contact makes work visible in terms of grades, which allow students to relate academic effort to shorter and longer term returns, teachers to set pressures and constraints on students by linking grades to certain kinds of performance, and administrators to regulate admission and participation in high-demand fields.

Even more profoundly, the standardized representations of student accomplishment produced by traditional grade-based accounting systems enable universities to communicate with one another about instruction in ways that maintain their control over the credentialing of competence. If a student wants to count academic work from another university toward a degree from Virginia Tech, Tech officials can look at a transcript and convert the courses to Tech credits. No knowledge or demonstration of what the student actually did at the other university is required. At the same time, with few exceptions, no amount of demonstration, testimonial, or evidence of learning or competence from nonuniversity sources may be considered in the conversion. The effect is to reinforce higher education's control over the definition of educational capital—credentials and other institutional markers—at national or international scales. In questioning credit for contact, CMI proponents were also questioning this institutional autonomy and opening a path for employers and state officials to follow in claiming increasing jurisdiction over the evaluation of the university's instructional work.

Universities can't be understood apart from the networks that link them with students, parents, legislators, regulatory and funding agencies, corporations, and other universities. One of the problems for any organization is to configure itself favorably in such relations, that is, define itself as belonging in a certain way to an "organizational field" (Dimaggio & Powell, 1983, p. 148). As Fligstein and Freeland (1995) put it: "The basic problem facing organizational actors is to create a stable world so that the organization can continue to exist. This necessitates the construction of an organizational field in which actors come to recognize and take into account their mutual interdependence" (p. 31).

In higher education the major lines of "mutual interdependence" regarding instruction are easy to discern (those regarding research are addressed by others, e.g., Rhoades & Slaughter, 1997, Slaughter & Rhoades, 2004): The state needs higher education to satisfy the demands of (relatively affluent) parents for mechanisms to help their kids "get ahead" (Brown, 1995). In theory the university also plays a role in producing a knowledgeable citizenry and an educated workforce (cf. Henwood, 2003, pp. 74–77). In return for this kind of thing the state gives its universities some money.

But how much money should it give and how is it to account for the instructional return on investment? Here the concept of output plays a key role in CMI advocacy. Twigg (1992), for example, argued that increasing instructional productivity in higher education is a matter not just of infusing "technology" but of emphasizing educational "outputs":

> What does it mean to increase productivity in higher education? Simply defined, it means either increasing output at the same cost and/or reducing costs while producing the same output. Currently, higher education places its emphasis on increasing inputs in order to produce the same or lesser outputs. We need to develop meaningful, sophisticated measures of what students need to know and be able to do as a touchstone for more productive education policies. Our goal should be a vast increase in productivity: more learning for more people at less cost. (p. x; see also Twigg, 2002, pp. 91–92)[2]

---

[2]The argument that the critical component in technology-based educational reform is an emphasis on objectives (as specifications of desired outputs) rather than technology per se, goes back at least to Skinner (1965), who suggested that the design of instruction, independent of the technical artifacts in which it's embodied, is the key to its effectiveness. Noble (1991) pointed out that "recent evaluations of the effectiveness of CBE [computer-based education] continue to insist that instructional design, and not the use of computers, is the pivotal consideration in the success or failure of CBE applications" (p. 82).

As Levine (2000) suggested (though he used the term *outcomes* when he meant outputs), this emphasis is closely linked to the struggle over the university's monopoly over the evaluation of competence:

> With the change in emphasis from institutional process to educational outcomes, degrees will become far less meaningful. A transcript of each student's competencies, including the specific information that the student knows or the skills that he or she can perform, will be far more desirable. Colleges now have a virtual monopoly on higher-education credentials. If degrees become less important, how will we continue to attract students in a world offering limitless educational choices? (p. B10)

The question is who controls the definition and assessment of these competency outputs? Its difficulty is compounded by the fact that the concept of output itself is ambiguous, even in domains such as manufacturing (e.g., Henwood, 2003). In the case of instruction it's hard to specify what students need to know and be able to do without knowing what they'll likely be doing in the future, and this is often unclear for college students. The relevant time frames are unclear as well—should outputs be framed in terms of weeks? semesters? As Strathern (2000a) suggested, the meaningful outcomes of university teaching may be emergent and invisible for years. And what are the contexts in terms of which outcomes should be conceived? The typical measures of academic performance (such as grades) rarely show the connections of school learning to competence outside school. Finally, many of the things college life produces—work habits, friendships, social capital networks, interests, dispositions, and tastes—are simply not registered in typical assessments (compare Strathern, 2000b, p. 218, with St. John, 1994).

These conceptual problems notwithstanding, the coupling of output discourse to CMI advocacy through slogans like those in the University Task Force's (1989) report became a basic element of CMI policy discourse in Virginia and elsewhere. A SCHEV (1993) report, for example, asserted:

> An input-based model, in which so many hours spent in a classroom entitle a student to a coupon in the form of credit hours, and so many coupons can be redeemed for a degree ... locks institutions into labor-intensive modes of instruction and says little about what the student will know or be able to do once that degree is in hand.... We need not lock all students into learning at the same pace in the same way. Virginia's colleges and universities can move away from "credit for contact" in numerous ways that reflect institutional diversity. Many highly successful industrial training programs or the curricula of several American experimental colleges and universities are not based on "seat time" accumulated by students. (p. 6)

How were such curricula and programs to get away from seat-time inputs while avoiding the conceptual difficulties of outputs? Basically they did so by introducing another kind of input. Instead of time and embodied labor, CMI was to be organized around inputs of prespecified instructional objectives defined at the level of the individual student. As Strathern (2000a) suggested, the substitution of objectives for outcomes shifts and compresses the temporal organization of instruction: "In teaching … you do not have to wait for the results years hence but can create a simulacrum of what the classroom should be producing (what its outcome or effect should be) through a map or plan … in the form of a set of indicators" (p. 3).

Instead of asking what a student actually does or could do and what it would matter in some broader context of life, one only has to look at the person in relation to the objective at one point in time. A certain score on a test, for example, or an end-of-course grade, defines the student in terms of the objectives and allows the output of instruction to be defined in terms of the sum of such snapshots (thus, as you'll see later, evaluations of CMI will give instructional outputs in terms of things like changes in a course's average grade). But note that these are not the outcomes of the instruction and they say nothing about what professors and students actually did.

The precedent for this substitition of reckoning by objectives for actual outcomes derives from corporate practice, particularly the scientific management approach developed in the late 19th and early 20th centuries, principally by the industrial engineer F. W. Taylor (see Braverman, 1974; Callahan, 1962).[3] Taylor argued that a basic problem for managers was that the complexity and emergent character of work made it difficult to see or understand unless closely observed over a long period. As Taylor put it: "We can see and feel the waste of material things. Awkward, inefficient, or ill-directed movements of men, however, leave nothing visible or tangible behind them. Their appreciation calls for an act of memory, an effort of the imagination" (cited in Miller & O'Leary, 1987, p. 251).

As administrative imagination is in limited supply, scientific management proposed to increase managerial control by making work visible in a simplified and temporally compressed form: as the deviation from some norm or standard. This allows work to be made legible in measuable, numerical metrics, in terms of which objectives can be defined. In accounting this translated into methods for monetizing "the individual person and mak[ing] them accountable by reference to prescribed standards of performance" (Miller & O'Leary, 1987, p. 241). As Miller and O'Leary explained:

---

[3]Few firms implemented all the tenets of scientific management (Edwards, 1979), and Braverman's (1974) account of it has been critiqued over the years, but it's undeniable that scientific management's influence as a rhetoric has been immense. Indeed, the celebrated managment consultant Peter Drucker, in the work in which he introduced the term "management by objectives," suggested that it "may well be the most powerful as well as the most lasting contribution America has made to Western thought since the Federalist Papers" (cited in Braverman, p. 88).

Accounting, in conjunction with other practices, serves to construct a particular field of visibility.... This process of rendering visible alighted on the individual person. More particularly it did so by surrounding the individual at work by a series of norms and standards. Through such norms and standards the inefficiencies of the person were rendered clearly visible. (p. 239)

In the workplace and in education this conception of outputs as the measurable work rendered visible by predefined standards or objectives was tied to shifts in who and where objectives were defined: from workers to managers distant from the site of production (but cf. Burawoy, 1979). Similarly, the key implication of the policy emphasis on outputs in higher education instruction was not any change it entailed in instructional practice (in that teachers have long used objectives), but a shift of power over the definition of objectives—what students need to know and be able to do—to actors outside the university such as employers, the state, or other educational consumers. The university's role is not only to provide instruction but to make it visible to these outside groups in terms that can't be monopolized by higher education.

One way to think about how the demonstrations described in chapter 1 and the accounting systems described in this one were articulated with each other is to see them both as reference systems. Aesthetic reference systems are internal to groups whose members define their identities in terms of the system and claim a monopoly over its use. Accounting reference systems are interpretable and usable by a wider range of groups, in part as a way of making their different activities commensurable—the distinction, perhaps, being one of scale if we think of accounting as a corporate aesthetics. In any event, in the early CMI efforts at Virginia Tech these two systems of reference became complexly intertwined.

Aesthetics

Change ventures that gain impetus as aesthetic projects are guided by attention to the relation of an object or act to some ideal or model of how it should look and work instead of its actual functions, uses, and consequences for some specific system of practice (Bauman, 1984, p. 7; Bourdieu, 1984; Jakobson, 1960, p. 356; Welsch, 1996). In aesthetic development the reference points for products or practices are defined not by potential users (e.g., students) but by other producers whose identities (like those of the developers) depend in some way on the type of object being developed.

This is not to say that developers don't think of users and uses, but that there's an aesthetic element in all professional work (cf. Gagliardi, 1996). We have to make our work visible not only for the people who supposedly need it or might use it, but also for the political and cultural audiences who evaluate its form and appropriateness and ultimately fund it. These latter audiences can be the most influential: Developers' images of uses are shaped or tethered by theory to aesthetics of how a good piece of software should work, what a good objective should look like, what a good web page contains, how information should be presented on a PowerPoint slide, what a good test quiz looks like, and so on.

Within such reference systems demonstrations are performances that make innovations visible and evoke some set of potential uses. Thus as Hakken (2003) explains, "the many technology demonstration projects whose raison d'être has become self-perpetuation. In a nation that tends to see technology as a 'good thing' in itself, such 'demonstration effects' are a real problem with AIT [automated information technologies] projects" (p. 294).

Organizing change around an aesthetic reckoning point helps buffer it from the consequences of early failures, which can be recast as problems of alignment (people using things the wrong way) rather than problems with the aesthetic itself. An aesthetic frame also gives developments (which may not show their effects for a long time) a chance to come to fruition, and thus gives groups time to coalesce around products and practices before they have to be proven in the field. Finally, by allowing development to proceed for long periods without anyone having a clear understanding of what's being accomplished relevant to the imagined target system, an aesthetic component allows people to discover new uses.

Accounting

If aesthetic reference systems are central to the identities of particular groups, accounting systems make the activities of those groups commensurable with those of groups and organizations with different professional aesthetics. What makes good teaching may be defined by instructional aesthetics, but what makes particular versions of teaching, such as those associated with CMI, good state policy depends on how they're transformed into the categories of the state (or more accurately, how they're made visible to administrators in terms of the categories that administrators use to register the heterogeneous domains under their control).

This translation is a critical mechanism for making one's efforts visible to the actors who control needed resources. It also allows one to set up and contrast one's agenda with a foil. Sometimes the foil is simply the past—you make your work visible as superior to previous versions of it. Sometimes the contrast is given an identity of its own—credit for contact— and constructed as the problem to be overcome. Accountability, as this argument suggests, is not simply about aligning work with some set of

standards, it's about making formerly disparate practices commensurate
and comparable, reconstructing the categories in which those practices are
conceptualized, and replacing or undermining an adversary (which may
have been generated or given an identity by the accountability system
itself). The most effective way to do this during the development of CMI
was to appropriate an already existing metric for representing instruction:
financial accounting.

3

Seeing Instruction Through
the Lens of Finance

The major incentive for change within Virginia higher education is money.
——*A Case for Change*, Commonwealth of Virginia Commission
on the University of the 21st Century (1989, p. x)

The technology initiative is the first comprehensive effort to change the cost function of
education.
——Vice-President of Information Systems (1995a, p. 1)

Whatever the motivation for introducing the equipment, the purchase must routinely be
justified in economic terms. But justifications are most often made by people who want
to make the purchase, and if the item is desired enough by the right people, the justifi-
cation will, in the end, reflect their interest.
——Noble (1984, p. 217; cf. Strassmann, 1997, p. 309)

The ability to measure financial performance is itself a social construction.
——Fligstein (1990, p. 298)

The story of how finance came to dominate university decision making
is too complex to treat in depth here (see Rhoades & Slaughter, 1997,
Slaughter & Rhoades, 2004), but some background is required. Simplifying
greatly: In the 1980s the U.S. government began cutting funding for social
programs, shifting responsibilities for social services to the states, and
privatizing formerly public functions. Cuts in federal taxes in the 1980s
moved tax burdens from wealthy to middle- and low-income groups. These
cuts and an economic slowdown generated by tight-money fiscal policies
shrank government revenues at the same time military spending acceler-
ated. The national debt quadrupled between 1980 and 1992 (Phillips,
1993; Sklar, 1995), eating up revenues in interest payments and stoking a
policy hysteria for balancing the budget—which in the United States
meant cutting social programs other than Social Security and Medicare.
Federal contributions to state and local budgets dropped even as federal

mandates required states to expand their roles in funding social programs (Benjamin, 1995; Phillips, p. 132). When the United States moved into a recession in 1989 and 1990, tax revenues in Virginia dropped for the first time since the 1930s whereas costs for Medicaid, K-12 education, and prisons increased (Miller, 1994). As in other states, cutting funding for higher education and other social programs became a way to balance the budget (Benjamin, 1995). A 2% cut in the 1989–1990 general fund budget for higher education was followed by three rounds of 5% reductions between 1990 and 1992. Whereas enrollments continued to rise at state universities (Carlisle, 1991, p. 1), higher education's share of state appropriations dropped from 14.5% in fiscal 1990, to 12% in fiscal 1994 (Hsu, 1995),[1] and did not rebound quickly when the recession ended (Virginia Tech Alumni Association, 1993, p. 3).

The recession didn't cause these cuts. As McSweeney (1996) pointed out, "a crisis—economic or other—is never a crisis in itself" (p. 206). An event or circumstance is "defined as a particular type of crisis in relation to a specific set of beliefs about what characterizes the world" (McSweeney, p. 206). Budget deficits and funding reductions in public programs are political choices, not natural catastrophes. In Virginia, elected officials chose to avoid tax increases (though state residents had a light tax burden compared to residents in surrounding states and to the nation as a whole) to maintain the support of conservative voters and the corporate business community.

Colleges and universities had limited options in this political climate. They responded to the initial funding cuts by shifting costs to students: Median tuition went up 63% from 1990 to 1994 (Hsu, 1995), and financial support for students declined (Mumper, 1996). Whereas tuition paid for 37% of instructional costs at Virginia Tech in 1989, it paid for 51% in 1993 (Miller, 1994, p. 6). During this period, like universities across the country, Tech implemented across-the-board cuts, froze salaries and hirings, slashed operating expenses, and offered retirement incentives. As Slaughter (1998) put it, "universities maintained revenues by increasing user costs, by private-sector investment, and by commercialization" (p. 223).

The state's emphasis on finances increased the concentration of decision-making control (albeit over decreased resources) in the hands of campus administrators. As early as 1989 state reports had urged a "decentralization"

---

[1]Although university leaders usually emphasized the size of the total state drop in higher education appropriations (around 20% over several years), universities have other sources of revenue, and the actual budget losses for particular institutions varied greatly. Between 1990 and 1993 Virginia Tech had a net loss of about $28 million, or 7% of its overall budget ($423 million in 1993).

of state functions that effectively translated into their recentralization at the level of the university:

> The Council of Higher Education and the central agencies of state government should change the way they do business and the way they build higher education budgets. Decentralized, autonomous operations with post-audit accountability, exception reporting, and a clear set of expectations, rewards, and penalties will put administration of higher education firmly in the control of those employed to do it: the presidents and their senior staffs. (Virginia Commission on the University of the 21st Century, 1989, p. 21).

In the early 1990s such recommendations began to be put into practice. Tech administrators defined the state cuts as a productivity problem, and defined productivity in financial terms. An administration planning memo circulated in early 1994 argued:

> The commonwealth of Virginia will continue the gradual privatization of its system of higher education, shifting costs from the taxpayer to students and their parents, though the pace at which this shift occurs will slow during the Allen administration [Allen was Governor of Virginia from 1994 to 1998]....
> Real growth in faculty and staff salaries can be achieved only through growth in productivity (where productivity growth is measured in revenue per employee). For faculty, this means increased productivity in those teaching, research, and outreach activities that increase institutional revenues. ("Assumptions for Phase II Action Plans," p. 1)

FINANCE DISCOURSE

Of course, business rhetoric is nothing new in higher education. Early in the 20th century Veblen (1957 [1918]) suggested that university administrators:

> dilate on the high necessity of a businesslike organization and control of the university, its equipment, personnel and routine. What is had in mind in this insistence on an efficient system is that these corporations of learning shall set their affairs in order after the pattern of a well-conducted business concern. In this view the university is conceived as a business house dealing with merchantable knowledge, placed under the governing hand of a captain of erudition, whose office it is to turn the means in hand to account in the largest feasible output. (p. 62)

What has changed since Veblen's time is the way corporate practitioners and their educational acolytes conceive "the pattern of a well-conducted business concern." The dominant corporations of the early 20th century were vertically integrated, production-oriented enterprises such as automobile manufacturers.

At the end of the century the dominant corporate form was one in which financial profiles rather than product or market were accorded primary importance by managers and analysts (Fligstein, 1990). The story of how this came about is well known. The breakdown of post-World War II international monetary agreements in the late 1960s was followed in the 1970s by international inflation, and then a worldwide recession. At about the same time global financial systems were being deregulated and international markets and financial activities became increasingly mediated by electronic flows of information managed by finance specialists (Martin, 1994). Institutional investors (e.g., pension funds) became increasingly powerful, and corporations increasingly raised capital through bonds or equities (Barnet & Cavanagh, 1994; Lash & Urry, 1994). These developments contributed to a new international business system in which organizations were treated by officials and investors as if things like assets, debts, cash flows, stock profiles, and the like, taken together, "sum[med] up all that is important to know about any given firm" (Fligstein & Freeland, 1995, p. 34; see also Barnet & Cavanagh; Lash & Urry; Martin; Strange, 1994). Financialization was thus both a strategy for making the organization visible and a tool for controlling it.

The use of this tool to compare and evaluate vastly different kinds of firms within the corporate sector laid the groundwork for similar uses in nonprofits like universities. Financial metrics became increasingly important as state funding dwindled and became less predictable, as corporate "benchmarking" consultants gained influence (Larner & Le Heron, 2002, p. 763), and as market-oriented educational policy was "borrowed" (Halpin & Troyna, 1995) back and forth between Britain and the United States.[2] Slaughter (1998), for example, noted that university administrators making cutbacks in the 1980s and 1990s:

> used a rhetoric similar to that of corporate CEOs, a rhetoric that stressed crises, the need for tough decisions, increased productivity, and maintenance of competitiveness. This was the rhetoric of the private sector, of markets, a rhetoric that privileged fields such as business and management, engineering and computer and information sciences, fields that were popularly associated with potential for market growth and rescue from recession. (p. 271)

---

[2]Thus between 1993 and 2001, and without explicit reference to the document, Virginia Tech implemented almost all of the following ideas articulated in the 1985 Jarratt report in Great Britain, which "recommended that, as part of the process of re-inventing themselves as enterprises, university faculties be broken up into private sector-style 'cost centres' and that they be managed through 'the centralisation of executive control, the linkage between budgetary and academic considerations, and the decentralization of accountable budgets to the lowest level'" (Shore & Wright, 2000, pp. 67–68). It is quite possible that none of the administrators involved in the decisions at Tech knew of the Jarratt report.

Tying CMI to this widening discourse of financialization was in part a matter of imitation. Administrators follow other administrators, especially those in organizations like one's own and organizations that seem to be more successful or politically favored (Dimaggio & Powell, 1983). When I asked TW, the director of Tech's Center on Excellence in Undergraduate Teaching (CEUT), where the push for "technology as a solution to teaching reform" came from, he replied in 1999:

> It's a national movement.... It seems to me the vice presidents of Information Systems at Tech have been influential. Erv Blythe, and the guy before him who ended up being the president of Educom ... Bob Heterick. So there's a lot of folks who have their fingers on the pulse of what's happening around. And I think a lot of what we're driving to do is, is motivated by a fear of being left out, left behind. And, also just the need to shift from a mainframe-based system to more of a distributed system. And I think a lot of the early stuff had goals that were way beyond instruction. It was just, you know, life really has changed dramatically in the past 8 years here–with respect to the access to technology and the way we work day to day. So, gradually, as those needs were satisfied, then people began thinking about instruction ... more programming related to instruction, more emphasis on doing web pages, and then distance education starts to creep in. And the idea of how the university is going to market itself, the share we're going to have of that emerging market. And I sense that there is a real fear that if we aren't there, that something really bad is going to happen, in spite of the fact that we're a largely residential campus, and plan to be that way for the next number of years.

Such mimicry is a consecrated managerial strategy. As one leading consulting firm put it in recommendations to universities regarding Instructional Technologies and CMI:

> At the end of many hours of discussion and frank assessments of the industry's [higher education's] present condition, participants in the first annual Coopers and Lybrand Learning Partnership Roundtable on the Transformation of Higher Education in the Digital Age reached the conclusion that major change was inevitable. Those institutions that do not envision the future and their unique role in it do so at their own peril.... Absent simple answers, what can be done to develop a strategy?... Our advice? Forget traditional strategic planning processes, adopt best practices from other industries, expect some failures, and above all, strive to build core competencies for a new future. (Kidwell, 1997, pp. 1–2)[3]

Adopting best practices from other industries requires some mechanism of commensuration to allow university practices to be compared to those of

---

[3]Coopers and Lybrand later merged into PriceWaterhouseCoopers, a global "professional services company" heavily involved in promoting CMI in higher education.

government bureaucracies or for-profit corporations. As the measurable, synoptic representations par excellence, financial terms were efficient tools for this task (Espeland & Stevens, 1998, pp. 314–315). The result was that during the 1990s universities, as Strathern (1997) put it, "were re-invented as financial bodies" (p. 309) and descriptions of educational practices were increasingly embedded in phrases held together by finance-related terms such as "'performance,' 'quality assurance,' 'discipline,' 'accreditation,' 'accountability,' 'transparency,' 'efficiency,' 'effectiveness,' 'value for money,' 'responsibility,' 'benchmarking,' 'good practice,' 'peer review,' 'external verification,' 'stakeholder,' and 'empowerment'" (Shore & Wright, 2000, p. 60).

These kinds of categories allowed administrators to represent university functions in ways that made them easier to oversee and compare (Scott, 1998, p. 11; Slaughter & Leslie, 2001). A "finance perspective," as Fligstein (1990) called it, involves "ruthlessly evaluating" the contributions of organizational units to the larger firm's profits and goals, investing further in those that are profitable, disinvesting in the others (Fligstein, pp. 238–239; Espeland & Stevens, 1998, p. 338).

As we'll see, this mimicry of finance approaches is not necessarily voluntary: The state also "coercively" (Dimaggio & Powell, 1983) induces subordinate organizations to adopt practices by creating a context where, as Clegg (1990) put it: "if agencies want certain resources then they will have to do certain things, adopt certain practices" (p. 228). I'll add this qualification: What is copied in these cases may be ways of representing practice rather than the practices themselves. McSweeney (1996), for example, argued that the migration of corporate finance categories from private to public (including university) sectors in Great Britain amounted less to the borrowing of corporate practices than to a mimicry of a "theoretical model" (p. 210), a process variously described as "conceptual inflation" (Shore & Wright, 2000, p. 59) or as a "domaining effect" (Strathern, 1992) "whereby the conceptual logic of an idea associated with one domain is transposed into another, often with unanticipated outcomes" (Shore & Wright, p. 20; but see Vidovich & Slee, 2001). In other words, what are imitated or transposed across domains are ways of accounting for practice.

HARD TIMES AND RESCALING

Take all that as a hasty and incomplete account of how finance-based arguments came to dominate the pallet of instructional accounting. The meshing of such arguments with CMI was not new. The inventor of the first modern "teaching machine" considered it as much an economic as an educational innovation and looked sanguinely to the troubles of his era, the Great Depression of the 1930s, to boost its prospects: "Education is the one major activity in this country which is still in a crude handicraft stage. But the economic depression may here work beneficially, in that it may force the consideration of efficiency and the need for labor saving devices in education" (Pressey, 1960 [1932], p. 51)[4]

Whereas Pressey thought that economic constraints would make teaching machines more attractive to resistant educators, the education funding cuts of the early 1990s found policymakers in Virginia already predisposed to embrace them. Years before the 1990–1992 recession, Gordon Davies (1986), the head of Virginia's SCHEV, attacked what he called "the ideology of access": the idea that state universities should be comprehensive, autonomous sites of instruction. Like Pressey (1960), he looked to an economic downturn to foster change:

> The ideology of access has led institutions and their patrons to expect that virtually every academic program should be offered within commuting distance in each region of the state. Against the pressures that result from this expectation, state boards often can only stall, delaying the inevitable on the chance that something–a state budget crisis, for instance–will cause the pressure to subside. (Davies, 1986, p. 93; cf. Davies, 1997, for an expanded version of this argument)

Echoing instructional television's early centralization agenda (Goldfarb, 2002; Stoddard, 1957), the argument against access envisioned an educational geography in which decisions about curricula would be centralized at the scale of the state. Instead of each university functioning as a self-contained curricular universe, each would specialize in certain fields and provide programs in those areas across the state. State education officials in the early 1990s saw CMI as the way to make such a scheme feasible. Erv Blythe, who succeeded Heterick as Tech's Vice President for Information Systems, recalled that he was asked around this time by someone at SCHEV for an example of a computer-networked class at Tech. When he responded by describing an English course (one of a handful developed with a Sloan Foundation grant in the early 1990s), the SCHEV official's response was:

> They said, "But this is the reason the state ought to be directing that. Virginia Tech shouldn't be developing an English course on the internet. That ought to be UVA [University of Virginia]. Virginia Tech ought to be doing, you know, Engineering Mechanics or a Statics course or a Dynamics course." ... It's sort of like, to me it's the old Royal Licensing idea. That you get a license to do Dynamics [laughs].

---

[4]Metaphors for contrasting CMI to older instructional formats (e.g., CMI is to face-to-face instruction as film is to theater) are impressively stabile. Pressey's (1960 [1932]) sneer about "handicraft" modes of teaching was still being used by CMI advocates 70 years later: "U.S. higher education remains what Bill Massy and Bob Zemsky have called a 'handicraft' industry in which the vast majority of courses are developed and delivered as 'one-ofs' [sic] by individual professors." (Twigg, 2002, p. 89).

Technology was to make this licensing scheme possible through its imagined capacity to overcome distance cheaply by capitalizing instruction.

CMI AS THE CAPITALIZATION OF INSTRUCTION

At the end of chapter 1 I mentioned a conference organized by JM where faculty were demonstrating their early CMI work to top administrators. JM explained the context for that conference:

> This is now August of '92. Within a month after that, we started to look at how could we broaden this program of helping faculty start looking at technology in a more programmatic, systematic way. And in the fall of '92 commenced the initial sketches of how a universal, across-the-university faculty development program would be put together, how would it work, what would it cost, how would you finance it, et cetera.

The reference here is to Tech's Faculty Development Initiative or FDI. When Blythe succeeded Heterick as Vice President for Information Systems in the early 1990s, one of his early projects was to equalize faculty access to computer equipment (to make sure it didn't all go to, say, engineering—unequal access remains a common problem in U.S. universities; cf. Lewis, Massey, & Smith, 2001, p. 130). Instead of just stuffing new computers into offices, however, the idea was to train faculty members in their use: To get the computers, professors would have to go through workshops (the FDI) that would introduce softwares, technological capabilities, and in later years provide exemplars of good instructional practice and design.

Blythe recounted that the FDI idea was already being mapped out within the Educational Technologies unit in late 1992 when it came up in a conversation about budget requests with staff from an Appropriations Committee of the Virginia legislature:

> I was talking about some networking thing; and they said, "What are you thinking about these days, where are you spending your time?" And I started talking about ... faculty access to technology issue, and talked about this program we were talking about. We had no idea how we were going to finance it.... And out of the blue, in December, this individual called me and said, ... "We would like to fund a pilot project for about X-dollars.... If you could get to us by tomorrow, a proposal ... we will put it in the hopper and see what happens." ... We got that in the next day, and then ... they called me up in March and said, "Hey, by the way, we funded your pilot program."

As noted earlier, this was a period in which the legislature was cutting higher education appropriations. As JM explained, getting this new funding depended on the implicit assumption held by some legislators that money for technology now would save the state money in the future:

Remember on your time line, the university is going through massive budget cuts right now, and restructuring calls are in the air. And we're out here suggesting we reallocate, reinvest in teaching. And there are people saying you use technology to save money. We do not answer that directly. We just keep going. Because we were quite certain that you would not save money. Not maybe ever, but certainly not in the short term. [JN: Can I interrupt? Who was saying that you use it to save money?]. That was coming out of Richmond [the state capitol].

As Blythe explained, he and the higher education supporters in the legislature never claimed that the plan would actually save money, although they were aware that some legislators supported it on that assumption:

[The] reasoning [of some legislators] was that if we can capitalize the cost [of instruction], we can turn what's currently a huge annual operating cost burden into a capital cost.... There were people who voted for that [reason]. Voted because they were thinking, this is about capitalizing the cost of education. They were looking for a way to spend less over the long run.[5]

Besides providing a snapshot of the origins of one of Tech's signature CMI programs—the FDI—this episode shows how a finance perspective rests on more than simple calculative rationality. Finance is also a rhetoric of justification for advocating lines of action in domains that are new to or poorly understood by participating actors. It reduces strangeness by translating situations into calculable terms, regardless of whether decision makers actually possess or understand the evidence needed for such calculations. Administrators can claim that spending money will save money in the long run, justify program cuts with claims of financial exigency, as in the case described here bank on digital technology's aura of fiscal efficiency to mobilize support. None of this need be (or in some cases could be) supported with evidence. As Blythe explained:

We never presented it that way [as a cost-saving measure], and the people who actually called us and asked us to put it together didn't see it that way. They believed, genuinely, that we needed to spend more, not less money on education. But ... they also knew that at that particular time, they would not be successful in spending more for education if it looked like the same formula, you know—that you could get more in something new, but you couldn't get something additional in along the old paths.

---

[5]These legislators may also have been looking beyond cost savings: Capitalizing instruction is a first step toward disaggregating teaching from research and would give the state more influence—at the expense of faculty members and their institutions—over which is to be emphasized and how it is to be pursued.

This strategy of surfing over the misconceptions of the budget cutters and instructional capitalizers to get support for new higher education projects was obviously effective, but it arguably invited a kind of policy blowback. That is, whereas the people close to CMI development may have been less than sanguine about its money-saving potential, national advocates (e.g., Twigg, 1996b; and Blythe's predecessor at Tech, Heterick, 1995), along with the key people shaping state and university policy, employed that rhetoric to mount attacks on traditional approaches to instruction and thereby place new pressures on university funding. A SCHEV report circulated in draft form in the fall of 1992 and officially issued in January 1993 (i.e., during the period when the FDI funding described previously was being cultivated) portrays CMI as a money saver that enables faculty to teach more students:

> Conversations with people around the state, with legislators, students, parents, interested citizens, and faculty themselves, indicate that some faculty, particularly at major universities, should teach more. But much more pressing is the need for faculty in general to extend the reach of their teaching to include more students. This can be accomplished without loss of quality only by re-conceiving the entire enterprise: by teaching differently, by using faculty time differently, and by taking advantage of modern technology. (SCHEV, 1993, p. 6)

A month later, in February 1993, a policy memorandum from Tech's Provost and Academic Deans called for using digital technologies to accomplish "structural changes" in the university:

> There is clear evidence in ... state-level reports that policy makers expect technology to be deployed not only to enhance student learning but also to increase faculty productivity. Other sectors of the economy are moving quickly to restructure their organizations and to make much needed productivity gains. Higher education is under considerable pressure to do so as well. (Provost and Council of Deans, 1993, p. 2)

The assumptions and terms articulated in Tech's 1989 report (University Task Force, 1989) thus passed through the bowels of state policy to reemerge as administrative dicta at Tech, invoked to justify internal reallocation decisions, specifically investments in CMI.

ADMINISTRATION BY SURFACING

Digesting teaching and learning into financial terms makes them more transparent to administrators (e.g., Tapscott & Ticoll, 2003) by substituting narrowly defined indices for complex, context-dependent processes (Strathern, 2000b; cf. also Scott, 1998). But to the extent that such indices leave out critical aspects of instruction, reliance on them involves what

Whitehead (1967) called the fallacy of misplaced concreteness, "mistaking the abstract for the concrete" (p. 51). Whitehead continued, "The disadvantage of exclusive attention to a group of abstractions, however well-founded, is that, by the nature of the case, you have abstracted from the remainder of things. In so far as the excluded things are important in your experience, your modes of thought are not fitted to deal with them" (p. 59).

Such exclusions produce administrative pictures that define the terms one can use to talk about a thing in public. The focus becomes secondary measures of a system's activity—grade averages, for example, or the marginal cost of teaching students in a given format. As in auditing practice the surfaces rather than the activities they stand for become the units of public account. Power (1994) explained:

> Audits generally act indirectly upon systems of control rather than directly upon first order activities.... What is being assured is the quality of control systems rather than the quality of first order operations. In such a context accountability is discharged by demonstrating the existence of such systems of control, not by demonstrating good teaching, caring, manufacturing or banking.... What is audited is whether there is a system which embodies standards and the standards of performance themselves are shaped by the need to be auditable. In this way, the existence of a system is more significant for audit purposes than what the system is; audit becomes a formal "loop" by which the system observes itself. (pp. 19, 36–37)

Instead of close surveillance (Foucault, 1979) or a Taylorist regulation of instructional practice (Noble, 2001), high administrators really don't want to know how professors teach or students learn. They want statements that can be reported to governing boards and disseminated in newspapers and promotional literatures. To take one example, a National Governors Association report offered the following evidence for CMI's value in "upgrading" professors to "add value" to their universities (cf. Miller & O'Leary, 1987):

> Given the demographics of the existing postsecondary teaching workforce, such state investments in instructor upgrades may be increasingly necessary. A development program in Virginia showed that professors could even become better instructors in traditional classrooms after they have taught a distance learning course. Faculties were provided with special training and the assistance of an instructional designer prior to teaching the distance learning course. They received training in pedagogical techniques and in the use of instructional technology, as well as a curriculum design specialist's complete review of the material to be covered by the course. Assessment results showed that when such faculty returned to teaching in traditional classrooms, their student course evaluations improved. (National Governors Association, 2001, p. 15)

Student course evaluations don't tell one anything about teaching or learning. Whatever changes in them might mean, they are not proof of more or better learning. They are, however, convenient tools for comparing courses or suggesting changes in them over time.

The progress of change efforts depends on the success people have in using such systems of accounting to make their products look worthwhile. Many CMI innovators have done this effectively—framing themselves in financial terms, surfing over misconceptions about cost savings, and justifying technologies in terms of their effects on traditional accounts of instruction like course grades. The downside, of course, is that anything not registered by the accounting system remains outside the picture—and this would include most of what professors and students do.

4

Public Appearances

The American's conception of the teacher who faces him is: he sells me his knowledge and his methods for my father's money, just as the greengrocer sells my mother cabbage. And that is all.

> —Weber (1946, p. 149)

To maximize the economics of scale, we will create on-line, high enrollment, core curriculum courses which will affect thousands of students each semester both on and off campus.

> —Vice President of Information Systems (1995b, p. 1)

But why should Tech administrators and higher education policymakers have been so concerned with teaching? Research universities, after all, give priority to research, and the budget crises of the early 1990s should have intensified this emphasis. Across the United States administrators were breaking universities into individuated units and shifting resources toward those with the most potential for financial returns (Reed & Deem, 2002).[1] Slaughter (1998) explained:

> Leaders of public research universities developed supply-side policies of internal resource allocation.... First, they moved state dollars to fields of study and departments that were close to corporate, research and high-end professional markets in the larger society; second, state resources were very often concentrated on departments that were already highly funded; third,

---

[1]Some institutions adopted revenue-based budgeting systems in which departments or schools are treated as profit centers and must calculate their revenue (some percentage of the tuition of majors and enrollees in courses, plus grants and contracts minus overhead) and costs (salaries, building rent, equipment, etc.). Decisions about programs and personnel are based on the surplus or deficits the departments produce (Hess, 1999; see Wilson, 2001, for a variant in which departments are taxed and then compete for funds to be centrally redistributed). Paulsen and St. John (2002) discussed "incentive" budgeting in relation to university teaching; Lasher and Sullivan (2004) provided an overview of higher education budgeting.

resource dispersion among departments increased, with the rich getting richer, as it were, and the poor, poorer. (p. 225)

Slaughter (1998) showed that when "faced with losses in state revenues, public research universities moved expenditures away from instruction and toward research and administration" (p. 223).[2] Departments that brought in a lot of external funding received more resources than departments that taught lots of students but acquired less external funding (Slaughter, p. 230). According to Slaughter, "fields of study and departments regarded as close to the market flourished, while other languished. These resource allocation policies increased differentiation and stratification within public research universities" (p. 210).[3]

The reason this scenario didn't take hold immediately at Tech–although it would eventually—is that there are political as well as financial markets, and the two aren't always well synchronized. In early 1990s Virginia, simply shifting resources and administrative emphases to research was problematic. The large tuition increases that university administrators had used to buffer the effects of early state budget cuts came on top of a decade of conservative attacks on higher education's supposedly declining standards, too liberal professors, and too easy courses (e.g., Anderson, 1992; Bloom, 1987; Geiger, 2004, pp. 94–96; Huber, 1992; Lauter, 1995; Tierney & Rhoads, 1995). The result was intense political scrutiny that mutated into public criticism. In late 1993 a consortium of 27 newspapers across Virginia simultaneously published a 5-day, front-page series titled "A College Education: At What Cost?" Among other things, the series attacked the state's universities for allowing professors to spend their time doing research in tenured luxury while teaching only two or three courses per term:

---

[2]Decreasing funding for teaching-intensive areas doesn't mean that administrators dislike large courses, it may mean that they're using cheaper forms of instructors–hiring adjuncts, for example, or reducing the number of graduate assistants allocated to such courses. Hess (1999) pointed to another scenario in universities using revenue-based budgeting, where "profitable" professors—those who teach large numbers of students—"are very desirable ... if they leave, a replacement for them can be justified based on the teaching revenues they generate, and that replacement can come in at a less expensive junior level" (p. 29).

[3]The ability of the organizational unit to describe itself in financial terms becomes crucial in such a milieu. At Virginia Tech, when the College of Engineering was asked to prepare for a potential 5% budget cut in 1995 (tuition increases for out-of-state students, who accounted for almost 40% of Engineering's student body, had begun to produce a sharp drop in their enrollment numbers; Blake, 1995; Slaughter, 1993, pp. 272–273), the college responded with a report showing that it returned $9 million to the university (through tuition and research overhead): "If it turns out the engineering college is earning for the university, 'it could be a very significant factor in allocating resources in the future,' [the president of Virginia Tech] said (Blake, p. D7).

Professors from at least four Virginia universities [including Virginia Tech] spend less time in the classroom every week than most people spend in their office every day, an analysis of faculty schedules shows.... Considering classroom time alone, this means the typical UVa [University of Virginia] faculty member ... gets more than $300 for every hour in the lecture hall. "Good Lord!" said Gov. Douglas Wilder. "The pure data does surprise me.... This is it?" (Walzer, 1993, pp. A1, A6)

That same month, Representative Rick Boucher, the U.S. house member for the Southwestern Virginia district where Tech's main campus is located, and at the time Chairperson of the Subcommittee on Science of the House of Representatives Committee on Science, Space, and Technology,[4] published an opinion piece in *The Chronicle of Higher Education*, a national higher education periodical, that criticized universities for neglecting undergraduate teaching:

Universities must define a new mission that maximizes their contributions to society. They must respond to the challenge to do more with less–to operate more efficiently during times of constrained budgets and to select what they wish to be in this era when they may no longer enjoy the luxury of being all things to all people. Universities must identify their comparative advantages and focus on what each one does best. Above all, universities must reaffirm– by action, not by rhetoric–that education is their primary mission. A report from the President's Council of Advisors on Science and Technology notes that "many higher education institutions ... are turning away from their education mission, particularly undergraduate education. Universities should reemphasize teaching in all its aspects, both inside and outside the classroom. In doing so, many institutions will have to curtail some of their research activities." (Boucher, 1993, p. B1)

Such criticisms were used by legislators and others to argue for further reductions in funding: "State officials, hearing about little-used programs and teachers who don't teach, say colleges can do more with less" (Intress, 1993, pp. A1, A5). Teaching, in short, had become a public relations problem for university administrators: It was visible, but in the wrong ways.

One response was to change its appearance. The 1993 planning document for Tech's CEUT, for example, emphasized the need for a big sign that people could see as they drove through campus:

Teaching must be valued and rewarded if higher education is going to survive the crisis of confidence so prominent in the mass media. The public in

---

[4]Boucher's committee chairmanship at the time gave him considerable influence over CMI-relevant issues. Earlier in 1993 he had introduced legislation, shaped through lobbying by the major higher education CMI consortium EDUCOM, to create a "National Information Infrastructure" (DeLoughry, 1993b, p. A15).

general and state legislatures in particular are anxious to know that teaching is given high priority on campuses receiving public assistance.... The symbolic importance of CEUT must not be underestimated. Visitors to the campus may know nothing more than the fact that physical space on campus had been reserved for a center devoted to teaching, but a prominent sign indicating the existence of such an office sends an important message.[5] (Committee to Plan the Center for Excellence in Undergraduate Education, 1993, p. 5)

In early 1995 Virginia Tech's president, Paul Torgersen, unveiled "The Virginia Tech Pledge," passing out copies printed on vellum paper to faculty assembled at a campus meeting. The Pledge declared:

As a land grant university, Virginia Polytechnic Institute and State University has three missions: teaching, research, and public service. None is more important than the instruction of undergraduate students. Few of life's experiences are more fulfilling or rewarding than one's undergraduate years. We hope to add further satisfaction and value to a Virginia Tech undergraduate education with this pledge of quality and constancy. Therefore, with an underlying love of learning and education, the faculty, administration, and staff of Virginia Tech give this commitment to all students. (Torgersen, 1995, p. 1)

Parents and policymakers were promised, among other things, that costs and tuition increases would be controlled "through effective teaching, the application of information technology ... and administrative efficiencies," that "undergraduate lecture classes will be taught by full-time faculty, with few exceptions," and that "our most distinguished faculty will teach undergraduate courses".

Finally, SCHEV itself took a prominent seat on the PR bandwagon, proclaiming in a 1996 policy paper that:

Of this much we are sure: the citizens of Virginia want to know that they and their children have access to the best faculty available. They want to know that, except in rare instances, faculty teach. They will not support institutions in which the teaching is done by graduate students or part-timers while the full-time faculty is off doing something else. (Commission on the Future of Higher Education in Virginia, 1996, p. 9)

According to CEUT director TW, such pronouncements helped convince faculty members that university administrators were making a genuine commitment to improving undergraduate instruction:

---

[5]CEUT evolved into much more than a sign. I merely point here to some of the thinking behind its creation.

It seemed that we saw increasing pressure on the undergraduate mission and what it was accomplishing, and support for that part of the mission.... And maybe that says something in itself that, you know, in a crisis mode you can do things that maybe you couldn't get done at other times.... There are a lot of things happening at about that time. I mean, it would be impossible for anyone to escape the idea that something big was going on that essentially moved the emphasis, maybe not from research, but at least pumping up the possibility for considering instruction as an important thing folks did. And the idea that there were real resources put behind it.

But if giving teaching a high public profile helped defend higher education from accusations of unresponsiveness to students, it carried its own political liabilities. Here I draw on Hawkins' (1979) observation that American universities developed two contrasting rhetorics of justification in the late 19th and early 20th centuries. One, in response to complaints that universities were elitist organizations squandering public monies, stressed their teaching function: "To the challenge for justification of the privileges claimed by universities in a democratic society, 'we teach' was perhaps the principal response" (Hawkins, 1979, p. 301). The other rhetoric, in response to competition from other knowledge-producing organizations (e.g., private corporations), stressed the universities' contributions to research (Gittell & Sedgley, 2000). The problem in Virginia, at least for a brief period in the 1990s, was that attacks requiring the "we teach" response–coupled with budget reductions and downsizings–were coming to bear at the same time as the corporatization of research and changes in intellectual property rights were requiring universities to reemphasize their roles as research-generating institutions aligned with external markets (e.g., Lee, Green, & Brennan, 2000, p. 117; Usher & Edwards, 2000, p. 264). As Hawkins suggested, the "we teach" response is politically treacherous in such circumstances:

To the extent that university spokesmen emphasized teaching in response to challengers, they subtly undermined those who made the creation of knowledge a defining characteristic of universities and whose primary allegiance was to research. If the university rested its case before society solely on its role as teacher, then by implication other institutions might as well control the search for new truth. (Hawkins, 1979, pp. 297, 301–302)[6]

---

[6]One can see the oscillation between these defenses of state higher education in the fact that by the end of the 1990s, as the state economy expanded and tuition freezes depressed the price of Virginia Tech in relation to comparable institutions, President Torgersen's "Virginia Tech Pledge" disappeared from the university web site. In contrast to the emphasis on teaching in the pledge, the university's 2001 strategic plan emphasized the need for acquiring contract and grant monies, and addressed instructional issues almost entirely in terms of online, distance education.

Too obvious an emphasis on research, then, could make the university look like an egghead palace abdicating instructional responsibilities, but too heavy an emphasis on teaching undercut the university's claims to be a patent-generating vanguard of economic progress. CMI seemed to offer a solution to this quandary: If one could do it cheaply enough and with large enough groups of students it would boost instructional productivity while leaving professors more time for research.

COSTING

Looking affordable depends a lot on how you do the accounting. Costs, like other financial representations, are constructed measures (Hopwood, 1987). Speaking of the interactive video project described in chapter 1, JM recalled that inexpensiveness was a key theme of the early demonstrations: "The salient thing was to be able to do it cheap. We were doing the whole thing for like $2,000. And everybody else at that time was spending $10,000. That alone got us a lot of conference presentations. We were the evangelists of cheap and we went all over the place doing that."

This figure of $2,000 leaves out the cost of faculty time. As MS explained (and duly noted in technical publications, e.g., MS, 1985), he had put "hundreds and hundreds of hours of work to produce this one lesson, in effect.... The bottom line on that project was that I think we spent about— we, JM and I—spent about 500 hours of time to produce half an hour of instruction."

This exclusion of faculty work from cost reckonings was not unusual. The university's official evaluation of an early, Sloan Foundation-funded effort to create online courses came up with the figure of $16,500 (mainly wages for a manager, technician, and programmer) as the cost of putting a large microbiology course online. The time devoted to the project by the professor, who was cited as claiming it would have taken 5 years to do the work alone, was left out on the grounds that "economists would not factor his [the professor's] salary into the equation since this [putting the course online] would be considered part of his 'normal working duties,'" a common argument professors have since begun to resist (e.g., Carnevale, 2004b). In this the evaluations explicitly framed the argument for a corporate audience, emphasizing Tech's labor pool and technical infrastructure for faculty training:

> Analysts from the corporate world would note that the total cost is quite low for a project of this magnitude. The low costs result from the availability of a skilled labor pool (primarily graduate assistants, including the production technician who was paid as a wage employee), the exclusion of software and hardware (owned by Educational Technologies), and the pre-existence of a powerful and robust network infrastructure, which the university has

constructed over the years. Also excluded was the cost of faculty training (the Faculty Development Institute, or FDI), which provided the initial opportunity to develop the project. (Taylor, Moore, & Roy, 1997, p. 5)

But if making instruction visible as a cost was relatively simple (especially when the cost of the professor is deleted) this is only half of the necessary calculation. CMI, cheap or not, makes fiscal sense only if it lowers teaching costs per student, something that usually means increasing the ratio of students to faculty.

BIG PEDAGOGY

Bigger courses are by definition more productive than small ones—that is, they process more students with fewer faculty, thus saving the university money and boosting departmental productivity statistics. Big courses make it possible for a select group of professors to teach smaller courses and devote more time to research and writing.[7] And their (usually) harsh grading regimes make them useful for weeding out or winnowing the number of aspirants in oversubscribed subjects. For such reasons big courses have been used in U.S. universities for a very long time. The educational historian Rudolph (1977), for example, asked, "What possibly could have been achieved with such enrollments as these at Harvard in 1903 that might not better have been accomplished by chaining students to their desks: Economics I (529), Government I (376), Geology 4 (439), and History I (409)" (pp. 232–233).

A hundred years later Virginia Tech offered hundreds of these jumbo courses. According to one account there were "as many as 50 classes each year with at least 300 students, 140 classes of 150 to 300 students and 170 classes of 100 to 150 students" (Zack, 1998, pp. B1, B3). Although some critics (e.g., Perley, 1999) were predicting that CMI would lead to the creation of such huge courses (and this was indeed a stated aim, as one of the quotes at the head of this chapter indicates), at Tech it actually gained impetus as a strategy for dealing with problems created by big courses that already existed. For example, it seemed that whereas students in such courses were receptive to the idea of instruction as an exchange reducible to financial indices, their professors were unsettled by the decline in deference attending such a relationship. According to one newspaper account:

Many professors say they are convinced there has been a loss of civility at the state's largest university [Virginia Tech] for reasons they don't fully

---

[7]Some professors enjoy teaching very large classes (Bartlett, 2003; Stanley & Porter, 2002) and in some such classes students attend and are attentive. Good studies are lacking of how students learn in such classes.

understand. "In terms of lack of respect, in terms of disruptive acts in class and those sorts of things, I think it's considerably worse than it was 10 years ago," said biology professor Jack Cranford, chairman of what's been dubbed the Climate Committee. "It's in the larger classes in the lower levels." "Students are almost demanding instead of asking and being polite," Cranford said. "It's: 'You're here to serve me. I'm paying my way, and you've got to do your job.'" ... When Tech professors invited students to talk about rudeness in class, some were as surprised by the response as they were appalled at the behavior. "I'm paying for it. Why should I go to class if I don't want to," said Steve Schneider, a fourth year student from Fairfax who also happens to be president of the Student Government Association. (Zack, 1997a, pp. A1, A2; cf. Bartlett, 2004)

At the same time, some students were apparently upset with the low or failing grades common in these courses. Administrators had a list of what they called:

killer courses ... where there were so many students who were failing. Ah, another area that we looked at was when there seemed to be a problem with retention rates. Ah, another was if there were these large lecture sections and it just appeared that there were very few people who seemed to be performing well at all–not necessarily failing, but, you know, one A and all Cs.

The speaker quoted here is AM, the same AM mentioned in chapter 2 as the state official instrumental in importing language on CMI from Tech's 1989 report into state policy discourse. After serving from 1991 to 1995 as SCHEV's. Associate Director for Legislative and External Relations, AM came to Tech as Associate Vice President for Learning Technologies and Director of Information Technology Initiatives, and in that role headed the University's Center for Innovation in Learning (CIL), a unit set up in 1996 to provide and administer funds for CMI-based course transformations targeting these high-enrollment, killer, core courses. As AM recounted:

It seemed plain, in the first year, then, that what we ought to do was offer faculty the opportunity to integrate technology with high-demand core curriculum courses, because that's where the majority of our students were.... [The grants] were mainly invitational. Because when we sent out the RFP people seemed not to know what to do with the RFP. And so, with [the then-Dean of the College of Arts and Sciences'] help, we focused on where the high-demand core curriculum courses were that he knew people were struggling with, and, and, you know ... large lecture courses where people were struggling with having the kind of learning results they wanted. So that's the way we sort of identified the first people we asked to submit proposals.... The second year, we decided that we still needed to focus on high-demand core curriculum courses, but by that time it was clear that there were high-demand upper level courses where there were still large lecture sections and students not being served very well and that we thought might benefit from a little work in this arena.

"In some cases," AM explained, "high demand would be 500 students in a lecture section, in another it would be 200. Usually it's above 100." By this standard, then, Virginia Tech had a lot of high-demand courses.

As already noted, the ability to teach a lot for less, or more for the same, is a critical justification for CMI. As early as the 1950s, Ford Foundation planners had argued that instructional television would make it possible to teach elementary school classes of 175 students and secondary school classes with 200 to 500 students (Stoddard, 1957). By the end of the century, distance learning industry groups were forecasting online courses with enrollments of thousands (Carnevale, 1999b). With jumbo courses already standard in higher education, by the 1990s Educom Vice President Caroll Twigg (1995, 1996a) was advocating a "1% strategy." Claiming that as few as 25 courses—1% of the total number offered—accounted for as much as 44% of a university's total enrollment, Twigg argued:

> It is difficult to change an entire institution, an entire culture. But if we decide to increase the learning productivity of not 2,000 courses but of a mere 25—approximately one percent of the total—we can make a substantial contribution to controlling institutional costs. Should our institutions develop a strategy for helping "the faculty" or for helping the faculty in those 25 courses who teach 44 percent of the students? Should we have a strategy for acquiring multimedia materials for all courses regardless of student enrollment or for the 25 courses? Should we be thinking about redesigning all courses by integrating technology and new pedagogical techniques or should we think about reengineering 25 courses to produce the most effective learning experiences possible for students? (Twigg, 1996a, p. 6)

Twigg's (1996a) numbers, based on a study of one Florida community college, quickly became corporate dogma. Without citing a source, Kidwell (1997, writing for Coopers and Lybrand) claimed that "the creation of a mere 25 courses would serve an estimated 80% of total undergraduate enrollment in core undergraduate courses" (p. 2) and Means (2000, at PriceWaterhouse) asserted that "25 to 30 courses constitute more than 80% of undergraduate education" (p. 2). Gordon Davies (2004), a senior advisor to the Education Commission of the States (and earlier AM's boss as Executive Director of SCHEV), advanced the similar if less grandiose claim (echoing his earlier quoted critique of access) that:

> More than half of all college freshmen and sophomores are enrolled in the same 25 or 30 courses, like introductory math, English, and psychology. Individual colleges or entire systems should standardize those courses—their design, teaching, tutoring, and student assessment—freeing faculty members to serve as mentors and advisors. (p. B20)

CENTRALIZING TRANSFORMATIONS

As Davies' (2004) comments make clear, whether or not 1% is a reliable figure, the strategy of focusing CMI on big, lower division courses meshes with the idea of standardizing and centralizing its development. From an administrative standpoint, knowledge of instructional technologies that develops through the efforts of individual innovators is scattered, ad hoc, geared to idiosyncratic needs and interests, and hence not easily shared or duplicated across the university. Authors writing in publications of the Educause consortium (e.g., Barone, 2000) referred to this as a "boutique" or "Lone Ranger" approach: Each project is unique and uses nonstandardized courseware or tools created or customized for the particular situation (as in the case of the interactive video project described earlier). Such efforts "do not scale and are not sustainable because each is dependent on its creator" (Barone, 2000, p. 3). Although not rejected outright, Lone Ranger approaches are considered insufficient as an organizational strategy: Self-motivated, entrepreneurial faculty may do well on their own, but most professors are risk aversives (Barone, 2000; see also Bates, 2001, pp. 72–74; Bates & Poole, 2003; Olsen, 1999a, p. A65; Young, 1999) who, left alone, will keep doing the same old stuff. Without using this terminology, administrators at Virginia Tech shared the belief that some central coordination of CMI efforts was needed. As JM recalled, by the mid-1990s:

> I think there was some perception that ... we're spinning our wheels, and there's a lot of people doing a lot of work, but there's no focus to it. And the number of dollars to support that work was flat, actually starting to go down. So we needed to find a way to kind of marshal some development resources, some new monies, and address major strategic course issues–to improve the core curriculum, for example.

It was hoped that the CIL, as it dealt with killer courses (and over time expanded to deal with less lethal offerings), could serve as a central funding unit for monitoring and coordinating CMI-based course transformations. In the words of AM, the CIL was:

> sort of our first effort at a strategic focus and more one-stop shopping, because that was the other complaint we were hearing, that it was just all over the waterfront, and there were all sorts of people doing all sorts of things, and that there were some people sitting right next door to each other in the same building inventing the same thing–and they would benefit from knowing that they were right next door to each other, not having to do the same thing over twice, two and three times. And so we were trying to find a way to facilitate the easing of some of these challenges.

According to its web page the CIL would centralize the course transformation process by providing "related infrastructure, technical support and assessment of results in targeted curricular areas," and by "coordinating communications and developing partnerships focused on integrating technology in learning" (Center for Innovation in Learning web page, p. 1). More importantly, it would provide money. In its initial year (1997), CIL grants ranged in size from a few thousand dollars to over $70,000, and a total of over $1.1 million was allocated to 48 faculty. In the years since, the number of projects funded has dropped and the level of funding has fallen to a still considerable $400,000 and $450,000 per year.

Part II of this book examines three CIL-supported projects, each of which approached CMI in a different way. One was a project by professors working in the veterinary medicine program to produce a CD-ROM for a Veterinary Pathology course. The second was Virginia Tech's most widely known effort at CMI, the Math Emporium, a large-scale effort to replace traditional math courses with computer-mediated instruction. The third case was an effort to transform a course from a traditional lecture format to a web-based or completely online format. This last was a collaborative effort undertaken by an assistant professor and instructional designers. All three projects involved the use of CMI in courses that continued to offer face-to-face, on-campus instruction. This mixing of online and traditional course elements is the norm: Even among students taking completely online courses the majority at Virginia Tech simultaneously take on-campus courses (Carnevale & Olsen, 2003, p. A31). Still, the reader is advised that online programs where instructors and students never see each other, although composed in part of instructional elements like the ones examined here, may raise issues not addressed here.

II

LOOKING AT CMI
IN VARYING
INSTRUCTIONAL
LANDSCAPES

5

Seeing Teaching as Work

With Sandi Schneider

> *It is well understood that the pursuit of excellence and rewards in teaching is a fool's game. One must turn his or her attention to research or administrative chores if one is interested in following the smart money.*
>
> —Lewis (1996, p. 145)
>
> *I brought this up, you know I brought this up in one of the faculty meetings.... The faculty orientation meeting. A couple of Associate Provosts were there, our Dean was there. And I said, you guys are telling us, basically, that ... it is an equal balance between teaching, research, and outreach. What our departments are telling us is that research is way up here, and then teaching. Then outreach. And teaching—basically you're expected to do it well. It's not even, it's not even, it doesn't even count, no matter how good a teacher you are that's the way you're expected to be, but it's the research and the money you're bringing to the department.*
>
> —DS
>
> *The fears and risks associated with new technologies are unevenly socially distributed.*
>
> —Woolgar (2002, p. 15).

As part I suggests, a basic task of administration is to fashion surfaces that make the organization legible in a certain way to outsiders while keeping the substance and complexity of its core operations opaque. One side effect of this work is that administrators can come to rely on these surfaces themselves. This is one reason that, as Becher (1994) points out, "there is a tendency ... for administrators to lay down uniform specifications to be observed across the whole range of departments, even where these are clearly inappropriate" (p. 157). In practice, however, even uniform specifications and pressures mean different things in different sectors of the university (cf. Trowler, 2001). At Tech, for example, there was a general pressure on faculty members to use CMI and specific assumptions about its uses were embedded in training like the FDI, but whether and how it actually got used depended on whether course offerings were restricted to the department's own students or provided as "service" to students in other programs, whether the field was "hard" or "soft," "applied" or "pure" (Becher; Biglan, 1973; Hativa & Marincovich, 1995; Neumann, 2001; Neumann, Parry, & Becher, 2002). The ways professors used grants from the Center for Innovation in Learning (CIL) grants depended as well on how their lines of research were viewed by funding agencies and corporate markets, on whether or not they had tenure, whether they could choose the courses they taught or had them assigned, taught the same courses year after year or changed assignments frequently, or taught graduate as opposed to undergraduate students.

All these things interacted in complex ways and sometimes produced counterintuitive results. For example, course transformations take faculty members away from the research and writing on which promotion and tenure depend, but untenured professors are usually more susceptible to administrative pressures and are sometimes assigned the jumbo courses targeted for computerization.[1] As JM observed:

> I would rather put a lot of emphasis on working with faculty after they're tenured. What confounds this, to some extent, is … kind of where the bar is in terms of what's expected of most faculty now. It requires everybody to— not everybody, but many people seem to have to do something with technology, whether they're tenured or not.

CONTENT ATOMIZATION AND DISAGGREGATIONS OF TEACHING

According to some technology advocates, however, pressures to do something with technology don't necessarily create problems. In fact, CMI should help even new faculty members use time more effectively. The argument works this way: Assume that content can be atomized into small, discrete, hierarchically sequenced units—an idea common to behaviorist

---

[1]Senior professors may teach big, lower division courses as well. JM explained, "Some of the most productive work [introducing CMI] has been done by full professors and career associate professors, that are going to be associates till they retire, and they know it. Many of the faculty that have been really up-front have been faculty who, I think it's fair to say, whose career, research career, has peaked." Some senior faculty welcomed the chance to concentrate on teaching. As one explained, "I liken myself to a closet teacher, one who had to repress many of his desires for many years because it wasn't politically correct to show enthusiasm towards teaching."

psychology and related ideologies such as programmed instruction.[2] In an article written for a handbook of research on instructional technology, several Tech professors (including JM's dissertation advisor) stated this assumption as follows: "Complex learning involves becoming competent in a given field by learning incremental behaviors that are ordered in these sequences, traditionally with very small steps, ranging from the simplest to more complex in the final goal" (Burton, Moore, & Magliaro, 1996, p. 49; see also Skinner, 1968, p. 21).

The focus of instruction is changing individual behavior. Progress is defined in terms of a student's or trainee's level of performance on the prespecified goals or objectives. Thus: "A curriculum is a sequence of content units arranged in such a way that the learning of each unit may be accomplished as a single act, provided the capabilities described by specified prior units (in the sequence) have already been mastered by the learner" (Gagne, 1967, p. 23).

If one further assumes that teaching can be divided into separate subprocesses, some of which are routine (and thus machinable) and others interpersonal, it follows that teachers should be able to off-load the routine of instruction to the technology and focus more on teaching's rewarding, interactive aspects. Skinner (1968), for example, suggested that teaching machines "should free [the teacher] for the effective exercise" of more "intellectual, cultural, and emotional contacts" with students (pp. 26, 27). The Ford Foundation's early efforts to promote instructional television similarly argued:

> The most effective use of such media is within an instructional strategy which, while taking away the teacher's basal expository role by assigning that to the media, frees him/her to assume the role of diagnostician of, and prescriber for, individual student strengths and weaknesses within the varying disciplines.... Convince a teacher that it's not exposition to the total class which is the essence of his/her professional being, but rather the highly skilled one-to-one and one-to-small-group relationship of teachers to pupil(s) ... and you make a convert to instructional TV. (Berkman, 1977, pp. 102–103)

The 1989 Virginia Tech University Task Force report endorsed the idea:

> In large enrollment courses, the replacement of some or all auditorium lectures and demonstrations by video presentations available (on-line or off-line) via the

---

[2]Such ideas, of course, are quite old, with direct connections back to early 20th-century scientific management and before that to arguments about the division of mental labor in the works of Babbage, the early pioneer of protocomputers (Babbage, 1971, pp. 175, 191; cf. Callahan, 1962).

student's own computer (modified to serve as a television set, or Compu-TV) will free faculty time for course development and revision and for individual and small group discussions and remediation. In small enrollment courses, interactive video, software tutors, and CD-ROM will allow more informal interaction, effectively extending the studio model of supervised individual work beyond its traditional applications in art and architecture. (p. 3)

An October, 1993, Tech planning document echoed these arguments, suggesting that by drawing on "the powerful computing and communications technologies now available" the university could:

develop a more diverse environment for teaching and learning–one that transcends our heavy reliance upon the traditional paradigm of course credit for classroom contact. We do not need to abandon the traditional lecture/lab methods of instruction, but rather to supplement these modes with other modes that will ultimately require less intensive faculty effort. (Accepting greater responsibility for our own destiny, 1993, p. 6)

At the peak of technology enthusiasm in the late 1990s, CMI advocates were claiming again that "with their new on-line courses [professors] can spend more time planning and facilitating learning and developing higher order thinking skills and less time presenting content" (Gillespie 1998, p. 39) and that faculty members would be "less concerned with identifying and then transmitting intellectual content and more focused on inspiring, motivating, and managing an active learning process by students" (Duderstadt, 1999, pp. 7–8). Instead of teaching we would have "technology-based delivery and instructional support systems" (Wallhaus, 2000, p. 23).

Once the functions of teaching are imagined as segmentable in such ways, it's a small step to thinking they can be spread across different people:

State-of-the-art courses employing multimedia components can be designed by expert teams of knowledge specialists and instructional technologists and then sold to individual campuses. Similarly, the information dissemination function of lecturing can be done by authorities captured technologically, thus eliminating the repetitive aspects of course instruction and freeing professors for more creative aspects of college teaching. (Baldwin, 1998, p. 10; Bess, 1998; see also Bess and Associates, 2000)

VOLUNTEER OVERTIME

Variants of the schemes hinted at in the litany of preceding quotes have already come to pass: Community and technical colleges, for example, are now buying online courses developed by other schools, and technology foundations are giving grants to help institutions build repositories of such courses (Carnevale, 2004a). Such practices, however, do not yet seem to have extended far into research universities, and the experiences of the professors I interviewed belied forecasts of saved time and increased efficiency.

For at least the first 6 months of an effort to shift her lecture course to web-based instruction, DS, then a new, untenured professor, was working, by her estimate, "65–70 hours a week, up to 80 sometimes," with the course transformation effort taking up "probably ... more than 50%" of that time. Like many new professors, DS had been assigned a large survey course to teach. She'd gotten involved with CMI in the hope of finding:

> a system so that I can streamline my teaching methods, so that I don't have to worry about, "okay, how do I go about preparing a lecture?" "How do I go about picking topics?" I know how to do that, I am trained out to do that, so all I need to bring is my creativity, and that is the fun part. And this way I wouldn't have to worry about teaching that much and devote more time to my research. So that was my thought.

Things turned out differently. About 6 months into it she commented, "So far I have been doing this by overtime, working overtime. But I'm trying my best to be able to balance it, without having to put in those extra hours. But I work an outrageous number of hours. So that's the way I've been handling it, putting the extra time in."

Although he worked on a smaller scale CIL-funded project—developing a supplemental CD-ROM for his veterinary pathology course—another professor whose work I examine, JR, recalled:

> The amount of time that went into developing it is about in the tune right now of about 2 man-years—very high intensity—a lot of effort—there is a tremendous amount of image that's in there as far as pathology specimens that had to be acquired and scanned things that have been brought together—it has been very intensive—I would say that much of the labor has been borne by teams of students who needed the skills and the study and it also helps their pathology training a lot doing this. The amount of time allocated to do the project here was "you can do it when everything else is done, on your spare time." There was zero, zero change in faculty activity plan in regard to this little activity.... I think that many people are finding that this is just another thing they throw on the pile.

A third faculty member whose CIL-supported work I discuss, FQ, a mathematics professor working with Virginia Tech's Math Emporium, called this additional work "volunteer overtime" and suggested that it's an unacknowledged but critical component of CMI efforts:

The state board of education hasn't said, well, you know, we understand that in order to bring computers into the courses, that's a lot of work for you faculty, so we're going to reduce your teaching loads. They haven't done that. So, it's sort of running on volunteer overtime and that sort of has a limited future–it sort of has a limited present, not just future–in something like a production environment we're dealing with here where you have just thousands of students taking courses. You know we just cannot expect enough volunteer overtime to computer enhance all those courses for thousands of students.

Volunteer overtime–unrewarded or administratively unacknowledged work—is ubiquitous in professional as well as wage occupations (Fraser, 2001). Its particular association with CMI work is not unique to Virginia Tech (e.g., Carnevale, 2004b, Marine, 2002, pp. 68–69; Phipps & Merisotis, 1999), and its costs vary for differently positioned professors. For the tenured, volunteer overtime can be a strategic investment, for the untenured a risky gamble.

For example, major design projects can require more time than universities typically allocate (cf. Lowgren & Lauren, 1993). In a November interview DS described how intense the design work had been since the beginning of that year: "We started, maybe, in [the previous] February. That's too short of a time. Too short of a time. Because we worked day and night since February. And we're still just barely meeting—making ends meet." She explained that she thought she could "afford it so far, but I'm trying to pull back from, you know, many–I'm enjoying myself very much, but at the same time I'd really like to work it out so that I'd have more time for myself."

She did eventually pull back. During the second year of the redesign effort the department chair who had initially encouraged this work was replaced by a chairperson who put more emphasis on grant writing, research, and publication:

He said, for example, I think, by the first year ... finish publications from your Ph.D., by the second year begin publishing from Tech. By third year ... you need to have external funding on the way. Fourth year, established. So ... he had it clearly demarcated, what his expectations are.... I'm expecting that he will make allowance for those of us who started in a different venue. Because with the other head of the department, she would say, you know, just start publishing whatever you have done, but ... she never put a deadline on it. So, my concept was by tenure I need to have, you know, number of publications, and that's what I'm planning to do.

The new department chair told DS not to spend too much time on CMI work: "He's of the mind that—'Don't ask for a Cadillac if you can do it with a Beetle' ... And he's also concerned about the time that I'm spending— he thinks that it will be at the expense of my research."

The chair then rewarded DS with a second 250-student section of the course: "He said that other person [a tenured faculty member] didn't want to teach it any more, and so he gave it to me." And he took away one of her two graduate assistants: "I used to have two graduate assistants, now I only have one for this course. So I have to rethink the whole procedure."

As this and the other cases suggest, CMI development isn't the frictionless substitution of one delivery technology for another, but a simultaneous reconfiguration of the social relations into and out of which the technological artifacts are constructed.

INTENSIFICATION AND ARTICULATION WORK

Technologies, or more properly technical artifacts and tools, have long been densely embedded in university teaching. As Rudolph (1977) points out, the lecture itself was a kind of early technology replacing the recitation. Like CMI now, it was taken to have inherent effects—indeed, many of the same effects critics have more recently attributed to CMI:

> Lectures kept students at a distance, they could be repeated with small cost in time and effort ... [they] stretched the distance between teacher and student by turning over to someone else the responsibility of reading tests and papers. For students the advantages of lectures over recitations were also attractive: They did not have to be prepared, they could sleep, they could skip class and borrow notes or even purchase course outlines. Yet lectures opened up such a great gulf between professor and student that each learned how to act as if the other did not really exist. (Rudolph, pp. 232–233)

But if computer-related technologies didn't create the distance between students and professor, the asynchrony of teaching and learning, or the distribution of teaching responsibilities across multiple actors and artifacts, they do involve changes in what these things look like. They move the work of teaching around in different ways from earlier technologies like the lecture. As Cornford and Pollock (2002) observe of "virtual universities":

> Technologies are used to move the work of the university around. Most obviously, communications technologies enable this work to be relocated between different locations, linking up students, lecturers, researchers, administrators, technicians, funders, evaluators and assessors without the need for copresence.... The virtual university, then, is a new social, technical and spatial division of labor in Higher Education. (p. 90)

University administrators are giving this new division of labor at least two different forms. The first and most commented-on involves routinizing the tasks and regimenting the temporal organization of teaching (e.g., scripting content, demanding more and more of the same kind of work).

Studies of public school teaching (e.g., Apple & Jungck, 1992; Hargreaves, 1992; International Labor Organization, 1991) draw attention to a general "intensification" of instructional work in this sense (cf. Shaiken, Herzenberg, & Kuhn, 1986), and critics of CMI in higher education like Noble (2001) see changes in responsibilities for course design and instruction as evidence of a similar intensification and deskilling:

> At NYU [New York University] Online, for example, which considers itself in the vanguard of institutional change, a team of different specialists in course design, development, content, delivery, and distribution handles instruction. Where once a single professor would perform all of these tasks as an integrated whole, the detail workers now do their separate parts, with far less control over the process and substantially less pay—precisely the pattern established long ago with the shift from craft to industrial labor that culminated in the assembly worker of modern industry. (pp. 30–31)

This fragmentation and delegation of teaching to detail workers does occur in certain niches of postsecondary education, especially those trying to expand rapidly by recruiting part-time instructors to manage new courses planned and tightly scripted by teams of instructional designers and "content experts" (e.g., Farrell, 2003).

At Tech, however, it was more common to see a second division of labor, especially in transformations of already established courses. There, activities previously carried out by the faculty member (perhaps working with graduate assistants), and new work associated with the technologies, were redistributed across new categories of participants (instructional designers, web developers) and artifacts (CD-ROMs, web pages, etc.). The question is not whether these were good or bad moves—there are clear benefits to team planning and course development—but how they changed faculty work.

It takes time to divide teaching into routine and nonroutine elements. Faculty members, instructional designers, and technology specialists have to work out understandings and differences; create, debug, and update materials like PowerPoint slides and practice quizzes; find already created materials and get permission to use them; fit instructional plans into new formats; create new artifacts; and finally reassemble these elements in instruction. All this produces intensification in the form of what Strauss (1985) calls "articulation work": "First, the meshing of the often numerous tasks, clusters of tasks, and segments of the total arc. Second, the meshing of efforts of various unit-workers (individuals, departments, etc.). Third, the meshing of actors with their various types of work and implicated tasks" (p. 8).

Chapters 6, 7, and 8 examine different ways of organizing this meshing across different participants and departments. Taken together, the three cases illustrate how the articulation work of CMI development varied according to the strength of the academic discipline, the organizational context of the program, the faculty member's career stage, the types of students enrolled in the course, and the position of the course in these students' career paths.

The chapters do not describe teaching practices and are not evaluations of courseware, instructional designs, the professors, or the courses themselves (cf. Kane, Sandretto, & Heath, 2002). Rather, they rely on interviews with the professors to model their "practical logics" of teaching (Cochran-Smith & Lytle, 1999; Scott, 1998). Practical logics are experience-based strategies that people develop as they work over time with "similar but never precisely identical situations requiring a quick and practiced adaptation" (Scott, pp. 315–316; cf. also Cochran-Smith & Lytle). In the case of teaching, practical logic refers to knowledge of how instruction works in particular settings with specific kinds of topics, students, resources, and constraints. Practical logics need not be formalized or derived from research on pedagogy. They could be based on the faculty member's own experiences in school; on instructional ideas congealed in textbooks, problem sets, or standardized labs; or on observations, suggestions from peers, or trial and error. Some parts of the logics may be easy for professors to articulate, others difficult. As this implies, the professors may not formulate these logics quite the same way they're described here, or they may have changed since the interviews were conducted—my account, in other words, is at best partial and incomplete. Why proceed with these shortcomings?

One reason is that CMI development efforts usually rest on the erasure of such logics. Computer-mediated instruction projects are willy-nilly attempts to formalize teaching, whether in terms of standardized pedagogical structures like programmed instruction or the assumptions embedded in softwares and communication networks. These "modes of ordering" (Law, 1994, pp. 107–112) effectively frame older approaches as unsystematic and disordered. As Berg and Timmermans (2000) observed in a study of diagnostic protocols in cardiac-pulmonary resuscitation (CPR), "with the production of an order, a corresponding disorder comes into being" (p. 36). They continued:

> Physicians emerge as "poorly calibrated" decision makers. What should be fought [according to the formalizers] are "informal, nonquantitative interpretations" and "ambiguous language." What should be mistrusted are criteria and guidelines that remain "implicit," "hidden," and can thus easily be "inconsistent," illogical, nonreproducible, nongeneral, and noncomparable. (Berg & Timmermans, p. 45)

The language in CMI for characterizing the disorderly approach of professors to teaching was not as extreme, but as one instructional designer at Tech explained:

It's very difficult to tell faculty that they don't know how to teach [laughs] and many of them don't. And so a lot of our time is spent dealing with the aspects of teaching and learning. And providing them with the information background that typically education folks would have gotten in some of the ed psych classes and education classes. But so many of the faculty here have never taken an education class or a course on teaching. They're content experts.

Whether or not such descriptions are accurate or useful, a basic problem is that they treat professors' ideas about teaching as gaps to be filled rather than alternative understandings. This points to a second reason for attending to professors' practical logics: They supply the frames in terms of which CMI is organized and interpreted. Without understanding them there's no way to make sense of what faculty are doing with it or to engage with it in a principled way.

Making Disciplinary Objects Visible: Pathology on CD-ROM

WITH SANDI SCHNEIDER

There [are] very divergent views about the use of technology—I will say that my personal experience over the years is that technology tools may tend to be over-emphasized as a substitution for effective teaching. That it is—it almost seems that … it's a little better if your course is online or if you've got a videotape or a disc that the students can use than the experience they might get in the classroom.

—JR

Taking money from a source like the Center for Innovation in Learning (CIL) does not require one to follow its agenda. The political, economic, and organizational processes that engendered the grant program created generalized pressures for CMI use but they didn't determine the exact forms of those uses. A case in point: The two tenured professors discussed in this chapter used their grant to create a CD-ROM for a veterinary pathology course, not to maximize outputs, increase productivity in a 1% course, or apply instructional design principles. TC, who taught a veterinary histology course and was a corecipient of the grant, explained that budget pressures had in a sense triggered the development of CMI in histology, but didn't determine how he responded to those pressures:

> In the early 1990s we were being pressured by the university to cut costs for delivery of courses…. I had a handout that was about 165 pages of copied text with 20 to 30 line drawings that I cut and pasted out of various textbooks to illustrate different points. So when we started getting leaned on about cutting cost delivery and increasing efficiency, I got to thinking about how I would do this using computer technology and I went forward with the idea of creating an online site…. [I] wrote a proposal to CEUT [Center for Excellence in Undergraduate Teaching]. They agreed to provide a certain amount of money…. My department head went ahead and [supplemented

that] ... so that I could hire someone to buy out my time that I was teaching the course... so that I could concentrate on creating this web-based version of my notes.[1]

The CD project in pathology built on the one in histology. The two courses are conceptually related, students take them in sequence, and the professors teaching them collaborate. As TC explained:

> I also teach in the general pathology course with JR and in the interval between getting the CEUT grant and now we had decided that this would be a useful thing to have for pathology as well. So we applied to CIL for money to take his material and digitize all his images and create a pathology web site that would complement the histology web site.... So that way the student gets an opportunity to put normal and abnormal next to each other and compare the two.

JR explained that the CD project in pathology actually started before the CIL funding, and from its early stages had involved students in the development process:

> A group of students and I were sitting around after the end of my veterinary pathology class and I said to them, "How would you like this to be different, how could we expand or increase or improve your learning experience?" And I said, "If we developed a web tool or disc would that help you?" They said, "great," and I said, "Fine, here's some money," and I put out probably about $4,000, $5,000 of my own resources from a foundations account and got them started.

STUDENT ROLES

This student participation in creating and vetting the CMI artifact is one of its unusual facets. JR recalled:

---

[1]Although cost cutting was an impetus for the decision to shift from photo reproduction to digitized photos, TC discovered that the change carried a hidden price in the form of ongoing revision and updating:

> I went ahead and spent a total of 14 months on the first version, because I had decided from the beginning that one of the things I needed to do was generate all new images to avoid copyright issues.... So I went ahead and I photographed— I don't know how many hundreds of pictures—and I hired a student assistant to digitize them—talk about a thankless job—and that was the start of it.... I went ahead and wrote new text in the form of captions pages to go with those and just sort of assembl[ed] it into a linkage.... This basically took over my professional life. I mean it is like writing a book—you never get done revising it. I've been through at least two major revisions and a couple minor ones.

[I] said, "Here are my notes, here are my slides. I want you to go ahead and design a course." And so that is how the whole thing got started and it has gotten increasingly more sophisticated over the years.... It is generally quite easy to find [among students] the expertise and talent that can be associated with doing this, so we've not had the need to reach out. It is good for us to have people that are involved programmatically because when we are talking about content and the interaction of the students with content—the people that are doing the design and the scale-up are students.

Students could take on this role in part because the veterinary medicine program was relatively small, very exclusive, and tightly organized. Students farther along in the curriculum could look back on pathology and judge the course in light of subsequent demands. As JR explained:

There have been ... 8 or 10 students, over the years, involved with looking at the work product here and going through the process of how do we feel about this, what do you think, what is the language that you do it, what did you get out of it, how did you learn this technique, how could you learn this better, are you an auditory learner, or you a visual learning?... The thing that was really the driving question here was ... after they had the course—what do they think they've learned and then what was covered or needed to be emphasized or needed to be covered or emphasized in a different way.

The program could also be treated as an object of evaluation by students because most approached it not as consumers of information, but as postulants to a profession. As TC put it: "Many of them [the students] actually almost view this as a vocation—not just a job—it's like becoming a member of a religious community."

The professors could assume that students with such commitments would understand the pathology course in terms of its relation to other courses in the program, and see the program itself as meaningful by virtue of its alignment with the standards and practices of the profession. There were also extrauniversity reckoning points that allowed professors to telescope assessments and judge the effects of the courses over time:

We actually have a better measure of long term learning experience than perhaps other people do because our students in their third or fourth year take national and state board examinations in a variety of disciplines in veterinary medicine—surgery, medicine, pathology, bacteriology—and we get scores and get ranked on how our students perform on specific disciplines versus the national norm or average. (JR)

The professors assumed that the students would treat the CD as a durable resource useful across this longer time span: "I will be able look at their scores, which are going to be 3 years after they have taken the course, alright, but they will have the CD that they [the students] can use for review and see how they do on the national board exam." This explains how the CD was supposed to be useful, but why did CMI take the form of a CD in the first place?

VISUAL LEARNING

Pathology, according to JR, "is very visual." It demands perceptual discrimination skills and visual knowledge that can only be acquired by working directly with specimens (cf. Gibson, 1979). The role of the CD in helping students acquire these skills was to provide otherwise dispersed and hard-to-find images of tissues in a readily accessible form that students could connect to the things they were seeing in laboratory work. The CD itself contains this bit of dialogue:

> Can I just look at this and skip lab?
>
> Bad idea. This is a study companion, not a substitute for the laboratory. The point of making this monstrous undertaking is to show you what the lesions look like so you can find them on your own in your own slides. It is also designed to help you with the language of pathology, as it were, the seemingly stilted manner that is necessary when describing pathology on glass. Lastly, the histology part is designed to give you normal tissue to look at to help you understand what pathology looks like. (From CD-ROM "Quick Intro" JR & Burke, 2001)

The content of the course, then, was spread across the CD, the lab, classroom instruction, the textbooks, and also the students' senses as they worked with materials in the lab (e.g., learning to see with one's hands, a common locution in fields where tactile learning is important; see Rose, 2004). In TC's words, students ultimately learned from dealing with real tissue, not just CDs and slides:

> You could not possibly teach this subject online. That was one of the suggestions that was made to me early on.... And I've been doing this for 25 years and ... I know that you can't teach this subject online. You can supplement the material online but you've got to be there looking at it in a microscope, on glass, and you've got to have somebody who knows the material standing over you to saying, "Yes, that is what you are supposed to be looking for" or "No not that, look for this—here's some of the clues." The analogy I use for the students when I open the course is that it is like riding a bicycle. You can't really teach it to somebody, you can only learn it by doing it. And my job is to explain the theory of bicycle function and why they stay vertical on two wheels. And until they've actually gotten on the thing and fallen off a few times and figured out how to make it stay up they don't know what they are doing. Once they learn that they never forget it. This is the

same way.... I am constantly giving them new examples of whatever it is they're supposed to be seeing in that topic and fixing that image in the back of their minds. Yeah, that's a plasma cell, that's a liver section, that's a pancreas—so that when they get into the second semester and they start looking at stuff that came from animals that were dead for hours and handled badly—they'll have some idea of what they're suppose to be seeing and where the deterioration was.... No—you can't learn it from pictures.... I have a colleague, he is a gross anatomist but the statement is the same for histology, he has the saying that there is no substitute for getting your hands on a real-live dead animal. And it is the same for anatomy—everybody wants to use pictures and models—but unless you're actually in there moving stuff around and peeling back layers of muscle you really do not have any conception of what the three-dimensionality of it is.

This sensuous, three-dimensional quality of "real-live dead animals" defines a stable and predictable environment—insofar as basic animal anatomy and biology are stable—against which course activity could be made meaningful (cf. Hutchins, 1995, p. 137). The CD connected the spacetime of the classroom to that of the laboratory and was meaningful in terms of that relation.

What the CD did not do was change the professor's classroom contact time or alter the way classroom interaction unfolded. CMI advocates who assume that technologies have inherent properties that can only be exploited in "asynchronous," "online" environents might consider this a flaw (e.g., Weller, 2002, p. 10), but such judgments are backwards. It isn't that technologies have inherent capabilities or that there are sharply defined asynchronous and online environments in which these capabilities are best realized. Rather, artifacts like the CD are produced to fit already formed ideas of teaching. As Slater (2001) argues, distinctions between live and online have to be explained rather than assumed:

> The important question is whether new media users make a distinction between online and offline, and if they do, when and why do they do it, and how do they accomplish it practically? It is the making of the distinction that needs studying, rather than assuming it exists and then studying its consequences. (p. 543)

In JR's case, the distinction followed from his conception of teaching as a performance unfolding in interactions with students (cf. Sarason, 1979). As he put it: "I feel very strongly that part of the thing people get in the classroom is a performance. And I don't mean that in a derogatory sense. I think that my students learn because they have interaction with me." This is the way of thinking that we have to understand in order to understand CMI in veterinary pathology.

INDEXICAL INSTRUCTION

In JR's account, performance instruction depended on close proximity and "direct interaction" (cf. McWilliam & Taylor, 1998):

> I'm perhaps not the best person to ask about the use of [computer-based] interactive tools because I set a very high stock in direct interaction in contact with students and in fact like being in contact with them in the classroom or small group contact with them—I think there is no substitute for that as a teaching and learning tool. So what I have tried to do is develop learning materials, which are supplementary and adjunctive and reinforcing but not use them as a replacement for physical presence of teaching.

JR explained that he generated instructional momentum and engaged students by moving around the room and referring to particular objects or people. Going completely online would short-circuit these strategies:

> I'm notorious for doing a Phil Donahue show[2] when I go in to lecture.... I don't stand in front of the room, I've got a mobile microphone, alright, and I go around and walk around the room and we interact and I will question and we point to different points and will talk and I will joke—and I think a lot of that is missing from the online content.

In a performance approach students are not just an observing audience to whom content is delivered, they are part of the medium through which the professor guides the collective production of ideas and concepts. Instead of breaking down information into a sequence of scripted, task-linked steps, the professor works toward it by repeatedly sampling students' ideas, looping back, and recontextualizing ideas and questions in response to the students' emergent understandings and misunderstandings. Once a decision has been made to dispense with a rigid script, this kind of direct embodied engagement, with its potential for improvisation, detours, misunderstandings, and clarifications, becomes compulsory:

> The reason for these compulsions toward proximity is not the amount of detail to be handled in some technical or even simply cognitive sense. Enormous quantities of detail are routinely transferred as data bases across electronic networks. Instead, the key is that there is no set script or standing recipe for

---

[2]Phil Donahue was a television talk-show host in the United States known for walking among audience members with a microphone to solicit questions and comments.

arriving at an outcome. Unlike, say, ordering catalogue merchandise over the phone or sending inventory data through a computer link, things must be worked out along the way. (Boden & Molotch, 1994, p. 270)

One qualification is necessary: The effects of a performance approach to teaching depend on the nature of the program. It probably works best for programs in which professors and students share strong commitments to a field. As noted earlier, veterinary medicine students entered the program committed to professional practice. As TC put it:

I read some book on pedagogical technique and a lot of it just does not apply to vet students. You do not have to motivate these kids. They're here because by the time they could sit up this is what they wanted to do. They are the most focused people you'll meet in your life, much more so than medical students or law students or anyone else.

This picture of students with powerful commitments to the field points to another function of live instruction—the generation of feeling and identification.

FEELING AND IDENTIFICATION

JR illustrated this point by stepping outside the conventional frame of the interview and questioning his interviewer, Sandi Schneider, using her uncertainty about the direction of conversation to generate engagement and attention:

JR:	The thing that can't go online—it's easy to define for you … what was the last play you saw that you enjoyed?
Schneider:	It was a small play—I can't remember the title—it was a Celtic fairy story.
JR:	And how many seats in the theater?
Schneider:	Probably about 50 or 60.
JR:	Intimate.
Schneider:	Mmhmm small theater.
JR:	Theater—okay—how were the acoustics?
Schneider:	They were excellent.
JR:	Okay so you were in there and when the light went down you were ready for the experience. Do you think you would have enjoyed that play watching it on a computer screen?
Schneider:	It would have been a different experience—it would have been a very different experience.

The point is partly what was said and partly the dialogical way it unfolded. Consider how the exchange differed from JR simply saying, "The difference between performance teaching and teaching online is analogous to the difference between watching a play in a little theater and looking at a digitized video of it on a computer." First, the dialogue changed Sandi's participation in the interview: The timing of the questions required her to stay engaged and assume part of the responsibility for making points. Second, the questions encouraged her to think of theater-going experiences in terms of the ideas JR was developing. Sandi understood that JR didn't really care about her theater going. Both of them understood the exchange as demonstrating a point about something outside it: performance teaching.

For students who participated in these kinds of exchanges repeatedly over time, such questioning would provide a model of conversational and interpersonal styles that could be taken as characteristic of professionals in the field. The sociologist Goffman (1981) argued that the concept of "the lecturer" needs to be broken into at least three parts: the "animator" ("the thing that sound comes out of"), the "author" (whoever has "formulated and scripted the statement that gets made"), and the "principal" ("someone who believes personally in what is being said and takes the position that is implied in the remarks"; Goffman, p. 167; see also Irvine, 1996; Levinson, 1988). A lecturer is by definition the animator (Steven Hawking and lip-synchers excepted) and usually the author (though this doesn't imply originality—professors may think of themselves as conduits passively transmitting the facts of their fields, assigning problems or exercises from textbooks used by generations of students). The role of principal, however, is by no means a given. The speaker has to be able to convey affective commitment, passion, feeling, and emotion about the subject of the discourse. This is perhaps most powerfully accomplished in a performance approach.

Searching for words after the preceding exchange, JR suggested that "content" was what was would be left if one made a recording of the performance. Looking at the play on a computer screen "would have been a content experience—it would have been—it would have been a transfer effect but it would not have been a transfer of feeling and emotion."

PERFORMANCE, FEELING, AND PARTICIPATION

Feeling and emotion are not just for the benefit of students, they also keep the performer engaged. JR described the experience of:

> teaching an online lecture … and I was sitting in front of a screen doing a lecture on emerging diseases in horses—and horses are an area of interest for me and … it felt flat to me—it felt listless—I wasn't deriving the energy that

I derive from the classroom—all of those elements were missing alright—and, well, certainly people can transfer the information on a disc or sitting at a screen, they don't transfer the feeling of the performance.

The "feeling of the performance" is probably a function of its emergent quality and the sense of moment-to-moment uncertainty about what comes next and what the exact outcome will be (i.e., the "participatory discrepancies" from which the performance builds; Keil, 1994). As the actress Anna Devere Smith puts it: "Whatever you're creating has to be creative right there. You can't go and do it in rehearsal—or it doesn't count. You can't fix it.... The observer really is having to absorb a full human being" (cited in Kondo, 1996, p. 332).

Performance thus places obligations on the audience (the students) as well as the performer (the teacher). As the exchange with Sandi Schneider suggests, students can't be passive recipients of content deliveries, they have to participate in the instructional event. Performance, as Frith (1996) puts it, "depends on an audience which can interpret ... work through its own experience of performance" (p. 205). "Knowing the conventions of the form, serious audience members can collaborate more fully with artists in the joint effort which produces the work each time it is experienced" (Becker, 1982, p. 48).

All of the factors outlined here come together in performance: its emergent, unpredictable quality, the combination of the author and principal roles, the engagement of students, and the modeling of a professional manner and persona. Yet it is also important to repeat that the significance of these factors, indeed the viability of performance approaches to teaching, depends on the structure of the program and the organization of the curriculum. In a course full of students from a variety of programs, few of whom intended to follow the professors into the field, something like JR's performance approach might seem at best entertainment, at worst a distraction for students who just wanted to know what would be on the test.

CURRICULAR SPECIFICITY OF INSTRUCTIONAL PRACTICES

Veterinary pathology thus reflected an approach to CMI development that may be available only to practitioners in programs designed to impart strongly bounded professional knowledge to an exclusive group of students moving through a tightly linked set of courses. The grounding of professional practice in a well-defined body of problems and practices, and the deeper time frame of the program—stretching from introductory courses to professional examinations—made it possible to design a CMI artifact that could be indexed to multiple professional situations (e.g., lab work, board exams, etc.). This was CMI shaped to fit with rather than transform existing instructional practices. In chapter 7 I examine a case in which the fundamental disciplinary practice involved—solving mathematics problems—was preserved, but its communicative context was radically transformed through CMI.

Making Students' Difficulties Visible:
The Math Emporium

WITH SANDI SCHNEIDER

Emporium, n.... 1. a place of commerce; trading center; marketplace. 2. a large store with a wide variety of things for sale.

—Webster's New World Dictionary of the
American Language (1951, p. 475)

Keynoting the dedication ceremony was John Morgridge, chairman of the board of Cisco Systems, Inc. Morgridge praised Virginia Tech for its innovative approach in applying information technology across campus.... Morgridge also praised Virginia Tech's leadership in creating the Math Emporium. "The beauty of this technology is that it will allow us as a society to master the material," he said.

—Nutter (2000, p. 1)

"There's no teacher to confuse me" (quote from first-year student in a Math Emporium course, used as headline of front-page article from the Roanoke Times).

—Zack (1997b, p. A1)

In state policy discourses of the early 1990s, paying for more instructors in order to offer smaller classes was an example of a backward-thinking input orientation, not to be supported by a university intent on breaking molds. This put pressure on efforts, like one in mathematics, to reduce class size in some introductory courses by hiring more instructors. In an April 1994 memo to the dean of the College of Arts and Sciences, Vice President and Provost Fred Carlisle invoked the "credit for contact" language to define a mandate for big courses:

> "The resources allocated to your college are allocated to the college—not to specific programs or departments. This includes the special instructor positions recently allocated to the Math Department.... The critical issue is student learning—not class size.... An expectation has been set in Virginia that higher education would find ways to use instructional technology to 'break the mold' of credit for classroom contact." (cited in FQ, 1994, p. 1)

Perhaps class size wasn't the "critical issue" for the provost, but the press of growing enrollments in a context of declining resources created a real problem for the mathematics department. In 1994 alone, according to the department chair, enrollment in math courses increased by 1,800 students while the department lost 6% of its budget (Olin, 2001, p. 1). In a memo to other math faculty, FQ, the recipient of the CIL grant discussed in this chapter,[1] quoted the Provost's statement and added that:

> [The dean], in his meeting with the department May 3, said that he would not "terminate the experiment" [of small classes] without giving it a chance to be evaluated. But he was not willing to specify what sort of data would justify a further commitment to small math classes. Further his "nontermination" does not seem to preclude steady erosion, since we have already lost three instructorships. (FQ, 1994, p. 1)

The implication, in FQ's view, was that the small classes eventually would be abandoned, and other means—probably involving CMI—would be needed to deal with the large enrollment courses that would result:

> The administration is reluctant to be explicit about this, but "break the mold of credit for classroom contact" and "the critical issue is student learning—not class size" should make it clear that there is a bottom line. The bottom line is productivity: We must do the job using (on average) less faculty time per student credit. We must find ways to get students to learn (and give them credit) either on their own, or in larger classes. In math we have had experience with large classes, and generally found them unsatisfactory. The alternative seems to be courses with large self-study components. These have been tried elsewhere in the past, without much success. They have not been tried here, nor with the latest technology.

The idea of self-study courses using the "latest technology" had a specific source. Chapter 3 described how a last-minute proposal to the state led to funding for a pilot version of a Faculty Development Initiative (FDI) to train professors in computer use, ostensibly as a step toward "capitalizing instruction." Among the first groups to go through those workshops were the mathematics faculty:

> [Virginia Tech] instituted a program in which every faculty attended workshops every three or four years and received a high end computer, configured to their choice, after each workshop. The Math Department was the first guinea pig [for the pilot version of FDI], and that was when the idea

---

[1]Much of the description that follows applies to issues generic to the Emporium; some, however, refers to FQ's particular instructional logic, which may or may not be shared by others who teach at the Emporium.

> of teaching math in a computer-enhanced environment got its start.... During that first workshop, we were introduced to the computer program Mathematica. Then, in the spring of 1993, we began using Mathematica in two of our first-year calculus courses. (Olin, 2001, p. 1)

Setting up a technology-heavy "self-study" course required more, not less, funding, however, and as in the case of the FDI itself, computerization was a key to getting money in a time of cutbacks—in this case, from internal university reallocations.[2] The mathematics department's argument was that as it provided critical courses to other university programs, those programs should contribute financially to the proposed facility. Peggy Meszaros, who succeeded Carlisle as Tech's provost in 1995, recalled in 2002 that she first heard of the scheme when the head of the math department:

> called me and asked if a group of faculty could address the Deans.... And he said, "We've got a major problem in that we cannot effectively teach math students, and we've got statistics to show it. And we've got a possible solution, but it's going to take the university getting behind us to make this work. And we really need to make a presentation to the Deans." ... There must have been 8 or 9 [math professors] who came to that meeting, who absolutely did a fantastic presentation, which was very data based, as you would imagine, talking about the ineffective techniques they had been using, and the resulting student lack of success. And then they presented this idea. "We don't have enough computers, we don't have enough space. What if we did have a large laboratory ... space, and we could take some software that we're beginning to pioneer, and we could work with students on much more of a round-the-clock basis. It wouldn't be an isolated, chalkboard lecture." They had all of the right words to say to get people very energized. And it was a university issue because all of our students are required to take mathematics. Well, after that initial presentation, Erv [Blythe] and his people sort of put the pencil to the plan, came back, and told us what it was going to cost the university. And it was quite staggering. And then it was a matter of selling that to the deans, because it was going to involve all of us in taking a reduction in our base monies, including the provost's office and all the vice provosts and so forth, in order to put this plan into place. And those were, as you would guess, some very tense meetings. Of course, lots of arguments about why it won't work. But we did persevere, and it was put together very quickly.

What got put together was housed in the space of what had been a department store at a small mall near the main university campus. In this Math Emporium, as it was named, students could watch lectures on CD-ROM, work problems, take tests on computers, and get help from

---

[2]The Math Emporium cost "several million dollars" to set up, by one account (Williams, n.d.)—some coming from grants but most from with the university.

human assistants (mainly graduate and undergraduate students) who staffed the facility from 9:00 in the morning to midnight. All of this could be situated in the language of the 1989 report (University Task Force, 1989). One of the Emporium's main designers, for example, argued that "the instructional offerings we present through the Math Emporium here at Virginia Tech represent a first step in truly escaping the tyranny of the 'seat-time' paradigm" (Williams, n.d., p. 1). A 1998 letter from the interim director of the State Council of Higher Education to Virginia Tech's president applauded the Emporium as representing "one of Virginia's most innovative approaches to date for breaking the credit for contact model of delivering instruction." The Emporium "encourages us all to envision the future boldly as we build technologically integrated campuses across the Commonwealth" (J. Michael Mullen to Paul Torgersen, January 16, 1998).

From FQ's perspective, however, the instructional logic of the Emporium was more complex. In his words, the Emporium consisted of:

> five hundred machines and substantial staff and thousands of students taking courses.... This is a production facility. It's not a sort of hand-craft thing. Most of the people who tinker with technology in courses are doing hand-craft things and ... they're not particularly worried about efficiency or long-term effectiveness or how realistic it is in terms of a genuine model for proceeding. We have to be very, explicitly sensitive to that kind of thing because we can't afford to do things in an inefficient way. We have to be within budget or under budget if possible because in a way one of the objectives of the Emporium is to try to rescue the math department, and the students for that matter, from what would happen with all these budget cuts and so on. We're getting a lot more students and a reduction in resources, so the alternative to computer-based things was very large lecture sections ... and we know very well that that doesn't work particularly well. So this is an effort to do better than the 300- to 500-person lecture sections that are common in other universities this size but within the same budget. That's absolutely killer. We cannot afford to do anything that is more expensive than traditional instruction, and that imposes a discipline on us that most people don't have.... The only way that we can transform a course is to make it computer based and remove the classroom component completely. Because if you do both, if you do computers and the classroom, then it's more expensive than a classroom alone. Usually, considerably more expensive in terms of faculty time and things like that. So, just as purely, sort of brutal economic necessity we are focused on computer-based course ... that is not an extension or an enhancement of a classroom.

The economic justification for these investments required a system that could deal with larger numbers of students without increasing the number of faculty members working with them. As FQ explained:

Traditional courses, you get more students, you have to have more faculty, you know exactly how it scales. Here [at the Emporium] it scales rather differently. You can add more students without more cost. Once you have a course online, and you're maintaining it, which you have to do no matter how many students are in it, then a lot of it is [cost] independent of how many students you have.... This kind of a thing only makes sense, only works, if it's big. And it works better if it's bigger.

Public accounts of the Emporium, such as a 1999 story in *The Chronicle of Higher Education* thus emphasized both its size and efficiency:

"We could have done something smaller, I suppose, something less far-reaching," says Michael Williams, associate vice president for Information systems and research computing at Virginia Tech. "But I think the emporium was absolutely inevitable," he says, given the budgetary pressures the university has faced recently under a pair of Republican Governors.... "We have a Governor who tells us about every week that we're spending too much money, and that state schools are getting a free ride," says Mr. Williams. "There's no getting away from the instructional-productivity pressures."... "It's early, but I feel fairly confident that it will pick up steam," says Carol A. Twigg, executive director of the Center for Academic Transformation at Rensselaer Polytechnic Institute. Virginia Tech's emporium "is changing the labor requirements" for teaching linear algebra. In doing so, Ms. Twigg says, the university has shown that it can reduce its per-student instructional costs for the course from $77 to $24, a labor savings of $97,000 a year.[3]... The Math emporium has become a big draw. Officials from the University of Alabama visited last month, Pennsylvania State University's president came the following week, and University of Idaho officials arrived the week after that. (Olsen, 1999b, p. A31)

---

[3]In addition to the claims of cost savings, there were also claims that the technology improved student learning—or at least that average final grades had risen half a grade in such courses (Olin, 2001). A detailed evaluation of the linear algebra course mentioned in the quote from Olsen (1999b) article offers a more ambiguous conclusion. Hannsgen & Bradley (2001) traced grade patterns for the last 2 years of "traditional" math instruction and the first 4 of "redesigned" instruction (i.e., from 1995 to 2000) and found that "overall grades show no particular pattern of increase or decrease" (p. 1). Final examination scores did increase with the redesign (Hannsgen & Bradley, 2001 p. 5), although the data to not allow one to judge whether this was an effect of the new technologies and instructional styles or of closer alignments of course material to final test questions. Looking at grades for the first and last years of the data provided—admittedly an arbitrary spread—only nonresident foreign aliens and Asian American students had higher average grades in 2000 than in 1993. The average grades of African Americans, "Spanish Surnamed Americans," and "White, non-Hispanic Americans" declined (Hannsgen & Bradley, 2001 p. 14). Only the nonresident foreign aliens had averages above a B in 2000; both African Americans and Spanish Surnamed Americans had averages below a C. The evidence shows considerable fluctuation from year to year, which might be related to changes in the test.

WHAT KIND OF INNOVATION IS THE EMPORIUM?

The Emporium changed instructional "labor requirements" by redistri-
buting contact across software and helpers (themselves students) who
circulated through the facility as students worked. FQ saw the helpers as
the Emporium's distinctive feature:

> The real product is not courseware but the whole setup: Emporium, helpers,
> focus group procedures, etc. We are tempted to think of courseware as
> electronic textbooks. But traditional textbooks fit into an elaborate and well-
> developed established system. Here there is no standard context. To be
> successful the context itself must be imported along with the software. Note
> there is already a lot of software available; the supportive context would be
> the unique part of this offering. (FQ, 1998, pp. 1–2)

By this account, the Emporium was not online remote education but a
kind of technology-enhanced teaching and tutoring environment (cf.
Blumenstyk, 1999b; Goodyear, Salmon, Spector, Steeples, & Tickner, 2001,
p. 66). As FQ explained: "We are not developing online remote education.
We are developing onsite education because we have found that the help
aspect is absolutely essential—the personal, immediate help. And we have
tried some of these things online and they are not very successful."

According to FQ, "online remote education" hides instructional
breakdowns and failures. The reasons behind students' problems remain
invisible to the teacher or aide who sees only their cumulative result—the
student dropping the class or making a bad grade:

> Generally, when you get away from the campus, you tend to find students
> whose preparation is even more uneven.... You find people with much
> weaker backgrounds. You may find more motivation or you may not. But, one
> of the things that we have really become sensitized to here over the last
> decade or so is not so much what we do for the students who succeed in the
> program but what the students who fail miss out on. So an online thing can
> only be considered successful if you don't consider failures.... What tends to
> happen is that most of the people just drop out. They get stuck. They are
> basically on their own. They do not have the supportive classroom
> environment.

If one thinks of instruction as mere content delivery, the lack of a
supportive environment isn't necessarily a problem. But if the aim is to
help ill-prepared students get good grades, then by this argument a place
like the Emporium should offer place-anchored instruction and have the
capacity to flexibly focus attention on individual students when they have
difficulties. The idea of the Emporium, as least for FQ, thus wasn't to break
with contact but to allow its more flexible allocation.

An additional premise of this practical logic is that students' difficulties are understood as specific gaps in disciplinary knowledge: as evidence that students lack a particular mathematical concept or skill rather than evidence of, say, lack of effort and attention, or general stupidity. These difficulties can be made visible only by mapping them onto a discipline-defined problem repertoire:

> When students have trouble learning ... it doesn't show up in some sort of abstract way: "Attention, faculty, your learning model is wrong." It's very sort of nitty gritty. You know the students can't work this problem. You really have to go at that from a disciplinary way and understand it before you can abstract it to any kind of sort of course transformation, course generality thing. So, it requires faculty expertise. (FQ)

If one needs a thorough understanding of the mathematics to diagnose and respond to student difficulties, it follows that responsibilities for teaching, planning, and designing instruction can only be done by people with the requisite mathematical expertise—not by technology specialists or instructional designers (cf. Ausubel, 1968, p. 352). As FQ put it:

> The learning process really does have to be tailored to the material being learned. I think there are some useful generalities, like design the test so they can be used for task assessment. But then in each individual subject what you have to do to a test to make it useful that way is probably quite different. So, fairly quickly you hit the content issue.

If you imagine the mathematics taught in the Emporium as a kind of landscape on which math problems mark locations and points of orientation, CMI can be thought of as an instrumentality enabling students to set the pace and sequence of their movements. This implies a certain conception of learning:

> It's really different than they learn in a classroom. They're more actively involved in it. They have to develop their own learning strategies.... So, for instance, we have always thought of as the right sequence of events as that there's a presentation, there's some examples, there's some homework then there's a test. The student's don't do that. We find a lot of the students will go directly to a test before they're anywhere near ready for it. And they'll take the test. So, some of our really superb classroom people were very disturbed by this and they said, "Should we lock up the test so they have to see a presentation first?" But, really it's a better thing to do to think, you know, "Why are they doing that?" (FQ)

The idea embedded in this view differs from the view of learning as a function of movement through a specific sequence of small steps that produce skills or knowledge that can be measured through assessments involving applications to newly encountered tasks. In this latter view instruction should make it difficult or impossible for students to get access to assessment tasks without first traversing the instructional sequence. FQ's idea of giving students access to quizzes up front, allowing them to detour around the sequence and concentrate on the specific test requirements short-circuits these premises. It assumes that tests actually provide evidence of proficiency, that performance indicates competence, that being able to work a problem is proof one knows how to work it, and that there are multiple legitimate pathways to assessment tasks. In such a scheme, students can take quizzes iteratively, first to identify the discrepancies between their current ability and the test, and later as summative assessments to be entered in the course account book. As FQ put it, assessment events would thus also be instructional events: "Because we have tests available on the machines, they can take them as many times as they want, so why bother with homework? Go to the authoritative thing first. That's the way they think of it, so okay we'll go with that."

The idea of using assessments as instruction is not new (see Newman, Griffin, & Cole, 1988, pp. 76–89), though it's usually considered as a way for teachers to monitor student learning to guide future instruction, or as part of a method for encouraging student reflection (e.g., through portfolios). In FQ's vision, the relationship was more direct: The tests were ways of telling students what they needed to know. This role had implications for the structure of the CMI:

> Our tests have to be a little more clear than maybe they should. We can't really expect that the students have already seen it. It has to be something that at least they can understand well enough to get started when they first see it. The tests have to be comprehensive. We can't spot check because that creates an incorrect assessment on their part of what they have to do and guides them incorrectly. Also, when they start actually getting into the material, of course there are places for presentations and things like that but the reference, I mean the textbook, has to be less linear.... Our early materials, lab books and things like that, where somebody would make up a lecture, plan and then transcribe it—[were] very linear, and that was really not successful. What we see is students sort of skipping around, using things more in reference mode. So, that means our materials have to me more compartmentalized.

Compartmentalization of content seems to mean modular organization without a linear, hierarchical sequencing. Subject matter is a landscape across which students can move back and forth by variable routes:

> To understand what's going on on the page you shouldn't have to go far from that page, it should be linked or something like that. It should be easy to

navigate and in particular we have to get away from the assumption that if they're on page 99 then they read page 98: because they really don't use it in that mode. We have found things like there's a real difference between the way students use online materials and printed materials and it is still very important to have printed materials. But, they have to be more carefully designed to take advantage of what's different about holding something physically. (FQ)

In this logic, the temporal organization of instruction is driven by students' difficulties, not the internal structure of the subject matter. And this defines the problem. CD-ROMs and software can give students access to assessment items and control over the pace of presentation, but they cannot respond well to misunderstandings. Students would need help from people who could look at their work, listen to their questions, press them to clarify, and give assistance and monitor its effect. According to FQ the provision of such assistance was one of the main ways the Emporium improved on traditional instructional:

We have a lot of helpers out on the floor. And if somebody has a problem, we help them right away. One on one. Specific.... The stronger students who do okay in sort of any environment are okay ... if they were going to do okay in a classroom, they'll do okay here. The weaker students who have real trouble in a classroom have trouble here, but we can give them more personal help here than we could in a classroom.

But what if you don't have assistants, or not enough, or they can't handle the students' difficulties?

THE CIL-FUNDED EFFORT

The CIL grant was to help develop the Emporium's capacity for rapidly reconfigurating this help function, or as the proposal put it, to create a "remote help" system for a range of computer-based courses in the Emporium (beginning with calculus courses). As the grant proposal explained:

The [Mathematics] Department is converting many of its on-campus courses to computer-based formats to be offered in the Math Emporium. These will also be offered off-campus at sites including the Northern Virginia center and Virginia State University. This can be successful only if we can provide students with fast personal help when they encounter difficulties. Basic help can and should be delivered by personnel physically present at the work area, but economic considerations require most help, including specialized help in the Emporium, to be offered over the network from a remote location. This abstract point has been clear for some time, and the original course development proposals included videoconferencing and similar help facilities. However our understanding of what students actually need has evolved a lot over the last year, and the first guesses now seem off the mark. As a result development of help facilities is lagging behind courseware. It is imperative to get them back on the same schedule. This project will refine and field-test new approaches, and begin deployment when a successful system has been developed. (FQ, 1998, p. 2)

One problem, according to FQ, was that Emporium helpers did not always have enough mathematical expertise to deal with students' problems:

> Maybe most of our helpers are actually undergraduates, and they certainly wouldn't be qualified to teach the course, but it turns out that they are very good at helping with a lot of the problems that the students have. But then there are problems they can't handle—more specialized problems. So what are we going to do about that?... Well, we've tried to have faculty floating around, but you know if the faculty member is stuck somewhere talking to somebody or drifts into a tutoring situation, they are not available. This is a big place; how do you find them? I don't know. It wasn't working very well.

A second problem was that the students' work would be indexed to problems and images in materials that might be inaccessible to the faculty expert and the students themselves might lack the mathematical knowledge to explain their difficulties verbally: "The original proposal has a lot in it about visualizing materials that the students ... suppose they take out a textbook and we're trying to help them online, we're sort of lost. Or suppose they take out an assignment sheet or something like that, what are we going to do?" (FQ).

The CIL monies were thus to support the creation of a flexible communication system that would make professorial assistance more accessible to students without requiring an increase in the number of faculty members physically present. The idea was to add to and reconfigure the work of the helpers, not to replace or automate it with technology: "The driving idea of this proposal is a sort of expert online backup for the floor help. It really was not intended to be a sort of stand-alone thing" (FQ).

To give such help, as noted previously, the physically distant professor needed a way to see the equations, problems, and diagrams as students worked with them, and to talk to students. The CMI needed to address problems of visibility (enabling the professor to see what's happening elsewhere), the multimodal nature of instruction (the coordination of artifacts like textbooks, papers, pencils, and computer screens, with gestures, facial expressions, postural orientations, speech, and so forth; see Jewitt, Kress, Ogborn, & Tsatsarelis, 2001), and time (both the amounts needed to resolve a student's difficulties, and the problem of apportioning time among hundreds of students).

ERROR VISIBILITY

The first response to the problem of making student work visible at a distance was to look for software to do the job. As FQ recounted:

> So, I thought, maybe we could have some kind of netcam thing they could put it under, or a scanner or something like that. So we tried some of that. The net cams have too low resolution.... That just didn't work. It didn't address the problem. So, the software we tried ... we tinkered with Network Assistant for a while, but that wasn't satisfactory. So what we got was Timbuktu [a software program]. And that has facilities for visualizing the student's screen, controlling the student's machine and an audio link. So we tried doing that for a while, for a semester or so.

The goal here was to create a window onto students' work for the physically distant expert who would have two-way communication with the students: "We had a lot of computer labs that were in Mathematica and the students were having some technical problems with Mathematica and often the floor helpers would not be able to deal with that. So the idea was, we would have some Mathematica guru: me" (FQ).

This guru arrangement involved buttons and lights on computer stations that would let faculty experts signal their availability and allow students to signal for help. It turned out, however, that although it was possible to make a computer screen simultaneously visible in two places and create an audio link between student and guru, such arrangements weren't always sufficient for determining the sources of student errors: "I could connect to the student's computer and see the screen. I could type in stuff or move the cursor around and there was the audio link. Well that didn't work out all that well.... First of all, there are a lot of things that go on that it's very hard to get to diagnose just looking at a computer screen" (FQ).

Part of the problem was that the computer hookup wasn't really supple enough to allow complex communication:

> The interface was cumbersome, we had to locate 500 microphones. Using the microphones was awkward. The audio link was slow and patchy. If somebody spoke out of turn it would black out part of it. That makes it sound like better software would be the answer, but there were other problems too. (FQ)

One of these other problems was coordinating the professor's help with the helpers' efforts. As FQ explained: "I wasn't part of the interaction between the student and the original helper, and usually the original helper would go off and sort of leave me trying to figure out what was going on. They were sort of cut out of the loop."

It was the helpers who could move around, spend time with students, look over their shoulders, and question them to elicit the sources of their difficulties:

> These students tend to have trouble formulating what the problem is and when they do, they're usually wrong. That's the other thing we've learned about online coursework is that the human interaction with the students is mostly from the student to the helper and the task is diagnosis. It's not information delivery. (FQ)

Insofar as physical proximity is crucial for unscripted and ambiguous interactions (Boden & Molotch, 1994) the helpers were better positioned than professors to sustain instructional interactions in emergent, uncertain situations (cf. Dreyfus, 2001, pp. 59–61). They could gauge students' comprehension or frustration and draw connections between their efforts, explanations, body language, and timing. As FQ recounted: "After a while it became clear that the students would rather have an inexpert human helper who could watch their body language, listen to them, see them point their finger at the screen than have a really expert helper behind the screen."

In this analysis the problem for CMI developers was not so much to connect students directly to the guru, but to improve communications between the guru and the helpers:

> The next idea was that the expert help should really be a resource for the human helpers. So the human helpers would go and say, "Hmm, I don't understand what's going on here, let's tap into the expert." Then the expert would log on, but the expert would really talk to the human helper who would be watching the body language and the pointing fingers and reading the text material and so on, doing some processing, helping with the diagnosis aspect of it, and then when the problem was sorted out it would go back through the human helper. That way they could better fit the delivery or any kind of explanation. As soon as the human helper understood it, which usually was pretty quickly, then they could do variations of their own to help the student do it. That didn't have to go back and forth through the machine, that would be effective, and also the human helper would learn how to deal with that kind of problem. It was really supposed to be a hidden training experience for the human helpers. (FQ)

As it turned out, guru-helper communications, like those between professors and students, needed to be more supple than feasible versions of computer mediation allowed. The developers turned to less place-bound devices: walkie-talkies. As FQ recounted: "The next iteration was, and this is what I spent the CIL money on actually, is we bought walkie-talkies so the audio link wouldn't be through the computers, but via walkie-talkie with the helpers, and that put the helpers in the link. The helpers made it much more immediate."

MEDIATION AND MONEY

A big part of teaching is the coordination of "mediating artifacts"—the "structural elements … brought into coordination in the performance of the task" (Hutchins, 1995, p. 290). The CMI in the project described here involved successive reorganizations of task elements that included visualization software, communications technologies, human helpers, texts like quizzes, and so forth. In FQ's description, the final configuration of relations seemed to work pretty well:

> The helpers would call in and say we need help with problem such and such in such and such a lab and if it was appropriate the expert could use the Timbuktu to visualize the students' screen and do some diagnosis of the code-type thing or whatever was appropriate. But, with the human helper there interpreting body language and stuff like that and learning that seemed to be much more effective.

But if this was a workable system for students, it was not successful from an administrative standpoint:

> So, right about then, we quit. We discontinued the whole thing, because it was too expensive in terms of faculty time. We had not released enough resources and we couldn't do the kind of bookkeeping we needed to do. We couldn't say we need a highly paid full professor sitting in the back never looking a student in the face, or rarely, just available via walkie-talkie or something like that and that's going to be their instructional assignment. That's very expensive. We couldn't afford it.… Eventually we'll learn how to do this thing on the smaller scale, but right now the only way we can be sure it will actually work, and be effective and justify the cost of all the helpers and so on, is to have between 5,000 and 10,000 students and even that is not enough for the expert online.… We've phased out a lot of computer material in our regular classes, which means there's less demand for expert help.… We are not going to be able to have really significant computer interactions in the courses, and we won't be able to support the help that it would need. So that was the outcome of this project. That we learned how to do it, and then we discovered we couldn't afford it.

DISCIPLINARITY AND CMI

Tech's Math Emporium has been publicly lauded as an exemplar of good CMI in the national education press. *The Chronicle of Higher Education* profile quoted earlier in this chapter described its success in these terms:

> Professors who work in Virginia Tech's Math Emporium have always believed that it's a revolutionary way to teach undergraduates. Now they have data, they say, that backs them up. The percentage of students earning a grade of

2.0 or better in business calculus is up from 66 in 1996 to 78 in 1998, the second year the course was taught at the emporium. (Olsen, 1999b, p. A31)

Such evidence makes the performance of the Emporium visible in ways that administrators seem to find compelling. Tomlinson-Keasey (2002), for example, recited the evidence noted in Olsen (1999b) and claimed that the data "suggest that students learn as well as or better than, they might in traditional courses" (p. 139; see also Davies, 2004). Tomlinson-Keasey went on to report that "the Math Emporium concept and the associated redesign of mathematics instruction have been modified and adopted by the University of Alabama, the University of Idaho, and most recently by Riverside Community College" (p. 139).

As noted earlier, things like students' comments, numerical ratings of instruction, and changes in grade distributions are dubious indicators of teaching and learning. The university relies on them, however, partly because they're easy to generate and quantify, but also partly because of the way most Emporium courses fit into students' academic careers. Consider that in contrast to veterinary pathology the Emporium was providing disciplinary knowledge for a nondisciplinary audience (very few of the students were math majors). In the former case professors could index CMI-related tasks to a range of multimodal experiences spread across different situations (coursework, lab work, field work, etc.), and trace their cumulative impact on students. In the Emporium, by contrast, professors had only the test results for a term.

The contrasts just invoked distinguish a couple of course types. First, there are courses organized around disciplinary knowledge for students intent on entering the discipline. Most professional education would fit this description. Departments offering and professors teaching such courses could be expected to claim jurisdiction over instructional practices rather than cede them to designers or others. Courses would be situated in long time frames, that is, linked to other courses within the curriculum stream and to disciplinary endpoints outside the course, even though the latter might be years away.

Second, there are courses organized around disciplinary knowledge for nondisciplinary audiences. The disciplinary emphasis again implies faculty control over instructional decisions, but the nondisciplinary aspirations of the students change the relevant time frame to the length of the course, and linkages outside the course are to experiences and settings that belong to different curriculum streams (e.g., Math Emporium courses linking to engineering courses).

These differences in course forms and functions had implications for how professors used CMI. In veterinary pathology the CMI provided a long-term study tool for students but did not reorganize classroom action. In the

Math Emporium the CMI was focused on immediate, transitory exchanges but did not cumulate or take the form of artifacts that students would take beyond the course. Instead of disciplinary information, the CMI mediated instruction across professors, helpers, and courseware. The next and last chapter in this part of the book explores a third course variant, one common in large research universities: the introductory survey or distribution course designed to provide nondisciplinary knowledge to nondisciplinary audiences.

Making Lectures Visible:
Redesigning in Nutrition

The planning model ... treats a plan as a sequence of actions designed to accomplish some preconceived end. The model posits that action is a form of problem solving, where the actor's problem is to find a path from some initial state to a desired goal state, given certain conditions along the way.... Goals define the actor's relationship to the situation of action, since the situation is just those conditions that obstruct or advance the actor's progress toward his or her goal.... The plan is prerequisite to action.

—Suchman (1987, pp. 28–29; see also Agre, 1997, p. 141)

This chapter deals with efforts to transform a traditional lecture course of about 500 students (taught in two sections of 250), first into a mixed-format, part-lecture, part-online course (organized around PowerPoint slides and online web notes, illustrations, diagrams, and practice tests), and then into an online, self-paced course (an effort that never went beyond a summer prototype). The professor, DS, recalled that her involvement began when:

> The head of my department told me that there was a [CIL] grant for innovating, or whatever you might call it, one of the core courses [which DS was scheduled to teach]. And she said she wanted to nominate two classes from our department.... And so, I thought about being a new faculty member and being very interested in teaching. I thought, you know, this is a way to get it done once and for all, out of the way.... Anyway, to make a long story short, I thought about it and decided to take it, once I looked at the specifications of the CIL [grant proposal].

The CIL grant was written with and used to support a collaboration between DS and a unit called the Biological Sciences Initiative (BSI). According to its web page, the BSI was set up, as was the Math Emporium, to deal with rising enrollments and shrinking budgets:

Between 1991 and 1995, Virginia Tech's enrollment remained static. However, the number of undergraduates in the four colleges with life sciences undergraduates increased by nearly 50%, from 2,372 to 3,579 [this would seem to be over 50%]. Students in the life sciences are the largest disciplinary cohort in the University. This rise in life sciences majors coincided with a dramatic reduction in support for higher education by the Commonwealth of Virginia. Across the University, faculty and staff positions and instructional dollars decreased by about 15% over this same period.... The result was increased class size, inability of students to schedule courses required for their degrees, and lack of more specialized offerings. (BSI Webpage)

Instead of a big, centralized learning environment like the Emporium, the BSI strategy was to support course transformations through instructional design (ID), a frame for CMI development advocated at Tech as early as the 1989 report of the Task Force on the Impact of Digital Technologies on the Classroom Environment. Through the BSI, ID would be used to:

engage faculty members in the teaching-learning process, so that their expertise is transferred to students by taking advantage of learning theory, instructional design and educational technologies.... The BSI has employed the services of two instructional designers, whose expertise is available to all BSI-affiliated faculty members to transform their courses. (BSI Webpage)

The focus here is the practical logic of teaching implicit in DS's work, but as ID became a powerful influence on that logic a necessarily brief and incomplete sketch of it is required.

ID DEFINED

There are different approaches to ID (e.g., Seel & Dijkstra, 2004a), but a textbook identified by a BSI designer as exemplifying his approach gives a definition that includes many widely accepted elements. First, instruction itself is "the delivery of information and activities that facilitate learners' attainment of intended, specific learning goals. In other words, instruction is the conduct of activities that are focused on learners learning specific things.... Every learning experience that is developed is focused toward a particular goal" (Smith & Ragan, 1992, pp. 2–3; see also Gagne, Briggs, & Wager, 1992).

As this suggests, the idea is not to discover goals or outcomes in the course of instruction, or to change goals as the process unfolds. Rather, goals should be well defined and transparent to participants from the outset and correspond to what students need to know or be able to do to carry out prespecified tasks identified through an analysis of some domain of activity (cf. Twigg's [1992] definition of educational outputs). ID promotes instructional efficiency by tightly linking instructional events to these goals or objectives. Design is thus "a systematic planning process prior to the development of something or the execution of some plan in order to solve a problem. Design is distinguished from other forms of planning by the level of precision, care, and expertise that is employed in the planning process" (Smith & Ragan, 1992, p. 4; see also Seel & Dijkstra, 2004b, pp. 6–7).

In addition to helping DS define instructional goals and objectives, then, the BSI designers worked with her to plan the course, and assisted her in producing PowerPoint slides and quizzes to animate the plan. A description of the CIL-funded work written after the first year of the 2-year collaboration provides an overview of these aims:

> To improve learning outcomes the course objectives, content materials, and student assessment measures ... were designed to correspond to the course goals. The course lecture format was designed according to established principles of effective direct instruction to improve student learning. A course Web site, designed with features to support teaching and self-paced and interactive learning, was designed and developed.... Lecture outlines were developed and placed on the course Web site to allow students to reduce the extraneous cognitive task of taking notes during lecture and thus more fully attend to the concepts being presented in lecture. PowerPoint slides were developed and placed on the course Web site to provide the instructor with easy to update course materials and to provide students with tools for reviewing and studying course materials when and as often as they chose.

ID AS A DIVISION OF LABOR

In addition to honing objectives and shaping materials and assessments, designers help insure that projects are efficiently managed (Bates & Poole, 2003, p. 58). As one Tech administrator explained, instructional designers "have a managerial role: to move the entire instructional design process forward, trying to keep it on track. What we call a project management role." In this respect they belong to the category of higher education staff that Rhoades and Slaughter (1998) labeled "managerial professionals": workers who "do not fit squarely into the category of faculty or administrator but constitute an occupational type that bridges conventional categories" (p. 49). According to Rhoades and Slaughter

> They share many characteristics with traditional liberal professions—a technical body of knowledge, advanced education (and in some cases certification), professional associations and journals, and codes of ethics. Yet they also mark a break with the liberal profession of faculty, being more

closely linked and subordinate to managers and indeed being very much managers themselves. (pp. 49–50; cf. also McCollow & Lingard, 1996, p. 15)

The rise of managerial professionals in the instructional precincts of universities is part of a wider trend in which teaching responsibilities are being shifted from tenurable faculty members to staff in adjunct, part-time, or nontenure stream jobs (Roemer & Schnitz, 1982; Tirelli, 1998). As Rhoades and Slaughter (1998) put it, "full-time faculty are decentered, as part of the professional workforce and as producers and deliverers of curriculum" (p. 48).

This decentering is not uniform across the university curriculum—for example, it seems more likely to affect teachers of large, introductory, 1% courses than professors of upper division, graduate, or professional courses—and can be pursued in a range of ways. At one end of the continuum the University of Phoenix uses course development teams of content experts and instructional designers to create syllabi and teaching scripts for instructors who often have little teaching experience:

> When the lecturers actually teach the courses, they are free to add extras … but they must stick to the objectives outlined by the group–and they all teach from the same detailed syllabuses and faculty notes. The notes are so explicit that an instructor shouldn't have to do any lesson plans for the five workshops of four hours each that make up a full course…. The course designers carefully script each in-class activity for instructors and each out-of-class assignment for students. (Farrell, 2003, p. A10)

In another approach, instructional designers at Pennsylvania State University work as part of a centralized administrative unit to produce distance education courses using a standard template. The course is considered the property of the university, which through this arrangement can "maintain control over production and keep costs down" (Carnevale, 2000, pp. A37–A38). One Penn State administrator was quoted as recalling: "Before the standard template was developed, creating online courses took individual designers too long, called for too many bells and whistles, and often involved methods that could not be easily understood by another designer" (Carnevale, p. A38).

At Virginia Tech ID was less centralized. Although its concepts pervade Faculty Development Institute workshops, and instructional designers worked on staff for the BSI and other CMI-related units (e.g., the university's Institute for Distance and Distributed Education or IDDL), there was no design template, and as chapters 6 and 7 demonstrate, faculty members undertaking course transformations were not required to use ID. On the other hand, professors asking for help from BSI, IDDL, or the Educational Technologies unit would find ID or at least some of its basic assumptions hard to avoid.

ID AS A PEDAGOGICAL INFRASTRUCTURE

These basic assumptions derive mainly from behaviorist psychologies and procedural versions of behaviorism such as programmed instruction.[1] They include the idea that content can be segmented and sequenced, that instruction should be linked to immediate feedback, and that goals and objectives should be specified at the level of individual behavior. Smith and Ragan (1992), for example, defined "instructional goals" as "statements of what learners should be able to do at the conclusion of instruction" (p. 66). ID builds these premises into what designers understand as theory-neutral techniques and procedures (e.g., Snelbecker, 1999).[2] Conceived as a technical practice, ID provides an infrastructure for CMI work not only at Virginia Tech but at higher education institutions around the world. Hartman and Truman-Davis (2001), for example, claimed that "the prominent role of instructional designers" (p. 52) is one of two characteristics of the "leading institutions" pursuing CMI (the other being the integration of information technologies with instructional technologies). They argued that "the effectiveness of faculty development programs based on the central role of instructional designers often distinguishes institutionwide efforts from boutique efforts" (Hartman & Truman-Davis, p. 53; Bates & Poole, 2003). Recent publications on online learning frequently echo ID positions. Simonson (2000), for example, defined "learning outcomes" as "observable, measurable behaviors" (p. 31; see also D'Andrea, 2003). Ryan, Scott, Freeman, and Patel (2000), citing the consulting firm Coopers and Lybrand's

---

[1]Although the term *instructional design* (ID) didn't become commonplace until the 1970s, its practitioners trace their disciplinary ancestry back to psychologists working with the military on the selection and training of personnel during World War II. Educational psychologists like Robert Gagne, once employed as a writer of programmed instruction, later president of the military psychology division of the American Psychological Association (Tennyson & Schott, 1997, p. 4), and programmed instruction advocates such as Mager (1962), who was also involved in military training research (Molenda, 1997; Noble, 1991), were influential in the development of ID (and educational psychology generally) after the war (Dick, 1987, pp. 197–200). Assumptions about design and instruction that developed historically with behaviorism, sometimes as an explicit part of it, are now congealed in design practices that are understood by practitioners as neutral technique (cf. Waks, 1975). As Burton et al. (1996) pointed out, "many of the current instructional design theories use major components of methodological behaviorism such as specification of objectives ... concentration on behavioral changes in students, and the emphasis on the stimulus" (p. 58).

[2]Thus proponents argue that ID principles can be used with any theory of learning—behaviorist, cognitivist, constructivist, activity theory, and so on (e.g., Jonassen, Tessmer, & Hannum, 1999)—though certain basic assumptions do not seem to change. For example, the constructivist ID approach to integrating CMI into university instruction described by Bates and Poole (2003, p. 162) shares much with explicitly behaviorist accounts. For a useful account tracing the influences of behaviorism on ID practice, see Waks (1975).

criticisms that CMI efforts in the United Kingdom were "amateur" and unsystematic, recommended a "framework for course design" that closely tracks ID practices:

1. A description of designed learning outcomes (these are commonly expressed as course aims and objectives);
2. a specification of course content (describing knowledge and skills and desired learning experiences);
3. a specification of the tutorial strategies to be employed (issues covered here include sequencing of learning experiences, choice of media for delivering learning experiences and the role of dialogic interactive activities designed to encourage and reinforce effective learning);
4. the assessment strategy to be used (encompassing both formative and summative assessment aims) (p. 43).

The formalization of instructional content and process implied in such statements has implications for the social organization of instruction. Specifying goals and objectives allows designers to define a boundary between content and method and thus frame a division of labor. As a prominent early ID theorist explained:

> Possibly the most fundamental reason of all for the central importance of defining educational objectives is that such definition makes possible the basic distinction between content and method. It is the defining of objectives that brings an essential clarity into the area of curriculum design and enables both educational planners and researchers to bring their practical knowledge to bear on the matter. (Gagne, 1967, pp. 21–22)

Once this boundary is drawn (not always an easy task, as the previous two chapters show) professors can be defined as content experts. And once these content experts define objectives against which course tasks can be calibrated, the designers can assume their role as pedagogical experts and guide professors' instructional strategies (Reigeluth, 1999, pp. 7–8).

In practice, of course, things don't work this straightforwardly. As the BSI designers stressed on a number of occasions, their design alternatives were limited by externally imposed constraints, chief among them the large size of the course, which produced a design emphasis on practices suited to jumbo classes: lectures, detailed PowerPoint slides, and multiple-choice tests.[3]

---

[3]There were efforts at project work as well, which proved difficult and time consuming. Large class size does not, of course, necessarily imply the use of CMI. Bartlett (2003), for example, described the case of a professor teaching a 1,000-student course, relying in part on 15 undergraduate and 2 graduate teaching assistants. The effect is reportedly opposite in some ways to the division of labor envisioned by instructional designers: "By delegating most of the day-to-day administration of the class, Mr. Halgin is free to concentrate on content" (Bartlett, p. A14).

THE GOALS OF THE COURSE

As large, lower division survey courses are used by departments to generate enrollments and productivity statistics, they must be designed to attract students from across the university. The vast majority of students in the nutrition course, for example, were not majors in nutrition or dietetics. The course therefore could not presuppose any interest, knowledge, or previous coursework on the students' part, nor could it afford to delve too deeply into theories or research in the discipline. Too much biology or chemistry and students uninterested in one or the other (or lacking the background to deal with them) might stop choosing nutrition as an elective. For DS, then, the problem was to present nutritional science without focusing too much on the science. Inasmuch as this was a problem shared by nutrition professors teaching similar courses across the country—that is, a structural problem rather than one resulting from the context of this particular course— standard solutions had already been developed and embedded in widely distributed material. The course textbook, for example, neatly articulated a nondisciplinary approach to the subject:

> When you study nutrition, you learn which foods serve you best, and you can work out ways of choosing foods, planning meals, and designing your diet wisely. Knowing the facts can enhance your health and your enjoyment of eating while relieving you of feeling guilty or worried that you aren't eating well. (Sizer & Whitney, 2000, p. 2)

The main objective defined by DS and the instructional designers paralleled the textbook's: Students should be able to assess their diets in the terms of nutritional science and use the field's guidelines to plan better meals. This didn't mean the course was about meal planning and cooking, however. Rather, it was designed to provide students discipline-based information that they could apply to decisions about shopping, cooking, and eating. For DS, helping students use knowledge this way meant helping them use "critical thinking." At first, she "wasn't quite sure what critical thinking was. And it kept being brought up in meetings that I went to, in the evaluation form, and I realized that the kids themselves didn't know what critical thinking was about. So I tried finding out about critical thinking."

DS tried initially to encourage critical thinking by having students look outside the course for information relevant to nutritional science:

> I saw it [critical thinking] more of acquiring beyond what is in the classroom. Not necessarily applying to yourself, just more information. So that's what I did in class. I had the two sections competing.... Anyone who brought in a bit of information that is relevant to the class material gained an extra point for the whole class. So that was fun.

Through workshops given by the university Center for Excellence in Undergraduate Teaching (CEUT) she began to develop a different understanding of the concept: "They had sessions on critical thinking. Because even when people talked about it, I still, for some reason–[laughs] to me, critical thinking was thinking for yourself–it is thinking for yourself–but it's really more application of the knowledge to yourself. And I just didn't see it in that light."

The light from the university's instructional specialists illuminated critical thinking in terms of students "applying what they know [from the disciplinary frame presented by the course] to their lifestyles." In the context of the course, application meant evaluating everyday eating events in the language of the field. The main project in DS's revised course thus required students to "estimate their energy balances" and record and analyze their "food, beverage, and nutrient supplement intake" (breaking it down into protein, fat, carbohydrates, fiber, and various vitamins and minerals) along with their physical activity (to be analyzed "using the ACSM Physical Activity Guidelines"). Then they had to plan new diets.

MAKING OBJECTIVES EXPLICIT

Student work on the course project obviously took place outside official class sessions. It was those sessions, however, that provided the basis for the material on quizzes and thus the bulk of the course grade. DS explained how classes had been organized before she began to work with the instructional designers:

> I relied on the instructor's [guide], but any idea that came to my mind I just brought it into the class. So there was no, there was nothing systematic. It was creativity on the spot. I'd be preparing the lecture, some idea would come to my mind, and I'd do it in the class. If there was a word—I'll give you an example—I was very much into the origins of words, so I'd tell them, I'd look up the origins of words and tell them about them. This was taken out by instructional design as—I don't know what the explanation was. It did save me time. And I would encourage them—I created the idea of a bonus for anything that they'd research and bring to class.... That was my own. I was very much into animating some of my classes, some of my lectures. And I would have done it had I not worked with instructional design. Instructional design held me back from that. They said it would not add anything.... Like for example if I was doing the alimentary canal I would like to have some parts of it move right then and there, to show the peristaltic movement. I would like to do that. Just every now and then just throwing in something really crazy, just to wake them up. But I was told that that does not add anything to their learning. I believed that when a class is happy, meaning the students are happy—this is just my gut feeling—that they are more prone to learning. Instructional designers told me that is not the fact. Nothing proves that.

The practical logic implicit in this account focused (pre-ID) on the unfolding classroom event. That is, as DS could not assume that her students were interested in her as an exemplar of the field, and could not count on their professional ambitions to sustain attention and engagement, the orienting instructional frame became the problem of keeping student attention during class (and by extension, getting students there in the first place). Digressions about word origins, the use of multimodal forms like animation to engage different modes of perception, or "just throwing in something really crazy" can be seen as tactics for capturing students' attention. In this logic, teaching effectiveness would be defined by high student attendance and attentiveness.

The effect of the design effort was to get DS to focus less on students' enthusiasm and more on aligning her lectures with course objectives. The mechanism of alignment was PowerPoint software. Each lecture began with a slide listing the day's objectives, and when topics were introduced the objectives slide would reappear to help students situate the new information. Written in more detail than simple outlines, the slides included phrases like those students might take in their own notes, structured the subject matter into linear sequences of hierarchically ordered units of information, and formalized these sequences in a predictable visual format (cf. Sutherland, 2004, pp. 6–7; Tufte, 2003). According to the designers, standardizing the form of the slides and indexing them tightly to the objectives relieved students of the work of deciphering the mode of presentation—figuring out what they needed to attend to for future quizzes. The objectives supplied the frame of relevance, and redundancies in the formatting allowed students to concentrate on the content. According to DS, this structuring of the content was the main benefit of her work with the instructional designers:

> the organization, the systematic way of presenting. So the kids were always expecting, "Okay, I'm going to see a purpose, I'm going to see objectives." ... Instructional design had it [the objectives] incorporated into the actual PowerPoint so the kids had it all in one place. And ... they would repeat the objectives and highlight every different one.... It just made things more compact, more together.... The objectives for the class are always being mentioned. And as we go down the objectives list, the objectives page is being flashed again, and everything connects with those objectives.

DISCARDING DEADWOOD

Aligning lectures to objectives involved winnowing the material to be covered. Like many university professors, DS thought first of instruction in terms of content (Stark, 2002):

[I had] a tendency of wanting to give them [her students] everything that there is out there about nutrition. [laughs] ... The instructional design team has helped me quite a bit with that.... They put me on the spot. "Okay show us how this is going to—"Okay, what are your goals?" So I tell them my goals. Basically it's healthy living. Healthy eating. "Okay, tell us what, you know, this chemical reaction—how this connects to the healthy eating."

Content that cannot be explicitly calibrated to objectives is considered "deadwood," which Smith and Ragan (1992) defined as "information that is not essential or especially supportive in learning an instructional goal. Deadwood is often included in instruction when a content expert writes the instruction" (p. 65). In a course like nutrition, most of the chemistry and biology vital to a nutritional scientist's understanding of an issue would seem unnecessary from the standpoint of instructional designers and most students. The design process involves eliminating such material and writing instruction in a more direct and expository fashion. As DS recalled, "And if I can't explain it, it goes out of the window. [laughs] They don't give me enough time to think! If they gave me enough time to think I'd come up with a reason, but they don't give me enough time to think. So out of the window it goes and we move on." This conceptual defenestration was of a piece with tightening the connection of the remaining course material to the objectives. As DS added, "[The instructional designer] is doing a wonderful job with linking the information that I really want—sometimes even, I just know it's important, gut feeling, but I can't connect it, she finds very good ways of helping me and showing me how to connect that."

JURISDICTIONS

Abbott (1988) suggested that professions assert control or "jurisdiction" over domains of activity by colonizing task areas emptied out by external forces, or by seizing them from other groups or professions: "External and internal forces create vacant task areas and greedy professions. In the first case, environing professions and new groups will contest the open task. In the second, professions will search for new work at the expense of old neighbors" (p. 98).

As the preceding chapters illustrate, jurisdictional shifts in university pedagogy have proceeded unevenly. The political pressures described in part I of the book opened up teaching, long a poorly rewarded jurisdiction in many regions of the research university, as a vacant or vulnerable task area. CMI was the medium by means of which groups like instructional designers and technologists could make a claim on it.

Claiming a task area like teaching involves advancing definitions of the activity, the kind of knowledge it requires, and who controls that knowledge.[4] This can happen in various ways, but the one most relevant here involves splitting off certain tasks within a jurisdiction, defining them as technical matters, then shifting responsibility for them onto other groups. Latour (1996) suggested that from the standpoint of the group delegating tasks: "To simplify its task, every group tends to think that its own role is most important, and that the next group in the chain just needs to concern itself with the technical details, or to apply the principles that the first group has defined" (p. 67).

When groups can claim such technical details as neutral, bounded task areas, however, the "details" become media of jurisdictional expansion. Treating practices like constructing objectives, organizing content, and designing software as neutral, technical matters (Reigeluth, 1999; Snelbecker, 1999; Waks, 1975) turns them into "black boxes," that is, "stabilized tools," "no longer questioned, examined, or viewed as problematic, but … taken for granted" (Clarke & Fujimura, 1992, p. 10). The theoretical claims presupposed in these boxes are hidden and the teachers' practical logics are pushed out of view.[5]

The separation of content from pedagogy effected by this move can be examined as a philosophical problem (e.g., Segall, 2004), but it's also fundamentally about the control of teaching. Casting professors as content experts implies that there is a separate task area of discipline-independent pedagogical expertise that can be centralized and bureaucratically administered. But if, as Rhoades and Slaughter (1997) argued, "technology … is another means by which [university] managers can bypass faculty's bailiwick, the curriculum" (p. 20), this has been a contested process.

Although some professors were willing to share their curricular bailiwick (especially when it involved huge, lower division survey courses), others resisted the delegation of instructional responsibilities to people outside the discipline. One of the veterinary school professors characterized the ID agenda as unnecessary and impractical:

---

[4]Abbott (2001, pp. 136–153) differentiated processes of expansion and power in academic disciplines from those of professions, but for the most part his discussion of academic work did not deal with undergraduate teaching, which, especially in the case of large, lower division courses, is better understood as a professional work task than as a "settlement" organized around specific disciplinary cultures of instruction. This would vary within and across institutions.

[5]Psychology (or educational psychology) is in a sense a disciplinary base (certainly in a historical sense), but instructional designers see their work as independently grounded: The design of instruction, at least in some accounts, can proceed without any particular theory of how people learn, or as noted elsewhere can combine contradictory and antagonistic theories. Thus Ausubel (1967, pp. 4–5), an educational psychologist identified by one of the BSI designers as a key resource, was one of many educational psychologists in the 1960s who argued that "theories of teaching" were independent of "theories of learning" (see also; Reigeluth, 1999, p. 13).

I viewed [CMI] as something I would do myself.... We have someone who works with [us] ... from over on the main campus—so we have an instructional design resource [referring to BSI], but I have over the years developed my own view of how web sites should be constructed. And I went through an FDI course on instructional design and teaching techniques and I was, you know, tearing my hair out at the end of it. I was optimizing my objectives in the cognitive domain until I wanted to barf and I—all the edu-crat doublespeak really turned me off.... It wasn't terribly useful no—there were some interesting ideas in there, but people who have to do other things besides a 100% teaching commitment and who are on 12-month contract—the amount of time you would have to spend to implement some of those really cool ideas means you would never have any time for anything else.

In Mathematics, FQ argued that disciplinary jurisdiction couldn't be delegated because teaching and learning issues in math education were specific to the subject matter and their resolution required disciplinary insight:

You had said, should course designers or course transformers work with faculty to do these things?... Doing a computer-based course ... what you find out is that there are some programming problems, there are some presentation problems, but those are not the killers. Those are really small potatoes compared to understanding how students learn. When students have trouble learning or—our current learning model of the learning process isn't quite right, it doesn't show up in some sort of abstract way— "Attention, faculty, your learning model is wrong"—it's very sort of nitty gritty. You know the students can't work this problem. You really have to go at that from a disciplinary way and understand it before you can abstract it to any kind of sort of course transformation course generality thing. So, it requires faculty expertise. So that's going up. Coming back down is just as bad. The learning process really does have to be tailored to the material being learned. I think there are some useful generalities like design the test so they can be used for task assessment. But then in each individual subject what you have to do to a test to make it useful that way is probably quite different. So, fairly quickly you hit the content issue.

Instead of a single CMI agenda or movement, then, a mix of external and internal pressures—budget cuts and reallocations, circulating policy slogans, administrative centralizations, and capacity-building efforts—have allowed different groups and organizational units to expand and establish organizational bases in the jurisdiction.

MAPPING INSTRUCTION

The result is a variety of CMI forms and uses. In the pathology course, the CMI centered on an artifact that contained images indexed to professional objects and environments (e.g., animals and their diseases, lab apparatuses). Assessment of students was ongoing and multimodal (not just written tests, but lab performances, etc.), and cascaded across the students' tenure in the program. The CD had a utility beyond the particular course because of the program's extended temporal organization and because the CD made aspects of the actual work of veterinary medicine visible. These characteristics and the tight organization of the curriculum selected for and shaped highly committed students, some of whom could even participate in the development of the CD. The program itself became a (perhaps the) unit of instruction. In this context, the live, "performance" teaching put a claim on the whole student—one had to be bodily engaged, attentive, interactive—and made the whole teacher (animator, author, and principal) available as model or professional exemplar.

In the Math Emporium, FQ's CMI was part of an effort to create a flexible diagnostic circuit in which students would be visible against the backdrop of a standardized pedagogical environment (i.e., the math problems they were working). If the CMI in pathology made parts of the professional work environment (e.g., images of lesions) visible to students in a form they could carry across the years of the program, the object of the CMI in the Math Emporium was to make students' transitory difficulties with math problems visible to professors at a distance and to embed that visibility in a communication circuit that included the human technologies already in place (the helpers). Learning was defined by students' performances on the criterion task. Assessments could take place at variable times, and in some cases were repeatable (e.g., quizzes could be retaken).

In nutrition, the problem was to produce a course that would have indefinite extension—that is, link to a range of settings external to the institution rather than specific courses within it. The solution was to make it academically self-contained, neither presupposing nor entailing other courses, and to tightly align course material to tests and within-course uses. CMI was thus used to make content visible as a test-calibrated text. As in veterinary medicine, the instructional work was distributed across multiple participants in the planning stage, though instead of students, instructional designers helped the professor shape objectives, calibrate instruction to those objectives, and then translate the instructional content into stable forms that would be accessible to students outside the class sessions. This design activity involved extensive investments of time by designers and professor.

In each case, the kind of CMI that was possible and desirable depended on other characteristics of the instructional situation, in particular, the ways programs and administrative practices shaped the students professors worked with. Practical logics of teaching are geared to certain kinds of students, and students are in turn partly products of university admissions practices, financial aid policies, course-taking requirements, and the social and academic resources of the programs. This variability among students suggests that their study practices with CMI, the topic of the next section of the book, are likely to be complex and heterogeneous as well.

III

THE STUDENT GAZE

9

Making Coursework Visible
in the Frame of the Test

As it is, the professors give too many lectures and the students listen to too many. Or pretend to; really they do not listen, however attentive and orderly they may be. The bell rings and a troop of tired-looking boys, followed perhaps by a larger number of meek-eyed girls, file into the classroom, sit down, remove the expressions from their faces, open their notebooks on the broad chair arms, and receive. It is about as inspiring an audience as a roomful of phonographs holding up their brass trumpets. They reproduce the lecture in recitations like the phonograph, mechanically and faithfully, but with the tempo and timbre so changed that the speaker would like to disown his remarks if he could. The instructor tries to provoke them into a semblance of life by extravagant and absurd statements, by insults, by dazzling paradoxes, by extraneous jokes. No use; they just take it down.

—Slosson (1910, p. 520)

What is decisive in collecting is that the object is detached from all its original functions in order to enter into the closest conceivable relation to things of the same kind.... Collecting is a primal phenomenon of study: the student collects knowledge.

—Benjamin (1999, pp. 204–205, 210)

There's no typical student experience of CMI, and this chapter and the one that follows are limited in that they examine CMI uses through the eyes of students drawn from just one class, the nutrition course discussed in chapter 8. The picture would look different had the students been recruited from a different kind of course. The advantage of using nutrition, however, is that as a large, introductory course it attracted a diverse group of students, some in their first semester in college, others on the verge of graduation, in fields ranging from the liberal arts to computer science.

The focus is not what students thought of the course (e.g., Evans, Gibbons, Shah, & Griffin, 2004; Hamilton & Zimmerman, 2002; Hara & Kling, 2000; Kitto & Higgins, 2003; Kuh & Hu, 2000), but how they

describe its CMI—the PowerPoint slides and web notes. Although these are far from cutting-edge technologies they are commonly used by many college students, and their relative simplicity makes them useful starting points for analyzing a basic feature of most CMI—the mobilization of course content. As Cornford and Pollock (2002) suggested, "In order to become mobile, work must be transposed into a format that is compatible with the technologies in use. To achieve this compatibility, work must be untangled from its local constraints and stripped of its existing linkages" (p. 90).

Web notes and PowerPoint slides don't exhaust the possibilities for mobilization, but by examining their uses in nutrition we can begin to get a sense of what's entailed in untangling and stripping teaching and learning from their anchorings.

NOTES AND NOTE TAKING

Cornford and Pollock's (2002) formulation suggests that we can think of web notes and PowerPoint slides as technologies for turning academic content into "text." As Silverstein and Urban (1996) explained, "To turn something into a text is to seem to give it a decontextualized structure and meaning, that is, a form and meaning that are imaginable apart from the spatiotemporal and other frames in which they can be said to occur" (pp. 1–2).

Students have long encountered instructional materials in the form of texts—books, most obviously. Notes, however, were distinctive in being produced during class sessions by students converting lectures into texts for study (Armbruster, 2000; Dunkel & Davy, 1989). CMI seems to offer the possibility of changing this text-making in two ways. First, it can allow students to get notes without physically going to a class. Second, it can allow them to experience the class with already scripted notes in hand. The former is not a radical innovation—students have long been able to buy, borrow, or copy notes. Having notes produced by the professor before class available during class is more distinctive. According to some CMI advocates, having notes in hand during a lecture releases students from the "extraneous cognitive task" of writing as the lecturer speaks. The argument is that students can't think well about the meaning of what's being said if they're busy writing it down. Simultaneous note taking presumably interferes with concentration and distracts students from the lecturer's inflections, emphases, and paralinguistic cues, making it more difficult to catch the rhythms and momentum of the talk and stay mentally engaged. By contrast: "Automated capture can help relieve the students of the burden of copying down everything that goes on in the class, thereby enabling them to concentrate better on the lecture or take fewer, more personalized notes" (Brotherton & Abowd, 2002, p. 75).[1]

Some students in nutrition offered similar explanations when asked if they learned better writing notes during lectures or listening to lectures while reading already printed notes:

> Like I think that by printing them out on the computer, I learn better. Which sounds funny because I am not like writing it down, but when I am writing it down I have a hard time concentrating on what the teacher is saying and understanding and then also trying to write it down. Like I will be trying to like copy the notes from the like overhead thing or whatever ... and I won't be paying attention to what she's saying. And I won't understand the material. So the only way I learn is when I go back and look at my notes. And that's just like, almost like the first time reading them, like, "Oh, wow, she really talked about this." But if I have the notes printed out it's like they are in front of me so like I can follow on what she is saying, I can pay attention to what she is saying and I can just jot extra things down if there is something that is not on the paper. (Lee)

For other students the issue wasn't just whether notes were available beforehand, but the amount of information and pace at which it was presented. In classes where the lecturer's presentation was paced by the time it took to do something like write equations on a chalkboard, and in situations where lecturers intentionally paused or repeated things to let students write, students reported little difficulty:

> My organic chemistry class, you look at the professor, he doesn't have the notes on the web, he like goes over everything from the book.... Organic chemistry can be difficult to understand the concepts.... But he pretty much goes over things repeatedly for us to understand ... and then while he is going you are actually paying attention. You are writing them down. And he doesn't give slides, he is doing it while, like you know he is writing everything while you are writing it, just like easier for us to grasp it. (Kate)

Problems with note taking by hand were most pronounced in courses where professors used technologies—including older ones like overhead transparencies—to display lecture material as detailed, already written texts: "I had a professor who just put overheads up and like, you know, they

---

[1]Other higher education commentators compare the number of words than can be spoken across a particular duration to the number of words that can be read, and add the argument that prewritten course material is preferable to lectures because it allows a greater amount of content to be delivered (Green & Dorn, 1999, p. 60). Aside from reducing the lecture to a content-delivery device instead of an event for thinking, this argument would seem to apply as well to books as CMI.

talk and it's like a huge overhead with like a million words and you have to write it down. And when you are done, you don't know anything about what he said. It just went over your head" (Peggy).

Creating content representations like these detailed overheads, or the PowerPoint slides in nutrition, was a way for the professor to prespecify what would be covered in each class session. Indeed, making deadwood-filtered PowerPoint slides and notes tightly aligned to objectives and tests available to students before a class may have created a pressure to get through all the slides designed for the given class period. This could produce situations where students who tried to take notes by hand were simply unable to keep up:

> I think sometimes there would be, sometimes, it wouldn't happen all the time, there would be too much information and so in class we go through it so fast that you really don't get a good grasp on it so then you are stuck, like you know, doing it by yourself, you know, on your own time, which is fine, but I feel like we could spend a little bit more time and slow things down a little bit more in classes sometimes. Because I just remember her flicking through the things and I was like gosh like it was crazy.... That was sometimes though, that's not very often. (Laura)

> **Hattie:**   One time because I talked to the TA [teaching assistant], and she said, "Well if you are having a problem understanding or something like that you might want to try writing it down." ... And I tried that, and I kept up for a little while and then she just went too fast I was just like, "okay I can't do this."
> **Gloria:**   You know something that was hard, like if you did go to class and you tried to take notes, because at first like, at the beginning of the semester I went to class every time and I never printed out the notes because I knew that [if] I had them in front of me I would just chit-chat you know and not pay attention or whatever. Like sometimes it would be like they were talking real fast, even if you were abbreviating every word there's no way you get it down.
> **Hattie:**   Yeah, so if she was going to take the notes off the web she would have to go a lot slower too.

In addition to the sheer volume of information presented, pacing also depends on the novelty of the material:

> What matters [to the student] is how new and unfamiliar each communication is; how much redundancy with previous learning there is; how much he can count on what he already knows to help him take each step. Too many steps, each too big, all to be taken too quickly, will lead to a stumble—or to dropping off the pace, and maybe even out of the race. (Lemke, 2000, p. 267)

It might seem that web notes would make speed and novelty moot, as students would not need to worry about taking notes by hand. And in fact, when asked to show their notes for nutrition, students showed print outs of the web material, occasionally adorned with hand-drawn illustrations copied from the PowerPoint slides in class (see also Newlands & Ward, n.d., cited in Brabazon, 2002, pp. 121–122; Ward & Newlands, 1998, pp. 181–182). But what do such notes represent? It's unlikely that many students try to write down "everything that goes on in the class"—the task from which web notes supposedly relieve them (cf. Armbruster, 2000, p. 180). Imagine instead that courses are suspended between two coupled organizations of information. Benjamin (1978), writing in the 1920s, suggested that the scholarly book had already become little more than a moment in the relation of two sets of notes:

> Today the book is already, as the present mode of scholarly production demonstrates, an outdated mediation between two different filing systems. For everything that matters is to be found in the card box of the researcher who wrote it, and the scholar studying it assimilates it into his own card index. (p. 78)

Lectures, presentations, textbooks, and CDs can be similarly imagined as mediations between the "filing systems" of professors and students. The contents of a professor's "card box" are relatively ill bounded and dense in connections to field-specific issues and ideas (that is, full of "deadwood"). In nutrition the problem of preparing a lecture was to put this knowledge in a form that didn't presuppose information students weren't likely to have, to segment it into discrete chunks, and to shrink the segments to the size of PowerPoint slides.

The second organization of information—the students' card box—is thinner and corresponds to what students think will be required for future tasks. In nutrition the notes were keyed to course assessments and worked as media for detaching and storing instructional events in forms that could be reviewed, loaned out, copied, summarized, or combined with other mediating artifacts (textbooks, old tests) to prepare for the tests. As the experimental studies reviewed by Armbruster (2000) suggest, what seems to matter is not whether students take notes as they listen to lectures or have the notes beforehand, but what they do with them afterward: "The real value of taking notes is to have them available for review prior to performing the criterion task [i.e., the test]" (p. 179).

The fact that CMI can make material available in dense and complex forms for repeated and prolonged examination does not alter the students' need for the material to be thinned to the thickness of the criterion task. Rather, it reshapes responsibilities for thinning, allowing teachers to do more of it so that material comes to students already tightly indexed to the tests.

STUDYING

For a while during the 1990s, as CMI spread through the university and sunk into its infrastructure, Virginia Tech administrators justified offering introductory courses with high enrollments, lecture-based instruction, and multiple-choice tests by invoking Perry's (1968) stage-and-sequence model of college student development (derived from interviews with Harvard undergraduates between 1954 and 1963). One strategic planning document asserted:

> There is a large body of research which explains the development of higher order thinking in college students. The foundation of this scholarship was provided by Perry who demonstrated that students progress through predictable stages of intellectual development, from dualistic thinking, through multiplicity, to relativism, and finally to commitment.... Because students can foresee the basic outlines of the next stage only when they are ready to enter it, any learning stages more than one step removed are inaccessible intellectually.... This understanding of cognitive development impels a curriculum which is increasingly labor-intensive as students proceed toward graduation—lectures for freshmen, seminars for seniors in the most traditional form. Lower division students, who typically are functioning more toward the dualistic end of the spectrum, will be comfortable in lecture classes with objective tests. (Virginia Tech Strategic Plan, 1996–1998, § 3.1.2)

Aside from the fact that third- and fourth-year students take lower division courses along with first- and second-year students, the more fundamental problem with this reasoning is that developmental models (Jonassen, Marra, & Palmer, 2004; Nelson, 1999; Perry, 1968), ignore context, gloss over organizational diversity, and underestimate the flexibility of students' repertoires for engaging instructional situations.

As Entwistle and Ramsden (1982, p. 12; see also Entwistle, McCune, & Hounsell, 2002; McCune & Entwistle, 2000; Ramsden, 1988) argue, different study approaches reflect strategies rather than developmental levels or intellectual styles. In what they label a "deep" study approach students relate instructional tasks to personal interests, think about "the relationships between different parts of the material" (p. 137), and try to synthesize general meanings. In a "surface" approach students focus on memorizing for the test without interrelating the parts of the lessons or trying to connect the material to contexts outside class.

Which approach students employ, does not depend on their learning stage but on the kind of material the course deals with, how that material is presented and used, how work is assessed, "the type of a question given in a test " (Entwistle & Ramsden, 1982, p. 21), the way a task relates to tasks students encountered in previous courses (cf. Hutchins, 1995, on "task histories"), the anticipated difficulty of the required work relative to work in other courses or activities (cf. Becker et al., 1968), and the relation of the course to students' longer term ambitions (e.g., whether they are trying to get into medical school or to finish up a bachelors degree and exit higher education).

Take the case of Lynne, a fourth-year business student who enrolled in nutrition because it was a "1000-level" or freshman-level course. To her this implied she could boost her sagging grade point average (QCA) by making a good grade with little effort:

> I took it because it was outside the Business School, which 50% of my credits have to be and because it fit into my schedule at exactly 1:00 p.m. which was when I had time to take a class. And I went through and I said what BS [bullshit] class can I take at 1:00 p.m. that's a 1000- or 2000-level class that I don't have to spend much time on?... I am not going to remember it in January much less a year from now ... I looked at the syllabus and checked her announcements and I just looked to see when the test was and I showed up and that was it. That sounds really awful, but that was probably the best part of the class is that it was so easy and they were giving you an A for the most part so that it just seemed too easy. Which is a good thing. It's raising my QCA. (Lynne)

It was "easy" in the sense that a "surface" study strategy—looking over the textbook and using the web notes to cram for tests—could bring a good grade. For other courses, however, Lynne reported studying differently. In commercial bank management she worked "every night. I study at least an hour. I go to the teacher once, twice a week.... So there's a big difference." Why? Possibly because Lynne was a finance major and bank management meant something in her long-term plans. Nutrition didn't. Moreover, the form of presentation in bank management made regular attendance and attention necessary, whereas the web notes and multiple-choice and short-answer tests in nutrition were more forgiving of a surface approach (cf. Entwistle & Ramsden, 1982, p. 165). As Lynne explained:

Lynne: [In nutrition] everything is on the web whereas in banking it's a general outline and then you go to class and you figure it out. He's probably the only one like this, but he's very specific, and he never gives out real notes that you take in class, but yet if you are there you kind of absorb it, whereas if you are not, you have no clue what's going on. So it's virtually unskippable for the most part.

JN: That's interesting. What is it, so how do you take notes in the banking course?

Lynne: I don't…. For the most part unless something is written on the board, I don't. But if you are there and you understand–and then we also have a bank game which we are broken up into teams where we compete against each other and the economy playing a bank game once a week. So you put in the input and it comes out and whatever. I know it's retarded, but it's actually really helpful in learning. So it's a very much hands-on type of thing.

The picture of how programs of study and instructional forms shape study strategies is further complicated in this exchange from a joint interview with Elfreda, a nutrition major, and Yoko, a second-year biology major. Elfreda, for whom the nutrition course was a programmatic foundation stone, puzzled over how to interrelate the material—to study it in a deep fashion and really learn it. Yoko, for whom the course simply fulfilled a distribution requirement, argued that for such a course one just drills for the test:

Elfreda: They did like did Native American [dietary habits] and they did African American, and it was interesting to learn like, okay, this is this culture and this is that culture and this is that culture, but there was like maybe one like common thread, if that. Like you don't understand why you are like, if there's not enough detail to understand a lot about the culture, like if I just think off the top of my head I think of like the three sisters, like you know (grains) for like the Native Americans, then here talk on [slavery?] African Americans and how like they got to eat lunch a big meal because they were done with their work, and Native Americans was like, go with the land, you know what I mean? Like it's good information, it's great to learn about, but you are like, "Where are you coming from?"

JN: Where does it fit into the learning scheme of things?

Elfreda: Right, yeah and I think that's kind of shorted there too. Like you are saying okay well this applies to nutrition because–it's interesting, I see that it can. I see that it should but it just wasn't like, it didn't get there.

JN [to Yoko]:   You feel the same way or did you have a different take on it?

Yoko [to Elfreda]:   I can understand where you are coming from but when I studied I just like done it, and I just went through everything repeatedly. And I went through it until I felt comfortable with knowing everything. But I could see where sometimes it could be hard. But I just go through it and through it and through it.

JN: You go through the notes?

> **Yoko:**   Right. And I read the chapters too. And the chapters are usually a lot broader than the notes so if you read the chapter and then read the notes you can kind of tell what she's emphasizing I guess.
>
> **Elfreda:**   It's a good point where you are saying, like I agree with that but it's like I have a really hard time studying it right off, just like, like ... why and what is it okay, you know what I mean? So I get really frustrated easy with that type of studying but I am really glad that works for you.

Among other things, I want to suggest, these differences are differences in the destinations of academic work.

TESTS AS DESTINATIONS

Summarizing their research on students' strategies, Entwistle and Ramsden (1982) argued that "dichotomized descriptions of learning such as deep/surface could not be used to describe students but could be used to describe students in particular learning situations" (p. 159). What's a "learning situation"? In the main, CMI advocates depict technologies as making course materials and instructional events accessible to geographically dispersed participants: The learning situation is a bubble surrounding content and assessments. Technology produces "Cartesian transformations" (Thompson, 1948) of recognized instructional events—deforming their spatial and temporal coordinates, stretching them this way and that, without breaching their bordering membranes. CMI moves or expands the learning situation out of its campus-based physical space-time location, in effect refashioning the "contact" for which "credit" is supposedly given.

But students don't just move around outside a course or a campus. They move within its space and time. Their problem is to transport parts of the course from their original locations to later collection points. Some of these collection points can be outside the course, as was true for the pathology course, but many are inside—tests, most obviously. Tests are not evaluations for students, they're destinations. CMI may allow course materials to move in principle in all directions, but students move materials to such destinations for particular reasons. Nothing, in other words, stays "untangled from the local" or "stripped of linkages" (Cornford & Pollock, 2002).

The question thus isn't just whether study is deep or surface oriented, but where it's aimed. Students get help targeting from various sources. Information about courses moves through networks fostered by business associations, fraternities, sororities, athletic teams, engineering clubs, peer groups, and the like. Such networks also provide resources to help members study in course-appropriate ways. As one student explained:

If you are studying for a grade, which I do a lot of the times, you will just like, for example for my chemistry class, we have koofers,[2] why I guess there are koofers for most classes, but like I will go over and if I can do the koofer if I can do every question, I am satisfied. I will be like, "Good, I can do good on the test," you know. I don't go and like look at all the material and be like, "Oh, wait, do I know how to do every single thing here." Like it's not like I know how to do everything, it's like I know how to do the questions that she's going to ask on the test. So if you are studying to learn, I think it would be harder because there is more material.... Like for my nutrition class I will like read over it and get the basic concept of it and try, you know, as much as possible in the amount of time that I have to study. But if I am studying to learn it, I would be studying more intensely. I would be reading more carefully–not more carefully, I would be reading period. Like I would be reading everything. And like trying to know all the material and understand it and not just try and be like, "okay, well I know a lot of this stuff so I can get a decent grade on the test pretty much." (Lee)

Old homework problems, koofers, quiz reviews, and web notes tightly calibrated to test items allow students to anticipate how lectures and readings might fit into likely assessment forms. The effects on how students understand their own learning can vary. Earlier I quoted Lee explaining that the notes allowed her to learn more effectively. Paul, on the other hand, pondered the fact that:

The material is presented in the way that you are going to have to have it on the test or quiz. I am not sure whether that is best or not in terms of long-term learning because when you are presented the material in the form it will result in the test it's easy to become lackadaisical, like I see myself doing, "Oh, okay, I sort of understand it," and go on about it.... By organizing the information almost exactly the way it ends up being on the test or quiz, it ensures fairly good performance on the test or quiz by a student because the information is in our head the way it needs to be there. We can go to class, which stresses that, you know, you need to have this level of fat in your diet, and you walk in to take the test and asks you what level of fat you have in your diet. And because it's presented in a very similar manner, the notes are exactly what is used in class and that is what is lectured to, and that is what is in the book, and that is almost exactly the same form you find it on the test, the quizzes end up being pretty easy.

If students count good test performance as learning, this is fine. If their criteria for learning include longer term uses, the situation is less clear. Paul continued:

---

[2] *Koofer* is a Virginia Tech term for old tests, crib sheets, copies of old papers, and the like, used by students to prepare for exams or projects. These are sometimes made available by professors, and often they circulate among fraternities, sororities, or other student groups. A koofer in the use the student describes would be an old test.

My question about organizing it like that, though, is since it's almost spoon-fed to you and since its given to you so close to the way it's on the test or quiz, do I remember necessarily what is way back in the past? No ... because as I went through, the information was presented in such a fashion that all I had to do was understand it in that frame and didn't have to attack it and understand it in a wider context. And without that wider context it doesn't stick with me. It's just details and facts and figures and concepts that I memorized, the biggest of which I recall, but the smaller details which are certainly important in a nutrition aspect, I don't understand in terms of—I don't remember them, they just don't come to me by instant recall because since the information is presented so similar and you know that if I memorize the information on these slides it will get me a good grade on the quiz, that is how you attack the problem.

Students who sought more from the course than the grade—for example, students majoring in nutrition who might assume the material would be important to their later work—might find the web notes too tightly aligned with tests. Like Elfreda in the exchange quoted earlier, Boris, another nutrition major, had difficulty understanding the course material in a context broader than the test and found it confusing to study from the web notes alone:

So like I read over her notes like each page three times because she says if you know my notes you will do fine. Ha, for the first test that I did that, that wasn't true at all.... Like I didn't find that true. Like do you know what I mean? So next time I concentrated more, like you know, I did the notes, but then I also concentrated more on the book, but that got me really frustrated because it was just like that book is so detailed and not that it's a bad thing, but it's so detailed that I am like, "Whoa, what did I just read?"... She had asked like really specific questions [on the test] about the digestive system. Like, okay, well, you know, like she would give us a list of things and that would be like, "What stays in the small intestines and then goes down to"—do you know what I mean? Things like that. And like overall I understand everything. You know what I mean? But then sometimes it's like I know it, but it's so, like either her questions are detailed that I was more focused on getting in the overall, does that make sense? I am concentrating on trying to understand the overall that I am not getting the detail. Like even though there is a lot of detail to read like I guess I don't find that detail as important, but she does. Does that make sense? So it's like playing cat and mouse or something, do you know what I mean?

Like an arrangement of variably transforming mirrors the web notes and PowerPoint slides made visible an instructionally purified, deadwood-deleted version of disciplinary knowledge that students needed to anticipate the tests. The routes to other kinds of destinations were not so clear.

IF THE MATERIAL IS ALREADY MOVABLE,
WHY GO TO CLASS?

In courses like nutrition, which combined face-to-face instruction with CMI, students could use the latter to skip the former. The same class could be a lecture course for some students and an online course (save for test days) for some of their classmates (cf. Moore, 2003; St. Clair, 1999). As someone who chose to skip class sessions, Lynne explained:

> The whole idea of the Internet and all was great for people like me who don't want to go to class. For people who do want to go to class I think it was a little distracting because, I don't think people who went to class got rewarded. I mean, like everybody who skipped that class, and we all ended up with the same grade as the people who did go to class and diligently took notes and did all the right things. I mean, if I was one of those people I think I would feel pretty screwed over.

Other students, including many who did not skip, attested to the variability in attendance and its weak correlation to performance:

> A lot of people, I mean, don't go to class in this class. So and then the test day, you are, "Where did all these people come from?," you know? Like the whole room is filled. (Laura, who attended regularly)
> —A lot of people don't show up for class so it's like, you know, like, say, on Fridays are like, not even half the class is there. (Peggy)
> —It just amazes me, not only in that class but in other classes, how when you have exams it's just so full, you see people you have never seen. (Ethel)
> —Yeah I have a friend in the class who is a senior, he will be graduating in December … and he never comes to class but he does great in the class. He just must be that kind of a person you know.… I mean there are times like when I went to class like once, the vegetarian one, it was right before Thanksgiving so I am sure a lot of people had to leave and stuff, but there were like 10 people there you know, and I thought we should have gotten more credit for being there. (Marilyn)
> I know like probably five or six other people in that class and we are all the same way, none of us come to class unless there's a test that day or to turn in the project. All we do is we print out the notes the night before and cram. (Gloria)
> Nobody is ever there. The only reason I go is I feel guilty for not going. And I have classes all day it's not like I can just skip it and be sleeping or something like that.… So I just may as well sit there. But it is a waste of time.… On Fridays, we have like no class on Friday, in this huge room, and it's unbelievable how many people don't show up. And then test time comes along and everybody is there. (Hattie)
> Yeah, and then like my roommate she is in the same class as me, she never goes to class and her grades are better than mine.… Same class … same time

9:00 a.m. and she skips it. She hasn't gone, the last time she went to a class was so long ago, like three weeks ago or something. But just knowing that the notes are on the web she just gets them off of there and [Interviewer: And she's doing really well?]. Yeah. (Kate)

In addition to being a different course according to whether or not one physically attended, there were also differences in the accounts of those who showed up for class. Some spoke of DS as an entertaining, lively lecturer, whereas others insisted she simply read the PowerPoint slides. It isn't my aim here to sort out these claims (see the appendix for a discussion), but to point out that courses like nutrition are pools of situations, people, and materials to which students have differential access and out of which they construct substantially different instructional experiences. Some of this construction is done consciously and strategically, other aspects are emergent. These multiple versions of the course make it necessary to ask what it means for a course to be available to students anytime and anywhere.

Making the Course Visible
in Everyday Life

With wired classrooms, the time and place of instruction are transformed: education becomes available anytime, anyplace in the world. Like networked global markets, education becomes a 24/7 business.

—Taylor (2001, p. 258)

Let me tell you what I heard for 3 hours yesterday afternoon. I was in the "learning anytime anywhere" partnership grant-making session ahead of FIPSE [Fund for the Improvement of Post-Secondary Education] giving out $10 million this summer—they want modules. They don't want any traditional courses. They don't want programs. You can package the modules, but it has to be "learning anytime anywhere," which means asynchronous. (AM)

As students, we are asked to perform well on the tests, we are asked to perform well on the quiz, we are not asked to remember it 2 years from now even though that is the ultimate goal. That is not what we are asked to do. (Paul, computer science)

There are times when there is subject matter that I am extremely interested in that I enjoy reading about, that I think is fun, that I don't have to try to remember, that I like to remember. And then there are things that I can really care less about, that I am just memorizing to take the test. But I mean my philosophy is that, you know, especially college, is like a test. It's a 4-year-long test.... Sometimes you just have to memorize that information to take that test and pass that test so you can get the grade so you can get the QCA [grade point average] so you can get a job. Which isn't the most positive way to look at it, but there are just some things that you just have to accept. I am never going to need this again, but I have to know it now. (Molly, pre-med)

The claim that CMI lets students alter the temporal organization of school work and study anytime, anywhere depends on certain assumptions about the stuff to be studied: the "content." "Content" plays a key role in CMI discourse. Instruction is frequently defined as content delivery, for-profit distance education firms speak of "buying content," and organizations like the National Governors Association (2001) put out statements like this one:

Of the three main elements of e-learning—content, technology, and know-how—content is becoming predominant, with spending on content now overshadowing expenditures on technology by 5:1. The key future success factors for content providers are predicted to be large off-the-shelf libraries, large dedicated sales organizations, branded top-notch customizable content, and content that leverages the interactivity and personalization aspects of the Internet. (p. 9)

"Content is king," claimed the president of Teachers College Columbia, and universities "are in the business of discovering and disseminating content" (Levine, 2001, p. 144).

In these kinds of pronouncements, content refers to instructional artifacts—lectures on CD-ROM, video and audio clips, written materials, interactive software, and so forth—considered as analogous to entertainment industry content such as motion pictures and music videos (e.g., Blumenstyk, 2001; Duderstadt, 1999; Katz, 1999).[1] For some CMI advocates the fact that content of this sort can in principle be used by anyone with a computer and Internet connection means that traditional academic departments—along with teachers and even instructional designers—are becoming obsolete:

> In contrast to the realities of our educational past, the new paradigm and the capabilities of our on-line environment encourage options and choices for the learner in an unlimited learning environment. Learners proceed through a vast amount of content in an often apparently unstructured manner. Collaboration and cooperation are encouraged as are problem solving and critical thinking skills. (Gillespie, 1998, p. 44)

Such claims mesh with arguments that the private sector is increasingly producing and shaping basic research (Lee et al., 2000, p. 117; McCollow & Lingard, 1996, p. 13; Usher & Edwards, 2000, p. 264) and that employers (and the state) are increasingly defining the learning required for specific jobs. The workplace, in this image, would provide the objectives, and higher education faculty, as content experts, would supply the relevant knowledge commodities (Davies, 1997; Selingo, 1999). In such a scenario—and its accuracy is irrelevant here—distinctions between traditional educational settings and training programs would blur and the temporal and spatial parameters of learning would be opened to negotiation by students and the employers within whose schedules students would need to fit their studies:

> Educational institutions are no longer limited to educating individuals before they enter the job market. Community colleges and university systems

---

[1]It isn't just administrators or business consultants making these analogies. Professors have also used entertainment industry products as analogs for their instructional works in arguing for copyright on things like class notes and televised lectures (e.g., Blumenstyk, 1999a; Carnevale & Young, 1999, p. A41).

are taking a greater role in providing lifelong education opportunities while offering more short-term certification courses and extension programs. They are developing more customized training and education programs, working in partnership with private sector firms to promote training in areas linked to employment opportunities. They are also creating more contract training programs to capitalize on the trend toward corporate outsourcing of training services, and playing a more active intermediary role in the provision of corporate training. The knowledge and skills obtained by this contract training in turn feed into the educational components of the institutions. (Benner, 2002, p. 188)

CMI was supposed to play a critical role in these changes by providing instruction anytime, anywhere. In a 1997 paper written for the Educom Consortium, Carol Twigg and former Virginia Tech Vice President for Information Systems Robert Heterick (then President of Educom) argued that by 2007 "the vast majority" of higher education students "will not be pursuing a degree program; instead, they will be seeking to update their skills and knowledge base primarily in response to changes in the economy" (Heterick & Twigg, 1997, p. 1). Instruction in this context would consist of showing students how to negotiate work-defined content landscapes to acquire specialized skills for particular occupations (or more narrowly, particular projects at work). A National Governors Association (2001) statement on "Technology and the Learning Revolution" similarly argued:

As work-related tasks become more specialized, so too does the information a worker needs to complete those tasks successfully. The best kind of learning in this environment is learning that combines small, interchangeable bits of information to assemble personalized learning content. Technology accelerates and makes affordable the process of customizing learning by making it possible to store, re-use and re-combine these "learning objects." (p. 8)

The images presented in these scenarios harken back to programmed instruction's modularized course material calibrated to well-defined tasks in standardized environments (e.g., Carnevale, 2001).[2] The main difference is that the sequencing of the tasks would be generated by the requirements of the external (extraschool) setting. Anytime, anywhere in this respect

---

[2]Indeed, Doug Noble (1991) links notions of specialized, "personalized learning content" back to military training agendas:

For the trainee as well as the microworld designer, the "system" to be learned is not a subject matter at all, but rather the trainee's own "cognitive system": the "mental models" of physical and cognitive processes through which the trainee understands both the conceptual structure of technical systems, and his or her thinking and problem solving strategies in acquiring this new knowledge. (pp. 156–157)

refs to the needs of employers who want to have workers trained anytime, anywhere, rather than having to send them to school for sustained study.

THE FLEXIBLE STUDENT

By the mid-1990s this idea of developing CMI for a new market of flexible, off-campus, working students had become part of the argument for the Technology Initiative at Tech. A 1995 planning document from the university's Information Systems division made such a student visible through a "scenario" (Information Systems, 1995)—a kind of virtual demonstration—starring the fictional "Jane"—not a Tech student, but instead someone attending a local community college while working as a sales clerk and taking three classes online from Virginia Tech. In the scenario, Jane gets home from work at 6:15 p.m. one day, logs on to her computer:

> And notices that she has received e-mail from her microbiology professor at Virginia Tech.... Dr. Schultz includes in the e-mail note all of the class reading assignments, as well as pointers to additional reading material; all available over the net in electronic form. But Jane's child is crying in the background. (p. 1)

Jane is apparently a single mother.[3] She can't get the wretched child to bed until 10:00 p.m., at which time "She can really begin her microbiology class. Logging on to her computer again, she brings up Dr. Schultz's 'web page' on her screen, and explores the course materials in more detail" (Information Systems 1995, p. 1).

Noble insists that "this emphasis on the autonomy of the learner ... is not necessarily a departure from the overall objective of automated instruction" (p. 157). He cites military trainers arguing:

> Training is shifting from a teacher-centered orientation to a student-centered orientation.... This trend is particularly important where manpower shortages permit less and less use of expert human instructors. Students are increasingly expected to be self-initiating, self-motivating, self-pacing, self-assessing, and generally, self-reliant. The productivity of students, rather than the productivity of instructors, is becoming the focus in evaluating the success and efficiency of instruction (Fletcher, 1985, cited in Noble, p. 157)

"Learner productivity," Noble notes, does not imply "learner control," and "the view of students as 'autonomous systems' sometimes serves the purposes of automation and total control of the training process better than more directed conceptions of instruction" (p. 157).

[3]The majority of distance education students are indeed women (Kramarae, 2001). As Carnevale and Olsen (2003) note, the nontraditional distance education student is "personified as a single mother with a job and two kids who desperately wants to earn a degree and gain more marketable job skills, but who doesn't have the time to attend traditional courses" (p. A32).

Jane finds she's on a study team and e-mails her teammates, clicks her way to the university library web page for materials, checks in on a special collection of amoeba slides in Dusseldorf, performs "several experiments and makes a number of observations" (Information System, 1995, p. 1). This is all accomplished by 11:30 p.m.: "Feeling pretty excited, Jane decides to go ahead and take the first test. Still logged into her computer, she again connects to Dr. Shultz's Web page and begins the test. 45 minutes later, she finishes; within 30 seconds, the test is graded and she knows the results; she aced it with a 94!" (p. 1). Jane has finished the lesson in 2 hours and 15 minutes—less than the duration of a single face-to-face class session.

In such scenarios CMI allows students to fit coursework into the schedules and locations of family, work, and other nonschool streams of practice. Study is organized in segmented events involving insulated, self-referential information packages. CMI allows the frictionless articulation of academic work with activities like sleep and child care.

These temporally liberating benefits supposedly extend to students on campus as well as off. Hybrid courses that combine online and face-to-face formats—as in the nutrition course—are increasingly common (Young, 2002) and account for the majority of online enrollments at Virginia Tech (Carnevale & Olsen, 2003). As one Tech professor explained:

> Typically in a course where I would have 15 students online, 10 to 12 of them will be right here in Blacksburg. The others will be scattered all over.... Why do students who live in Blacksburg and can walk to my office want to take a course online? Because they're busy. They've jobs and they've got social and leadership kinds of activities they have to be engaged in, as well as another batch of classes. And the fact that they can do my course online and meet me in cyberspace once or twice a week and have real-time conversations about their writing and about the literature they've been working on, means that I'm reaching out to them in a way that, wasn't possible before.

As students have always been busy in these ways the distinctive contribution of CMI is presumably that it simplifies the coordination task by allowing academic work to be done at different times and locations.

On the one hand, then, CMI is supposed to unbuckle students from the temporal constraints of classrooms and courses, freeing them to move at their leisure across broad landscapes of content. On the other hand, CMI is framed as a response to the increasing temporal constraints of modern life. It allows people like Jane to get through the content by the shortest route, in part by helping her more efficiently substitute study for sleep. In the remainder of this chapter, I draw from interviews with students in the nutrition course to examine how this tension between anytime, anywhere and here, now, or never education played out on campus.

TEMPORAL ORGANIZATIONS OF STUDENT ACTIVITY

The Jane scenario centers on the use of CMI to vary the organization of academic work across multiple systems of temporal reckoning: the work day, the academic career, and parenting. Rather than transforming Jane's activities, CMI would substitute for them. The demands of her life are treated as modular and segmentable (rather than continuous and intertwined); the temporal ordering of activity is depicted as monochronic (linear, one stream of events at predictable tempi) rather than polychronic (multiple, differently rhythmed activities going on simultaneously; Hall, 1959). Time seems to be broken into relatively brief segments, organizable in terms of unique goals (getting the kid to sleep, passing the amoeba test). The goals are instantaneously given (i.e., no search or discovery processes). Social articulations (with fellow team members) are frictionless and require no time to establish.

Perhaps this is how it works. Two students in a distance education course, writing about their online experiences, seem to have been classmates of Jane:

> People in our stage of life, in our types of jobs, never have enough time just for the normal demands of life.... Times were stolen from my normal schedule—early morning, late at night, lunch hours at the office, weekend hours between doing the laundry and honoring our social obligations. Thank goodness the asynchronous aspect of the online environment lent itself to this kind of crazy schedule. (Hamilton & Zimmerman, 2002, p. 261)

The nutrition students, by contrast, reckoned academic efforts in terms of multiple time frames (the idea of a normal schedule being problematic, the lack of one a key to the ways college works), the most extensive being the undergraduate institutional career.

THE INSTITUTIONAL CAREER

An institutional career is a cumulative sequence of organizationally account-able experiences (courses, internships, etc.) that confer membership by credential in an institutionally consecrated category of person. Institutional careers in undergraduate education are mapped on academic program structures, and as at many universities Virginia Tech's programs were defined by "check sheets" that listed the courses for which students needed credit to receive particular degrees. Students used these lists both as course-taking guides and as instruments to measure their progress toward graduation:

The year 2000 checklist for HTM [Hotel and Tourism Management program] ... has what we need for the core curriculum and then the courses required in HTM and in the College of Human Resources and all the business courses we need. Then we have our list of electives. We have to have, I think, three electives from HTM and it gives us a list of about six or seven that we can choose from. And then we also have 2 hours of free electives I think.... Whether it's a prerequisite or one of the courses or one that I have to have to graduate, they all are. And my boyfriend was laughing at me when we were looking through those because he has all these open spaces [in his schedule] that he can take whatever he wants to take and mine is right down to the wire. You know, I have to take these this semester and these the next semester. And partly I guess it's because I came in one semester late and I am just a tad bit behind. I need to make up for that lost time. (Diane)

Students could get behind if they switched institutional career paths or were slow to commit to one:

On the paper [the check sheet] it has like all the classes you take your freshman, sophomore, junior, and senior year, and like for your freshman year it's like, it's tons of classes. Like that have to do with the major. So it's kind of hard like, I mean you should know, I mean it would have been nice if I knew last year so I could have, because ... like I took sociology and communications. And for my major I have to take psychology, so I basically took those two classes for nothing, and I have to go and take psychology. Which is a total waste of time for me ... it is like a waste of time for me to take sociology and communications when I don't need them in my major, which it would have been better if I had taken other classes because it would have been easier to graduate on time. (Lee)

The check sheets are less like prescriptive timetables (Foucault, 1979, pp. 149–156), then, and more like shopping lists—for students locked in an academic grocery where they have to buy something every semester, can't return or exchange anything, and where their early purchases can go bad if they buy without a recipe, develop an allergy to weed-out courses, or lose their appetite for a field. Whether you're on track or behind, or, as in Jasper's case, anywhere at all, depends on being able to plot your course taking to a check sheet:

The thing I think about all the time that has to do with school is this major. I have got to get a major down.... They give you this thing, you are in University Studies, and I go to see my counselor, you know, every now and then, and talk to her, and they don't really help you out. They just kind of tell you a little of this and that, and kind of point you in the right direction, but they will never tell, "You take this class, take this class, take this class," and I think that if it was up to me, and I got here on day one and they said, "All right you will be taking this class and you will take this class and go through in sequence just like this and then that is it, you come down and graduate and you are done." You know, that would have been great for me. Here I am now, I have all of these classes that are so random I don't even know what, I am just go in there and just ask them, "What does it equal [i.e., what kind of degree would the courses add up to]?" I am going to tell them, "What is this?" I don't know, that kind of makes it hard, you know, so then I get down to the point where I have got to sign up for classes, and I start talking to my friends, "Hey, you know, have you got any classes to take that you liked or that were interesting or you know?" I took Indoor Plants one time, someone told me that was an interesting class. It was kind of fun, though. And stuff like that, you know, I get classes. I don't know, I am not disciplined enough to sit there and say, "No I am going to do this, I have got to get a major right now and do that," you know. I just keep taking classes until they tell me I have to do something else, and then I will do it. I will pick something and, you know, loophole around it somehow. But hopefully I will get a major down here sometime and then you know it's kind of a worry, you know, you have got on your shoulders: Because here I am, I have been going to school now, this will be the third year, I am going to school, and I don't have a major. So now here I am for the past 3 years, I don't have any clue what I am going to do in life, you know, just sitting there, hmm, with a big question mark on the top of my head. (Jasper)

Students may find courses interesting in their own right (as Jasper enjoyed Indoor Plants), or for personal, idiosyncratic reasons (taking nutrition because one is interested in changing diets), but at institutional and organizational levels courses are meaningful only if students can plot them as locations on a graduation check sheet defining a temporally structured route to a particular degree. That is, check sheets are technologies for reckoning one's position in academic time—the temporal structures and endpoints built into institutional careers. As Munn (1992) suggested, such reckoning structures are ubiquitous tools that people use to "'tell time' to ask 'when' something happened, will or should happen—and to 'measure' duration—to ask 'how long' something takes, or to 'time' it" (p. 102). Check sheets, and at different scales syllabi and course assignments, serve as "ind[ices] of temporal distance from the accomplishment of certain purposes" (Munn, p. 104): getting a degree, passing the course, getting a desired grade.

Progress along these paths, however, does not imply movement toward understanding and knowledge. That is, events reckoned in terms of check sheets may be difficult to reckon to points outside school. Molly, for example, explained that she sometimes felt:

like when I am studying, it's sometimes like, "Crap, I don't need to know this, I honestly don't. It's interesting, but I don't need to know this." But then you just have to: You can't omit a class because it's something that in 10 years you will not need to know. Like there is not anything you can do to get around that. You have to do your best at it.... For example, this morning I learned about domestic violence and how often that it occurs, like once every 18 seconds is a statistic she gave us this morning. I will remember that. I guarantee you I will remember that. But say you know in 4 years I decide I will be a social worker, and I want to work with people who are victims of domestic violence, how am I going to know how to apply the definition of domestic violence in a statistic to that person?

Molly's sense of meaningfulness (the noncrapness of information) seems to be occupationally specific (no mention of the possible relevance of knowledge about, say, domestic violence, to one's actions as a citizen). This fits with her characterization of courses dealing with things she doesn't need to know as unnecessary detours, delays, and temporal dead-ends in the occupational trajectory. As a result, her uncertainty about the longer term or civic relevance of such information left her with only one way to make sense of the course: in terms of the grade. The dissipative object of academic work becomes a good score on the next test.

SEMESTERS, WEEKS, DAYS

Within the institutional career, students work with a cascade of temporal reckonings: Desired occupations are reckoning points for undergraduate programs, undergraduate programs for particular courses, the course for its required tasks and test, the tests for note taking and study. Take the case of Paul, the computer science major quoted at the beginning of this chapter: "Basically my class schedule is MWF [Monday/Wednesday/Friday]. I only have a single course on T/Th, which this year is a southern literature course taken purely for enjoyment and because it satisfies a requirement for my minor. MWF is much more focused on required courses."

Although not always accurate, the course-numbering system at Tech supposedly signals a course's difficulty, first- and second-year (1000- and 2000-level) courses being supposedly easier than third- or fourth-year courses. Paul used this mapping to shape the study-time demands of the semester and make it easier to maintain a high grade point average (GPA):

If I take predominately freshman- and sophomore- [1000- or 2000-] level classes [such as nutrition], my GPA will stay higher than if I branch out to take more 3000- and 4000-level courses. So I tended to stay towards that end of things simply because the CS [Computer Science] classes and math courses I have to take for graduation are fairly difficult and cause my GPA to decrease, and I have always had the goal of doing this combined graduate-undergraduate program knowing I needed to maintain a 3.5 GPA in order to do so.

Paul explained that clustering courses within the day made his schedule more efficient and brought it more into line with the temporal routines he'd encountered in the workplace (cf. Anderson-Gough, Grey, & Robson, 2001):

> In terms of my normal [Monday-Wednesday-Friday] schedule, my classes are stacked back to back to back on purpose. In past years I have found that by starting my courses later in the afternoon I was tending to stay up later at night, sleep in more in the morning and while I was able to get the same amount of work and be just as productive. Immediately preceding this semester I have been away at co-op for 9 straight months. And doing that, I got very used to getting up and being at work at 7:30 in the morning and going to bed at 10:00 to 11:00 at night, maybe 12:00 if my girlfriend and I went out to do something. So rather than having to switch my sleeping patterns back to what most people would consider abnormal–but for CS majors is a normal sleeping pattern–I decided to schedule my classes early in the morning. There I have nutrition at 9:00, geology at 10:00, engineering at 11:00 and CS at 12:00, at which time I am done for the day.

This schedule defined a temporal slot for pretest study—the hours before his string of classes—and turned the rest of the day into flexible study time (some of which might be spent catching up on lost sleep):

> MWF [Monday-Wednesday-Friday] normally I get up at about 7:00 or 8:00, depending on whether I have studying to do or not. If I have a test in the morning, I normally get up and spend 1.5 hours before I go to class as a final review. If I don't, then I will sleep in a little bit more in the mornings. After classes, which as I said I get out at about 1:00, I normally swing by Dietrick or Shultz [student commissaries] or somewhere and pick up some lunch and come back to the room. If I am tired, I will fit a half-hour to 45-minute nap in there and get up and start academics straight through until I call my girlfriend at 9:00 to 10:00, straight through until I go to bed at midnight.

This standardized routine was atypical of the students interviewed, most of whom varied their schedules according to weekly and semester-long rhythms keyed to test schedules and due dates for graded assignments. Molly, for example, a second-year student majoring in nutrition as a route to medical school, explained that she focused a disproportionate amount of time on chemistry, the course she found most difficult and the one that at the time was most important to her medical school ambitions. Her routine was shaped by the rhythms of assessment events:

> I always have labs due Friday, and I always do them Thursday night about 11:00.... It took me about an hour to do that graph.... I put the Y where the

X was supposed to be and vice versa and then I was talking to someone, I have a friend who was a chemistry major and I was talking to him on the phone and he was like I hate to tell you this, but it's the other way around. So I put about 17 points on this graph and extrapolated and done all of this other stuff and then I had to redo the whole thing, and it was not fun.... Chemistry is something I work probably out of all my classes the hardest at. I spend the most time on it, on a progressive daily basis. My other classes usually what I do is read every now and then so that when it comes time for the test I am pretty where I should be and then 2 to 3 days before the test really concentrate. Chemistry, I work a usual day for maybe an hour and a half and if it's a really hard chapter I work maybe 2 hours a day and that is during the week and then on the weekends, like a weekend before I have a test say Saturday afternoon from 12:00 to 4:00 I will sit down and do all the practice problems over again and look through all of my homework and all my class notes and everything I have highlighted in the chapters. And then Sunday it's an all day ... like 11:00 [a.m.] until I go to bed I sit there and review what this is, review what that is and go over the problems I don't understand. I call my friend, who is a chemistry major, and he tutors me and helps me out and then take the test on Monday and hope for the best.

Courses less central to the major or easier to approach with surface strategies usually required less time. As Paul explained:

My study time for nutrition is virtually nonexistent. It takes up very little time. It normally gets 2 to 3 hours, a day or 2 days before a test. That is the only time I spend engaged in the material. I find going to class and just reading the notes up on the web, the quizzes and tests are easy enough to where I don't have to spend that much time engaging in them so I simply don't. I have to prioritize, and if I can get an A without doing it, I don't.

Students' semesters are not temporally homogeneous or smooth, then. Academic work accumulates and gets compressed at grading points. Paul's routines shifted at such junctures to a system of temporal reckoning based on the difficulty of his courses and the types of assessments they used:

As we approach exam time, my schedule will begin to change. Come finals, I don't have a schedule. I sleep when I am tired, I study when I am not, I eat when I am hungry, pretty much I can be up from 4:00 in the morning to 8:00 in the morning. Go to bed when my roommate gets up, you know, whatever the pattern needs to be to get it done. I pretty much become a hermit, me and a bunch of books and some notes. And that takes a toll, but at the same time you only have to do it for a week or two so it's not an impossible task to pull out.

Because students take multiple, independently designed courses, requirements and tasks overlap in varying and unpredictable ways to make academic work polyrhythmic. Kate, for example, described her coming week:

> The coming, Monday, Tuesday, Wednesday, I have like papers, projects, due for like almost every class.... Like on Monday I have nutrition and you have to like do this, it's like a project on nutrition.... So we had to do like a 3-day evaluation of like what we ate for you know those 3 days. So that's due on Monday, that's also time consuming. And then ... I have like quizzes, a lab report, formal lab report due and a quiz in that organic lab on Tuesday. And I have this paper due for marriage and family dynamics on Tuesday. It's like everything is on paper. Then on Wednesday I have I think another, yes, I have another paper due on Wednesday for some other class.

And there are additional complications. One is that student experiences are shaped not just by courses but by family, friendships, jobs, and other kinds of networks, each with its own rhythms. The resulting organizations of time are varied, complex, and beyond my ability to summarize. A simple contrast, however, should be sufficient to illustrate how courses are stretched beyond their boundaries, how the timing of academic work is driven by assessment, how the rhythms of the day and week percolate out of the intersections of multiple activity systems, and most fundamentally how the course is a different course for different students. Table 10.1 describes Molly's schedule for a specific Monday in the middle of the semester she was taking the nutrition course.

The sorority provided the defining activity frames on this day. As Molly explained:

> I am in a sorority, and I am in charge of a rush party, and I have a committee and I am responsible for doing all the decorations, the skit, all of that good stuff. And I have a committee, and I have weekly meetings with them and so I had to call them and let them know when the meeting was that week and what they needed to do for it and what they needed to bring. Which takes a lot of time and then next semester I have, I am an executive officer so next semester it will be even more time committed to that.... The reason I joined in the first place is because I wanted to be involved in a group that not only did lots of social things, but also lots of community service and philanthropy events, which, I mean, contrary to most people's belief like an exorbitant amount of time is spent with community service, with philanthropy, doing that, raising money for this. And that is something I really enjoy, and I think is time very well spent.... That week [the one referenced in the time log in Table 10.1], I asked if I could switch the week that I was doing [the scavenger hunt] because that was homecoming week for the Greek system, and I knew I was going to be very busy outside of school, and it ended up not being

TABLE 10.1
Molly's Monday, October 12

7:10 a.m.	Alarm goes off
7:45 a.m.	Out of bed
8:00 a.m.	Shower
8:08-8:20 a.m.	Get ready, dressed, etc.
8:22-8:28 a.m.	Dry hair
8:35 a.m.	Out door
8:45 a.m.	Arrive in commuter lot
8:55 a.m.	Arrive in McBryde [very large classroom]
9:00-9:50 a.m.	Engineering
9:53-9:57 a.m.	Walk to GBJ, find seat
10:00-10:15 a.m.	Get and eat coffee, muffin
10:15-10:40 a.m.	Study!! for chemistry exam
10:40-10:45 a.m.	Go to Davidson 3 from GBJ
10:50-11:00 a.m.	Take general chemistry exam!!
11:54 a.m-12:00 p.m.	Walk to [a campus food court]
12:04-12:10 p.m.	Get lunch
12:11-12:36 p.m.	Eat lunch outside of Dietrich with friend
12:36-12:48 p.m.	Get mocha at Deet's Place [campus coffee shop], bathroom
1:00-1:50 p.m.	Nutrition course
1:52-2:00 p.m.	Ride home
2:02-2:15 p.m.	Return messages, talk to roomie
2:15-2:56 p.m.	E-mail Mom, friends, read e-mail
3:00-3:08 p.m.	Go to [tanning parlor]
3:15-3:45 p.m.	Tan
3:45-3:56 p.m.	Go home
4:00-4:45 p.m.	Nap and watch TV
5:00-6:00 p.m.	Shower and get ready
6:00-6:35 p.m.	Dinner (made by roommate)
6:38-7:00 p.m.	Dishes and clean apartment and room
7:00-7:15 p.m.	Change clothes
7:15-7:20 p.m.	Ride to [sorority] house
7:30-9:30 p.m.	Scavenger hunt (Homecoming week)
9:45-10:45 p.m.	Plan out week in planner (e.g., assignments and tasks)
10:45-11:15 p.m.	Call committee members
11:15-11:30 p.m.	Balance checkbook, access nutrition home page
11:32 p.m.-12:00 a.m.	Go online, check exam score
12:00-12:15 a.m.	Talk on phone
12:16 a.m.	Asleep!

feasible, which was fine, no big deal. But yeah Monday I went on a scavenger hunt with the fraternity that we were paired with, around to different places in Blacksburg.... I usually don't go out on Mondays, Tuesdays, Wednesdays, Thursdays—on Fridays I go out.

Students like Molly have to bend time to fit their academic work into the temporal requirements of social identities anchored in organizations, like sororities, that operate on the margins of the academic sphere. In this instance the sorority-fraternity system superimposed shorter term temporal structures (the time required for community service, the social activities Molly described), and longer term rhythms (possibly extending beyond the university years) mediated through friendships and social capital networks. Molly subordinated her usual daily and weekly academic routine (not going out on Mondays) to maintain her place in these longer rhythms.

In addition to such entanglements of time, the position of the course along the student's institutional career trajectory can shape daily and weekly temporal routines. Elvira, like Molly, was a pre-med student taking the same nutrition course (though in a different section). She was, however, a year further along on the path defined by the check sheet. Her time log, shown in Table 10.2, begins the same October 12th recorded by Molly.

Although Elvira's Monday and Wednesday schedules were identical she organized time differently on the 2 days. On Monday she did last-minute studying for an organic chemistry test and layered multiple activities into single time slots: Instead of skipping anatomy to study for the test, she studied during anatomy while presumably monitoring what went on in the class. After the chemistry test the focus of her time shifted to human anatomy, with a test on Wednesday serving as the next reckoning point. Whereas Molly fit academic work into the temporal structure of social activities, Elvira subordinated social activity to test preparation. She studied 5.5 hours on Monday and 10.5 on Tuesday, then skipped psychology on Wednesday to review her notes just before the test. Once the organic chemistry test was finished, the temporal borders of anatomy expanded— Elvira shifted time appropriated from other uses to test preparation for anatomy. Once that test was done, she shifted again: Attending a meeting for students interested in getting into medical school situated her in a temporal frame stretching from Virginia Tech to professional school.

ANYWHERE ANYTIME?

The pictures of temporal organization sketched here are unusually simple in that both Elvira and Molly, unlike the vast majority of U.S. college students, weren't holding down paying jobs (King & Bannon, 2002). Still, the time logs suggest that for most students things like jobs, identity-defining memberships in organizations, and the places to which one has access are inextricable from academic work. Students talk to friends while studying, watch course CDs in their apartments, and shape study time to fit social obligations. In the Jane scenario CMI was imagined as a tool that

TABLE 10.2
Elvira's Week

Monday		Tuesday		Wednesday	
6:30 a.m.	Woke up, showered, dressed, got ready for school	7:30 a.m.	Woke up, showered, got dressed, and got ready for school	6:30 a.m.	Woke up, showered, dressed, got ready for class
7:40 a.m.	Left for bus stop	8:30 a.m.	Left for bus stop	7:30 a.m.	Left for bus stop
8:00 a.m.	Went to food selection and preparation lecture	9:00 a.m.	Food selection and preparation lab: made cobbled apples, baked apple crisp, orange apple	8:00 a.m.	Food selection and preparation
9:00 a.m.	Nutrition lecture			9:00 a.m.	Nutrition: did a problem-solving activity
10:00 a.m.	Went to Hahn to ask Dr. X a question concerning a koofer problem	12:10 p.m.	Went to Wallace to pick up homework and class activities for nutrition class	10:00 a.m.	Went to Hancock, saw a friend, and talked for a few minutes
10:15 a.m.	Studied for organic chemistry test			10:15 a.m.	Reviewed human anatomy notes
11:00 a.m.	Psychology at McBride	12:15 p.m.	Walked over to Davidson for bus	11:30 a.m.	Ate lunch while reviewing
11:50 a.m.	Went to Burger King and took food to Hancock and studied for o. chem. test	12:40 p.m.	Got home, checked e-mail, and ate lunch	1:00 p.m.	Went to human anatomy and took the test
12:50 p.m.	Human anatomy and physiology in McBryde (studied for o. chem. test in class)	1:30 p.m.	Started studying for human anatomy test (reviewed chap. 10)	2:00 p.m.	Friend and I went to Squires for graduate and professional schools fair
				3:00 p.m.	Went to library to see the answer key for o. chem. test that I had on Monday

(Continued)

Monday		Tuesday		Wednesday	
1:50 p.m.	A friend and I went to Hancock, I studied a little and talked to my friend	3:30 p.m.	Went to friend's room to watch CD-ROM that explained the sliding filament theory and action potentials	3:15 p.m.	Went to Derring to pick up a timetable, friend and I sat there and talked
4:00 p.m.	Took o. chem. test			4:00 p.m.	O. chem.
5:00 p.m.	Went to Main Eggleston to visit friends	5:00 p.m.	Came home and studied notes on muscles	5:40 p.m.	Got home, checked e-mail
				6:00 p.m.	Cooked macaroni and cheese
5:20 p.m.	Went to McBryde for human anatomy review session	7:00 p.m.	Ate dinner and talked to my roommates	6:20 p.m.	Ate dinner with roommates, talked
6:30 p.m.	Went back to my apartment, talked to my roommates and ate dinner, checked my e-mail	8:00 p.m.	Reviewed and studied for human anatomy test	7:10 p.m.	Got ready to go to medical schools meeting
				7:15 p.m.	Left to go to McBryde
				7:30 p.m.	Medical schools meeting
8:00 p.m.	Studied for human anatomy test till midnight (chaps. 7–9)	11:30 p.m.	Roommate and I quizzed each other and reviewed for test	9:30 p.m.	Got home
				9:30 p.m.	Talked to my other roommate about what was said at the meeting
12:00 a.m.	Got ready for bed	1:00 a.m.	Got ready for bed	9:45 p.m.	Talked on phone
12:30 a.m.	Went to sleep	1:20 a.m.	Went to sleep	11:00 p.m.	Got ready for bed
				11:30 p.m.	Went to sleep

allowed the university access to students in the home and allowed students to add work into their schedules. For Molly and Elvira, by contrast, CMI was a way to extend the course and configure it flexibly with a variety of social contexts (cf. Fenwick & Tausig, 2004; Presser, 2004), that is, to complicate the learning situation.

A university campus, at least a large land-grant research university campus, is not just a site where lectures are performed, but an unusually concentrated social and material environment that can be flexibly reorganized. The social and material resources—not only the libraries, but also classmates from around the world, dormitories, sorority and fraternity houses that concentrate students, rooms for study, the restaurants, coffee shops, and student centers of the surrounding town, and so on—give students access to a diversity of ambitions and future expectations more densely packed than one can find almost anywhere else. Students who live or work on campus can borrow ways of doing things, look at a course from different perspectives, and sample a wide range of courses. Events and practices overlap and mutually define one another (see also Crook & Light, 2002, p. 164), and students, to some extent, can manipulate, discover, or create new configurations of structuring activities to deal with the multiple activities they're engaged in. Here's a description of part of a campus-based student's repertoire of study strategies:

JN: When you are studying for a hard course like the banking course or a math course, how do you study for it?

Lynne: With lots of paper, absolute silence, perhaps a little classical music, and I sit there and I have to rewrite all of my notes, I learn by writing it down because I won't remember it. And after writing it down, studying it, whatever. If I still don't get it, I usually start, I usually have like a study group with one, maybe two other people and talking about it out loud to make sure that I am still on the right track really helps. And if I still have no clue what I am doing, it's usually the teacher by then.

JN: How do those study groups get formed? Are those just formed from class to class or do you see the same students?

Lynne: I think business students—I have a person that's probably been in almost every single one of my classes since freshman year, so it's just knowing people and even if they have different sections of the class, as long as they have the same teacher, it's pretty easy to find someone.

What stands out in this account is the time and space Lynne has—for solitude or collective work, with a structured environment of music or silence, to write and rewrite and try new strategies if one doesn't work—as well as the people she has access to in various interactional formats: students in different sections of a course, peers with whom she's worked across multiple classes, and the variety of learning tools she could use, including writing and rewriting notes, talking with other students, immediate feedback, and so forth. Unlike the Jane scenario where CMI adds work to an already established daily routine, CMI for students like Lynne adds to the complexity of resources for reorganizing and reconfiguring such routines.

Implicit in this claim, however, is the idea of the campus as a separate space, a temporally and spatially bounded density of resources. But like a course, a campus isn't the same for all students, and some, like imaginary Jane, have heavy commitments outside its sociocultural and academic streams. For example, Jody, another student in the nutrition course, found work and home responsibilities constraining her studies:

> The problem really is I don't, I like to know what I am doing, where I am going to be, I don't know, like everyday. When I get up I want to know Okay this is exactly how my day is going to go, well the woman I work for she is just a spaz I guess. I mean she will call at like, I am suppose to teach on Mondays, that's the only day I am suppose to work … and she will call at like 3:30, "Can you come in to work today?" or she will tell me when I get to work on Mondays, "Oh you have to stay until 10:00 tonight because I scheduled something for you" … and I don't like that because I like to know what I am going to have to do. But because then like I will prepare: well today I am going to study for this and this and then tomorrow I can study for this and this. And then she will call and if I don't go in I feel bad because she might not have anybody else to come in or whatever. But then I don't get done what I need to get done.… Usually on the weekends I go home.… Last year I went home about every other weekend and now that I have my car here and I live in an apartment, I started going home on just Sundays and now I go home more often. I don't know. I have a bad situation at home so I go home a lot. My mother passed away when I was a senior in high school. And I have a younger sister who is 15, she is a sophomore now and my dad is there and my sister is there so I don't know. I feel obligated to go home you know.… My dad expects a lot more from me I think. I don't know, maybe not, maybe I just see it that way but I feel like I need to go home because they need me there. But then I feel like I need to be here and then I worry about stuff that's going on at home when I am not there.

Home and school are densely intertwined for Jody in ways that don't seem to hold for Molly, Elvira, or Paul. Yet Jody's unpredictable job demands and family responsibilities are tightly coupled and interactive in ways that don't resemble the Jane scenario. For Jane CMI works because activity streams are presented as linear and modular: Family and study can be disarticulated and separated—the logic of the scenario depends on this being a standard possibility—and on content being stable and identical when viewed from any position or relative motion.

It seems more plausible, however, that students' academic movements relative to one another create multiple versions of course content. Rather than making a course available anytime, anywhere, CMI makes possible an indeterminate but large number of courses which need not be closely related to one another. This variability and the ordering forces that generate it are simply hidden when students' work is translated into the standardized units of account (grades, course credits, money) that make instructional effects visible at the end of the term.

CMI and Organizational Change

Our choice is not technology versus no technology, but a wider determination of the concepts and the values that higher education should embody.

—Agre (1999, p. 39)

Changes in the division of instructional labor (e.g., the participation of designers), the kinds of materials students work with and when and where they can get those materials, the technical media for representing course materials (PowerPoint slides, web pages, CDs, digital video, online chats, etc.), and the administrative discourses used to talk about those media, do not necessarily imply changes in instructional logics, curricular structures, or the ways students study.

This isn't oversight or failure, it's a reflection of the fact that change efforts in education advance by strategically hardening certain positions and practices—treating them as if they need no explanation, description, or justification—and using them as staging points for innovation in targeted phenomena or processes. The targets and especially the innovations launched at them get the attention, but the rules and fields of play are critically important as well. Computers and courseware may fill the field of vision in CMI reforms, but their presuppositions (e.g., grading systems, objectives-driven logics, etc.) make their uses legible in ways that foreground certain issues and obscure others. Attention focuses, for example, on things like systems for storing lectures, visualizing student work at a distance, two-way communication, online chats and tests, animation, blogs, and so forth, whereas other things are buried in the background— for example, the large size of classes, the system of course electives, grading scales, and the like.

This continuity within change raises an obvious question about how a book like the one you're reading might inform the politics of instruction. Discursive controls, those that work not through detailed prescription and surveillance but by defining the presuppositions for action and shaping what counts as reasonable or even possible things to talk about or do (Bachrach & Botwinick, 1992; Foucault, 1980; March & Simon, 1958; Perrow, 1986) work especially well in organizations like universities that lack accessible histories and traditions of debate over core practices like teaching. Poor organizational memories make it difficult or impossible to reconstruct the development of instructional practices in one's own department, let alone the task histories that students bring to a class, and thus leave problems to be framed in the dominant aesthetic or accounting system of the institution.

Indeed, assumptions embedded in current practices gain much of their efficacy from the fact that the debates, arguments, and contingencies out of which they emerged get lost from view over time. Take, for example, the idea of organizing instruction around behavioral objectives. Originating in vocational and military training influenced by the scientific management movement (Neumann, 1979; Noble, 1991), objectives were widely adopted in elementary and secondary education by the 1960s (cf. Reiser, 2001b), spread to technology-based higher education instruction by the 1970s and 1980s (Reiser), and went from there to CMI. Key assertions remain relatively constant across this expansion, so much so that end-of-millennium state policy and instructional design theory can end up rearticulating World War I-era vocational training dicta:

> The question of the different speeds with which men progress can be met in two ways. By one method ... the man will be given a fixed amount of time, in which he can either go as far as he can.... This is essentially the method of the regular school; classes are carried for a given period.... The method of organizing ... that will best meet the needs of emergency training is undoubtedly that that provides for keeping the learner in the course until he is completely trained according to the "requisition for training" in his case, rather than in only partially filling the requisition in order to make time even. (Allen, 1945[1919], p. 228)

The same ideas reappear some 70 years later in arguments for the Math Emporium at Virginia Tech:

> If John sits daydreaming in a traditional classroom, the class goes on without him. If he sits lost in reverie in the Math Emporium, the computer in front of him patiently waits; there will be no progress, no completion of assigned tasks, until he does something—until he takes an active role in learning. In the same way, if Mary stays silent in a traditional classroom, bewildered because the Einstein in the front row answers all the questions before she can digest the information, the material may be lost to her. At the computer in the Math Emporium, however, no one answers the questions, so Mary must understand all of the material before going on the next level. (Williams, n.d., p. 1)

Instructional technologists give the point a slightly different inflection:

> The migration of manufacturing jobs abroad, the increasing complexity of equipment, and the current corporate restructuring movement's emphasis on quality combine to require ever-increasing numbers of employees who can take initiative, think critically, and solve problems. To meet this need in industry and the need for life-long learners, we must now focus on learning instead of sorting. But how can we refocus our systems on learning? Educators agree that different people learn at different rates. So, when an educational or training system holds time constant, achievement must vary, as has been the case in our industrial-age educational system ever since it replaced the one-room schoolhouse. The alternative is to allow time to vary— to give each learner the time he or she needs to reach the learning goals. (Reigeluth, 1999, p. 18)

Finally, university presidents envision these ideas as changes entailed by a changing educational marketplace:

> Colleges currently emphasize a commonality of process based on "seat time," or the amount of time each student is taught. Students study for a defined number of hours, earn credits for each hour of study, and, after earning a specified number of credits, earn a degree. With the increasing number of educational providers, the individualization of education, and the growing diversity of the student body, however, that commonality of process is likely to be lost. The focus will shift to the outcomes that students achieve. Time will become the variable and learning the constant. (Levine, 2000, p. B10)

The assumptions underlying this procession of claims—that instruction is for narrowly defined tasks for which objectives can be specified in advance, that learning is intraindividual and takes place only within the instructional setting under surveillance (i.e., seat time is the only time spent learning)— become harder to see over time, fading out of the picture as they move across institutional domains. A vocational training strategy turns into both cutting-edge math pedagogy and a cure for outsourcing, then into the inevitable consequence of institutional change.

Good ideas, of course, deserve an afterlife, and even dead ones have their zombie uses. The real problem is that as ideas and practices migrate away from the original contexts of their production the critical conversations that engaged them there don't always follow. The discourse of objectives and outputs expands across task areas and jurisdictions, becoming in the process entrenched, whereas critiques of it await independent recreation in each new domain. For example, although I've omitted intermediary steps, there's a clear genealogy linking the positions quoted earlier. By contrast, when Strathern (2000a) complains that administrators promoting CMI collapse "outcomes" (what follows from a series of events, what an organization does over time) into "objectives" (norms and standards defined at the outset), there's no organizational or political connection to the similar critiques that came before. In Strathern's argument:

> There is an inbuilt little gadget that gets over the problem that academics in higher education traditionally accounted for their output in terms of (student) generations—the reputation books acquired over decades or the success of former pupils in their middle years of life. The gadget means that you don't have to wait a generation or two. You can speed up the process. It is very simple: you turn the system of measurement into a device that also sets the ideal levels [of] attainment. In short, audit measures become targets (Hoskin, 1996; Macintyre, 2000). They collapse the is and the ought, continuing a long process that began when examination results became aims—when a high score is not simply how you measure up but is a level you have aimed and striven for. (p. 3)

Both observation and objection parallel earlier critiques by U.S. curriculum theorists of the use of behavioral objectives in elementary and secondary schools:

> A significant part of the framework of systems management is concerned with and is based upon the precise formulation of goals, on a microsystem level usually with the specification of behavioral goals. For example, a student's behavior is preselected before he engages in educational activity and this behavior is used as the end-product of the system so that feedback can be generated. (Apple, 1975, p. 117)

> Instructional success is defined in terms of the attainment of prespecified objectives and not, as would be at least somewhat more natural, in terms of the value of the results actually obtained. (Waks, 1975, p. 90)

What's lost by a lack of articulation with the past isn't academic genealogy—the point is not about citations or their lack—but an organizational one: the kinds of transdisciplinary and interorganizational networks, cadres, and practice schemes that sustain and propagate a perspective over time. There are various reasons why this happens, not least of which is the difficulty discipline-based academics would have pursuing an object of critique as it migrates across disciplines and domains. But part of the reason, too, is the absence of organizational memory I've referred to already and the resultant opacity of the mechanisms by means of which a loose, emergent, and multisited agenda like CMI develops.

So if it's possible to boil the flesh off what I've said so far and come up with a skeleton key of mechanisms for introducing CMI into the university, substituting a caricature in place of the portraits of the previous chapters, it would look something like this: Start from your professional base (like

ITV), make a claim on some new domain (like CMI), get allies and collaborators interested in some "boundary object" (Star & Greisemer, 1999) like the computer, build a demonstration artifact, put on some dog and pony shows, get other people involved in doing demonstrations, construct a public profile for your work group, and accumulate organizational resources.

Now get the actors on a larger scale interested: Develop binary contrasts that set off what you're promoting from some already existing alternative, real or imagined, and evoke a whole range of such contrasts—credit for contact is to genuinely independent study as input is to output, as synchronous is to asynchronous, as face to face is to online education, and so on. Never try to define these contrast terms precisely. Show how the innovation will solve some external or preexisting problem (e.g., declining resources) and simultaneously get or keep your organization on par with comparable organizations. If need be, open up your organization to the influence of more powerful actors, such as the state or the corporate sector (who may have been connected and influential previously in a different fashion or to a different degree). Such actors can soften up the organization for change agendas. Policy is basically a way to generate or signal vulnerabilities—openings for mobilization or incursion—in existing institutions. Circulating ideas, like credit for contact, through such external circuits makes them more potent in the local setting. In all this, however, try to keep control of the translation of your work into the categories of these external actors—do your own bookkeeping (or at least shape the terms in which others do it). On the other hand, if someone with money or power shows interest in your efforts for the wrong reason, don't educate them but instead try to surf over their misconceptions.

Make work within the domain of the innovation (e.g., using technology in instruction) a standard organizational expectation (e.g., course development and work with technology became items on Tech's template for Faculty Annual Reports). Create a central administrative unit to promote the innovation, but maximize involvement by allowing innovators to go in different directions. Provide centrally supported assistance for those most likely to need help and lack ready models for the kind of work entailed by the innovation (e.g., new faculty, or faculty teaching courses or in programs in which they have little personal investment). Allow variation but do not register it in any formal or systematic way in the accounting system of the organization: If programmatic differences exist, their exact nature, reasons, or consequences should stay out of public debate.

Within programs, if you've got an academically prestigious or powerful discipline behind you, close shop and keep tight control of the work. If you're on the outside of departmental structures, or weakly positioned in relation to them, claim compatibility with all theories in the domain of practice (e.g., all learning theories) and emphasize procedural and technical prowess. Within courses, design the CMI to fit the system of relations that produces its particular construction of students.

If students are defined by long-term, program-exclusive relations (as in pathology) design the CMI to move across time and the different situations in the program (and perhaps beyond it). Use the CMI not to render the course material as detached text, but to index it strongly to disciplinary contexts (as in the coupling of the CD with lesion images to lab and coursework). Use it to make elements of professional practice visible, keeping students oriented toward that destination. Draw on the program-specific knowledge of groups like students to keep change agents internal to the field. In general, attribute problems to external constraints, especially inadequate funding.

On the other hand, if students are short term and highly heterogeneous as a group, use the CMI to make visible the information they need to reach the exit point of the course. Shape the content into detachable text along the lines of entertainment industry content. In general, counter problems by questioning someone else's past or existing practices. The problem is always that there hasn't been enough change, that the potentials of the change agenda haven't yet been properly recognized or exploited.

None of this is bad, of course, but it does make it difficult to step back and reconsider what's outside the frame of the picture, and how that might need to change.

Appendix

Data Sources

Very few stories are narrated either to idealise or condemn; rather they testify to the always slightly surprising range of the possible.

—Berger (1979, p. 8)

This book is basically an effort to make sense of some aspects of the place where I work. Like most faculty members at Tech I get caught up in strategic planning, cost cutting, and budget worries. I periodically go through the very useful and informative FDI (Faculty Development Initiative) workshops, and I use a computer, keep an out-of-date web page, occasionally employ the university's course management software to post assignments and archive student contributions, communicate with students via e-mail, run a listserv for my professional organization, and on rare occasions conduct class sessions (or at least small group discussions) with geographically dispersed students via chat software. And I've been here long enough to remember when not all faculty had computers, and the university's computing capacity consisted of a mainframe.

Just as my own experiences and interests have evolved, so has the work that's ended up in this book. It did not begin with a hypothesis, and the various reports, notes, and interviews I've drawn on come from several separate endeavors corresponding very roughly to the three sections of the book.

The first, chronologically, really had nothing to do with CMI. It was early 1994 and I was using most of my time and mental energy studying an elementary school. The periodic announcements about state budget cuts (which had started in 1990, just months after I'd been hired as a tenure-track faculty member) barely registered in my mind, and the strategic planning going on in the College of Education where I worked seemed something best avoided. Here, for example, is a bit from a speech from our then-dean at a fall 1993 faculty meeting:

A few months ago, I had the opportunity to visit with a person who served as the public relations director for Disney, to discuss the development of a public relations campaign for our College of Education. She talked about the value of simplicity when formulating a mission statement, and cited the brief statements of several successful corporations such as Mayo Clinic, Delta Airlines, Disney, and McDonald's. The College Planning Steering Committee decided to rewrite our original mission statement so that it too was simple and focused when adopting the following statement: "The COE of Virginia Tech is dedicated to the creation and application of knowledge for the improvement of educational policy and practice."... We have many problems in the COE that have common goals or outcomes, much like Ford Motor Company with its array of automobile nameplates. We share a similar situation with Ford in that the college must remain financially competitive and prepare a gameplan that enables us to forge new pathways of quality and acceptance by our customers. Ford adopted statistical quality control and other quality assurance strategies, which included training requirements for all of its suppliers, and managed to become number one in sales in the U.S. in 1993, outperforming Japanese auto manufacturers. Reinventing the wheel highlights the story of Ford's planning efforts to produce a new product that would be responsive to the needs of its customers. Ford's planning initiatives were based, in part, on needs assessments that involved its customers and major paradigm shifts including the consolidation of research and production divisions to create a corporate signature. Ford has a better idea and that idea involves quality, economy, safety, and product value for everyone. The COE has to address similar issues....

My attention to this kind of thing perked up in January 1994 when the Provost, apparently not happy with our array of nameplates, decided that we needed to narrow our mission to deal only with issues related to kindergarten through high school. As he explained:

This [cut] is not really about enrollments, not really about weighted student credit hours, it isn't about any other standard measures you come up ... it's not really about quality–so much as, what I'm talking about today is the matter of mission and priorities, and in that sense a matter of focus, a real sharpening up of the college's fundamental purpose.

This sharpening allowed a 20% cut in the college's budget, sliced off programs like adult education and exercise physiology (supposedly not closely enough articulated with the K-12 mission), and forced the survivors to defend themselves as investments. Soon I was spending the morning in the elementary school, then driving to campus for afternoon restructuring meetings. Not long into this process the then-president of the college faculty association, TW (later interviewed as head of the Center for Excellence in Undergraduate Education) suggested that I monitor and archive the restructuring process. I thought this might be useful and thoughtlessly agreed. I wound down the elementary school fieldwork and spent almost

2 years attending restructuring meetings, generating lots of audiotape, and collecting memos, e-mails, and reports. The archive piled up. A lot of the material, it turned out, focused on the build-up to the Provost's announcement, that is, the university's early responses to the state budget cuts. This was the source of the information about financialization in Virginia higher education and Tech planning.

After about 20 months of intensive planning for restructuring the College of Education, Virginia Tech's then-president, Paul Torgersen, abruptly decided that instead of reorganizing it he would just dissolve it and merge it with the College of Human Resources. As he explained:

> There are a lot of colleges of education, schools of education out there. A [university governing] board member asked ... "Why do we even have a college of education? Radford [a nearby university] was set up as a teachers' college. It's 15 to 17 miles away, why don't you consider closing the College of Education?" Well, that's a very superficial sort of question. I read only a couple of days ago, a member of the House of Delegates who was reelected from Danville, was questioning whether we need all these colleges of education.... Part of it is symbolic. I'm sorry that you're caught up in this, but part of it is symbolic. What the university is doing is saying, "We had nine colleges, we now have eight." And believe me, that's going to be applauded across this Commonwealth like you can't believe. And the university needs that support.

Having been forced 22 months earlier to divorce supposedly irrelevant programs like adult education to "sharpen [its] fundamental purpose," Education was now in a shotgun marriage to departments like Hotel and Tourism Management and Interior Design. At the time I didn't think there was much point in continuing the archive—the planning that had been done was rendered irrelevant by the merger—or in writing anything up about it. I put the material in a file cabinet and moved on.

This is not to say there was no connection between the downsizing of the old College of Education and the university's CMI efforts. AM explained that some of the ideas for creating the Center for Innovations in Learning (CIL) came from efforts by educational psychology and instructional technology faculty (uncomfortable with the imposed focus on K-12 professional preparation) to expand their professional jurisdiction into the university's CMI efforts. As AM explained, the College's Instructional Technology program was already providing assistance for the then young FDI program:

> When I came here in November of '95, the education faculty–they were also in a state of restructuring themselves by this time–and they came and visited with us in Information Systems, proposing that there needed to be some better strategic focus on what we were doing by way of integrating technology

into teaching. And also a better means of incorporating in the faculty's work what we already know about what seems to work, or what doesn't work, in this arena.... And so we developed a white paper over a period of about 3 months I think, that said basically that we'd like to integrate what we know about teaching and learning, the research on teaching and learning, and what's working with our faculty, with a more strategic focus on what the university needs to do in this area next.... So, let's see–that occurred during the spring. And we sent in a budget proposal at the end of the spring, early summer to put out some grant money. And to pay a little bit for someone to help us with the assessment of what we were doing. And by October or November I believe, we had gotten a budget.

I mention this bit because it illustrates several methodological points. First, that you can be an engaged participant (as I was in the college's restructuring efforts) and not be aware of things—like the meetings AM referred to—that end up having longer term effects than the meetings on governance structures and curricula that seemed important at the time. Second, if this limitation on knowledge was true for me it was true in different ways of the people I quote in this book (granted that everyone quoted is better informed than me). All accounts are partial, and partial accounts can't just be added together or averaged to find the truth. The way everyone (me included) sees an event is a function of the larger patterns of events in which they've participated. Uncertainties don't resolve. Loose ends and ambiguities remain.

Then again, I had just been archiving public events, there was no research study, no particular problem or focus. I didn't get one of those until 1997, when I cotaught an introductory class on qualitative research methods with one of my colleagues, a revered professor of instructional design whose participation attracted students from the instructional technology program (students who otherwise rarely take my courses). One of these students was at the time working with the Biological Sciences Initiative (BSI), and she and a BSI colleague invited me to study their efforts. I had an interest in higher education and in an earlier work had focused on student learning (Nespor, 1994). I thought this might be an opportunity to focus on teaching. The initial idea was that we'd study both the nutrition course and a lower division biology course that was being put completely online. Unfortunately, the professor teaching the latter course decided he didn't have the time (at the time) for the BSI work and soon dropped out of the study.

My initial thoughts were that the project would be short and simple, involving mainly interviews with students, professors, and designers. With a small grant from the Center for Excellence in Undergraduate Teaching (CEUT) to support transcription, we commenced.

DS helped us solicit volunteers for interviews by offering extra-credit points to those who participated, which may mean there was some selection bias for students anxious about their grades or anxious to whine about the course. In the end, however, many students reported making good grades and having little trouble with it.

The time demands of participating were modest. We wanted to do two interviews: The first would be a one on one early in the term. The second would come at the end of the semester and would be conducted in small groups of two or three. We asked students to bring copies of class notes (some forgot), which we then photocopied. We gave participants the option of keeping a time log across a week and doing one interview instead of two interviews: The logs in these cases were used to structure a single interview.

I also interviewed DS twice, and the instructional designers and I had frequent unstructured conversations about the design process and BSI generally. The designers did some audio- and video taping of the class; and I did some sit-in-the-back-and-take-notes observation during the second year of the study. The designers also audio recorded a score or so design meetings they had with DS, and I made a video recording of DS and one of the designers sitting at the computer constructing PowerPoint slides for a lecture.

Chapters 9 and 10 are based on analyses of 47 interview transcripts (with 40 students) over the 2 years. In the interviews students were asked about how they negotiated the demands of the nutrition course and how the course fit into their larger academic experience: why they took the course, how it fit into their major, how they chose the major, why they came to Tech, where they saw themselves going afterward. We tried to be especially attentive to comparisons: When students contrasted nutrition to other courses (or when we asked them to contrast it) we tried to pick up on the terms and criteria they used and ask for more description. We asked them as well to talk about specific features and strategies used in the nutrition course and to describe how those differed from strategies used in other courses. The aim was to get them to be as concrete as possible in describing how they did what they did (rather than, e.g., asking them to make judgments or evaluations of course experiences or CMI in general).

Using interviews with students to talk about their own activities is tricky, using them to find out about a professor's practices is very problematic. It's become popular to talk about classrooms as communities, and maybe some are—certainly there are often cordial relations between faculty members and students—but at the end of the day, in most courses, professors are making students do work they wouldn't otherwise do, and rewarding or punishing them for how they do it. Undergraduate courses are often arenas of struggle. As Becker et al. (1968) put it: "The relation between students and university in this area [academic work] may reasonably be called one of subjection" (p. 7).

Although entertaining teaching, predictable assignments, and high grades can make it more palatable, most students don't like this relationship, and as noted in chapter 4 tensions sometimes boiled out in Tech's big "killer" courses. More often, though, these tensions stayed below the horizon and out of public view—until someone interviewed the students.

All of which is to say that when you focus on the specifics of tasks, study, lectures, and the like, you invariably run into students who disparage their courses and professors (no matter how good and hardworking they might have been), and at the opposite extreme can be enthusiastic about professors with good presentation skills and little to say (Marsh & Ware, 1982; Naftulin, Ware, & Donnelly, 1973). In fact you find situations where students give diametrically opposed accounts of the same course.

DID SHE READ THE SLIDES OR DELIVER A LECTURE?

Gaskell and Hepburn (1998) suggested that the course can be thought of as a "token," an object of negotiation and struggle that gets reworked across networks of institutional actors:

> The token is usually not passed unchanged from hand to hand.... The token is either ignored or taken up by people who see their interests translated within it. In the process of shaping it to their interests, these people usually modify the token. The path of the token is a product of the number and strength of the links that are established between it and a diverse group of other actors. It is not a product of an initial quality but of the subsequent actions of a multitude of others. (p. 2)

As tokens, courses can be simultaneously contextualized or made meaningful in different ways: Think of a continuum ranging from courses like those in veterinary medicine where access is highly restricted and numerous constraints tightly limit a course's contextualization, to introductory courses for nonmajors, like nutrition, open to a broad and indeterminate range of recontextualizations.

Some nutrition students, for example, felt that DS was a gifted lecturer who drew them into the subject matter with anecdotes and questions that revealed her expertise and personal interests. Laura, a senior microbiology major, said that she "really liked" how DS "doesn't just like go through the information and that's all she does. Like she stops and she asks questions and she just incorporates like, the class, like, to talk with her and stuff. And it just makes it a more laid-back kind of setting so it makes it more fun for me I guess." Similarly, Lee said nutrition was her:

> favorite class, so I try to go to it every day.... I am really interested in nutrition and I really like my teacher, DS, she's really good. So I enjoy, like, the teacher

makes all the difference to me. If I don't like the teacher then the class could be really easy, and I could do horrible in it. Like that's happened to me so many times.... [DS is] really, well she's a friendly person to begin with. Like she just seems really nice and she knows the material really well and can talk about it and get it across to me so like in a way that I understand it. She's not just like, sitting up there like, reading off notes or something, I don't know.

In a group interview several students elaborated:

Marilyn:	It brings it more into like real-life things rather than book work to memorize the stuff.... When we went over anorexia and bulimia, you know, she put it into a perspective for you actually think of a person being bulimic or anorexic rather than just studying a disease you know?
Peggy:	She told like stories from like friends that she had that had the problem and so you know and then kind of like you know made it sound like you know more personal or just you know more human than just reading the book.
Ethel:	She also talks about herself. I think she said [something about] her craving chocolate or something so she also brings her weaknesses into the lecture and her positive you know things that she does.
Marilyn:	Right, which I think is very good because you always think of a dietician eating pears and bananas all day. And that you know they have no flaws when it comes to eating and so knowing that the person who's lecturing to you has cravings as well and it's a little yeah, makes it more real.
Ethel:	She will ask us questions. She will want participation from us. She will ask us different questions, and she's not afraid for us to ask her questions and she's not afraid if she's wrong, you know, she will admit when she's wrong. And she will try to take the extra effort to, if we have a question she will always put it in the announcements on the home page. She will answer that question or answer it in class and she gives us opportunities for extra credit also, just little odds and ends....
Marilyn:	Especially like if she sees a class that's really empty, she will say, you know give us hints and stuff on like what she's going to stress on that test or whatever, she will be like hint, hint, you know. So you are kind of privy to extra information.

For these students, DS was an engaging teacher. According to other students, however, she simply "read" the notes on the PowerPoint slides. Lynne, for example, said:

[DS] pretty much read the notes for the most part. I mean she seems like a very nice person and she obviously knows what she's talking about, I have no doubt about that, but she seemed to me she had a few anecdotes but it was mainly from the notes, directly from the notes, and all of her tests were from the notes so it seems unless I really wanted to go and listen to her speak, which during my five classes Monday, Wednesday, and three on Friday, I just preferred to take the time as a lunch period or something. I had no interest in hiking all the way to [the building where the lecture was held] just to hear her speak about something that I could read.

Gloria similarly claimed:

> [DS was] reading directly from her overheads and I can read, so I could print it off the Internet if I wanted to.... She's reading verbatim like it's not even like she is really lecturing. She's just like, you know, the slide will show up and she will read it to us and we are like, okay, you know, we can all read, thanks. But I think it makes it a bit tedious and boring. Like if she would I guess customize it better to like just a lecture, to not sound like monotonous and like straightforward I guess.

Lynne, of course, was an inveterate skipper in the nutrition class and Gloria skipped some as well, which raises questions about the bases for their complaints. But even some students who attended regularly, like Hattie, claimed that the class was an oral rendition of the web notes: "She usually just basically reads from the notes so there's nothing [no notes] to take." As Kate put it: "She reads everything off the slides. She does that.... She just reads everything off the slides." Elfreda, an HNFE major (in this case, hoping to continue to medical school), explained that although she liked:

> the fact there are these slides and it's supposed to be a restructured course and it's interesting to be involved in that, but it's so dry. The class is really, really dry. I mean you look around and half of the people are sleeping and it's an interesting course. I mean you are dealing with nutrition every day of your life and it affects you in so many different areas.... And I just think it's kind of, I am not like putting blame on anyone I am just saying it's a really dry course. I just sit there going, okay and I just take my notes on my lecture thing and I leave everyday without getting that much out of it and I don't like doing that. Like if I am going to take a course I want to be like, even if it's something that I am not that interested in I want to try, but it's hard to, it's hard to know how to try.

Then again, some students thought it was alright that the professor read the notes. Boris, for example, said that DS "reads right from the outlines so you don't have to write anything down.... Like she really kind of just reads it verbatim. And then maybe she will add like a couple of things, but not—you know what I mean?—like you don't have pages of notes." At the same time, Boris also insisted that "even though she reads what her notes say, she makes it interesting. You don't feel like it's just verbatim, does that make sense?"

Does it? Consider Fig. A1, one of the PowerPoint slides that DS used in the class:

Now here's a transcript of an audio recording of DS referring to this slide during a lecture:

General characteristics of the RDA's. What are they? Recommended dietary allowances. What are their general characteristics? They are estimates. Please circle that word *estimate*. I know some of you are giggling because I am a little bit moronic using this pencil, it takes some practice [she's referring to a light pen she's using to point to words on the slide]. As the semester progresses, you will see that I become a little bit more adept. And it is for healthy people. Only healthy people. So that is a limitation. You can't use it for sick people. Why was it established? It was established by a government board that was put together of scientists. Why? Because the second World War when the United States decided that they were going to join the war, the second World War, and they were recruiting young men for the Army, a lot them did not qualify. Not because they were sick, but because they suffered from nutrition, nutrient deficiencies. They were anemic. Some of them had beginnings of goiter, which is iodine deficiency. Some of them had other B-vitamin deficiencies, lots of deficiencies. And that was kind of embarrassing to the government you know a great growing wonderful country and wealthy, rich, the richest country in the world with nutrition deficiencies? So they said, "Let's put together a board of scientists who know about nutrition so that they will educate the nation." They realized it was and because of lack of food, mostly because it was people did not know what to eat. There was already so much abundant food that people were probably eating more of one nutrient than another thinking that they had enough when they didn't. So that is why it was established in 1945 of a number of scientists who

GENERAL CHARACTERISTICS OF THE RDA

Are that estimates of the amounts of nutrients that should be consumed by **healthy people** to meet their nutritional needs
Established by the Food and Nutrition Board of the National Academy of Sciences
Begun in 1945
Updated every 5 to 10 years

FIG. A1.   PowerPoint slide, Lecture 6.

> collected all of the literature that was available on nutrients, nutrients are the different compounds that are needed essential for your growth and development and for processes in the body from your intro to nutrition lecture.

Not surprisingly, DS didn't literally just read the notes. So what do the differences in the students' accounts mean? I'm not really sure, which is why I'm talking about this in the methodological appendix. Here's what you can't do: You can't reduce the different accounts to differences in students' developmental stages. All you can do is look for a pattern that connects the students' accounts to other data you have. The bigger and denser the pattern, the better the explanation, though it's inevitably incomplete. Look at the transcript: The strip of lecturing associated with the slide (i.e., what she says while the slide is visible) begins with DS reading the title of the slide, then glossing its contents, using terms and phrases from the slide—"general characteristics," "estimates," "healthy people"—to index her speech to the visual display. She even explicitly directs students' attention away from herself and toward the notes ("please circle that word"), which acknowledges the printed versions of the web notes as mediating artifacts present in the instructional event, and signals that particular portions will be important for future tests.

To this point, DS arguably hasn't done much more than read the slide. But what follows—her explanation of how and why the guidelines came into being—clearly does add a lot. She creates a narrative in which she names agents, describes antecedents, suggests motivations, and locates the action in a specific historical context. In short, she supplies all of the modalities that sociologists of science say have to be stripped from statements to make them sound scientific (e.g., Latour, 1987). DS thus shifts from the simple provision of test-relevant fact to a kind of storytelling that she described in interviews as a technique for generating student interest.

Now situate this in the larger frame of the course. The slides, we've been told, are tightly calibrated to the objectives and the objectives to test items. This means, according to the rules of the game, that DS cannot use digressions to introduce testable material. It can't be interesting in that fashion. The narrative material about recruiting problems during World War II, in other words, is all deadwood, not only from an instructional design perspective but for students interested only in a good grade, who are basically signaled to disattend when DS moves away from just reading the slides. To do more than read the notes—for these students—would require differently written slides that would not include so much information—and an understanding that DS might verbally introduce testable material not on the slides. Meanwhile, students interested in the field could hear the historical information as interesting rather than as noise, and students like Boris could hear it both ways.

Something like that, anyway. The first methodological point is that students' interview accounts provide rich information about their reflective understandings of school activity, but need to be read critically and relationally, as accounts produced as much by their social locations and trajectories as by the topics discussed. The second point is that making sense of accounts is impossible without understanding the organization of the environment to which they're indexed, which requires evidence beyond what's available in the interviews themselves.

ORGANIZATIONAL PROBLEMS OF RESEARCH

Of course, there's another kind of methodological problem arising from students' remarks. DS was untenured at the time of the study. Some of the student comments quoted earlier, which I had not anticipated at the outset of the research, could be read in an unfair and damaging way.[1] On the other hand, people in her position are precisely the ones whose voices and experiences need to be heard as they're often the ones expected to do CMI development work. My resolution of this tension was to wait until the tenure decision had been made before writing up the student interview material—at least 5 years.

Partly for that reason—and also because some things about the nutrition course didn't seem to make obvious sense to me (Why was it so big? Why would it be dumped on a new teacher?, etc.)—I began in the second year of the study interviewing administrators who had been involved with CMI, as well as a new batch of students. As retrospective accounts, these narratives may be oversimplified and too linear (see Deuten & Rip, 2000), and one needs to be wary of what Becker (1998) called the "hierarchy of credibility," but I take them at face value as supplying an official version of events.

Over the course of that second year, the situations of the BSI designers who had encouraged my involvement began to change. They continued to conduct student interviews with students, but their work responsibilities with the BSI and decisions in their personal and professional lives led them to pull back from the study as it expanded in scope and dragged out in time. As the designers were collaborators in studying the design process, it didn't occur to me to try to turn them into research subjects after the fact and work up that material. Thus there are no quotes from or analyses of the transcripts of our conversations or the design sessions. The story of instructional design (ID) work at the university remains to be written.

---

[1]Not that this is an unusual risk created by the study: A publicly accessible web page carries student comments about professors at Virginia Tech, some of them much more brutal than anything heard or quoted in this study. (The page was taken down summer of 2005.)

Beyond losing that portion of the study, the downside of deferring publication and working alone was that it was hard to maintain intensity. The study went fallow and didn't really pick up again until 2001, when Sandi Schneider, a graduate student in instructional technologies, enrolled in a couple of my doctoral courses and there read some early drafts of what would become the chapters in part I of this book. As a class project for an ethnographic methods course I was teaching she interviewed eight faculty members who'd recently received CIL grants. This is where the interviews with JR, TQ, and FQ come from. Sandi's work reminded me how partial the picture I'd assembled from the nutrition course had been—here were programs where CMI had nothing to do with ID—and made it possible to address some new issues.

Along with DS and the nutrition course, the interviews from Sandi's work were selected to illustrate some of the diversity of CMI uses: from the addition of a technical component with little change in the professor's practice, to a transitional form with various CMI-based components influencing classroom practice, to a situation (the Math Emporium) in which formal instruction per se was provided via CMI and face-to-face work was contingent on students' difficulties. In writing about these interviews I obviously didn't worry about forcing the chapters into parallel forms, but I did try to maintain some continuity in focus and level of detail.

The lack of interviews with students in veterinary medicine and the Math Emporium is a shortcoming (although a number of the students interviewed commented on Math Emporium courses they'd taken). However, the object was not to study student learning (which would in any event have led far from CMI), or to describe how instruction actually unfolded (which would have transformed the professors into objects of scrutiny). It was to see how CMI fit into the professors' reflective analyses of teaching. You could think of part II of the book as a study of teaching ideologies and of part I as a study of the evolution of an administrative ideology.

A year later, 2002, I had two more instructional technology students in my methods course, but in this case for various reasons they couldn't come up with research topics on their own and asked if they couldn't do something with me. I wasn't doing anything it would make sense for them to work on, so I came up with the idea of beginning an oral history archive on CMI and IT at Virginia Tech. I'd realized doing the earlier interviews with administrators that some had been interviewed on the same or related issues by earlier researchers, and it occurred to me that it would be useful to have some sort of public archive, a collection of oral histories that would be publicly accessible. (Because of language difficulties the interviews my students conducted didn't turn out to be as useful as one might hope, and the oral history project is languishing). Although the interviews were not actually geared to the book, some of what was discussed turned out to be relevant and I have used snippets from the interviews with Erv Blythe, PM, and MS.

Finally, in 2002 or so, I started trying to write in earnest. The structure and focus of the book changed several times. In analyzing the interviews the students' academic careers were the unit of analysis. I asked what turning points they contained, how their direction shifted, how nutrition and other courses fit into these trajectories, and so forth. The interviews provided accounts of the students' strategies, which, however accurate they may be as descriptions of students' actual practices, do provide a picture of the named and generally recognized elements of students' study repertoires and how these vary for different kinds of classes. The object was not to generalize across the sample or to find commonalities or themes, but to look at phenomena like the course, CMI, and web notes from the standpoints of students, and use these models to complicate the pictures presented in the literatures of CMI and higher education.

It turned out that much of the student interview material was not necessarily related to CMI—discussions of selection of majors and so forth seemed generic to undergraduate education with or without CMI (a judgment I made based on comparisons with interview research conducted with undergraduates at a different university 15 years earlier). To spend time on these topics would have produced major digressions in the tone and structure of a book that already had a lot of twists and turns—and obviously would have lengthened it. So I left them out, at the risk of producing a limited, sectioned-out view of students that's not far from the kind of thing I complained about in the introduction. My only defense is that some of what I focus on usually doesn't get enough attention in writings on CMI or higher education generally, which makes this a contribution, albeit flawed.

The use and nonuse of the student interview material points to the way that this kind of work evolves. Unlike experimental or survey research, long-term fieldwork on ill-defined, heterogeneous phenomena cannot always identify its focus prior to the beginning of the research. The unit of analysis in part I, for example, was the whole trajectory of CMI from peripheral to centralized agenda. Although I knew some parts of that trajectory at the outset, I had no way of knowing what that whole thing would look like. Things that seemed like they'd be critical at the time later came to seem like digressions, whereas other things that had seemed marginal at first—like the early interactive video project of JM and MS— took on increased significance as the book evolved. What makes them significant is not that they were typical in some way, but that they occupied crucial positions in the path or network of relations out of which CMI emerged, that they connected a range of events and phenomena.

This points to a basic methodological operation. Exploring initial empirical questions—for example, why was someone putting lecture notes on PowerPoint slides for a big course with hundreds of students in it?— quickly leads you to realize that before you can find the answer you first have to address other questions: Why was anyone offering a course on this topic, why was the course so big, where did the ideas that professors and designers used to structure the slides come from, and on and on. Because you don't know at the outset what kinds of things you're going to find or need to find out about, the work has to evolve. You can spend a lot of time with a topic just figuring out if you need to spend time with it: Do you really need to investigate the history of the mainframe computer's use in research and instruction, or describe in more detail instructional television, to contextualize the rise of CMI at Virginia Tech? Or think, for example, of AM's description of early sources of the CIL cited earlier in this appendix. Some of the efforts she described provide possible lines of explanation for the local influence of specific approaches to ID on FDI (and elsewhere in the university). Should I have followed this up? Should I have interviewed the participants (one actually was interviewed and was asked about the CIL, but mentioned none of this), or excavated the position papers? I chose not to, not because it didn't seem interesting—one of the irritations of doing this kind of work is that there's always much more that could be said about almost anything you write about—but because I had limited resources, my aim wasn't an exhaustive history, and this looked like a detour that wouldn't substantially change the pattern I was already seeing. It's possible this was a mistake—there are probably others here—but one of the advantages of doing research on named, public institutions is that there's a good chance you'll be corrected; it encourages (I hope) counter or complementary histories.

In short, the idea is not to describe everything, but to describe the networks of practices and assumptions that had to be in place to make the event of interest possible or necessary (Becker, 1998). In Ragin's (2000) terminology, the descriptive explanations that emerge from such a process are "fundamentally configurational. Different parts of the whole are understood in relation to one another and in terms of the total picture or package that they form" (p. 68; see also Diesing, 1971, 1991; Kaplan, 1964). The better explanation is the one that can connect more phenomena in meaningful and interesting ways without sacrificing their complexity. Such explanations are inherently fragile. There's a "house-of-cards" quality to the whole thing, such that "the character of the 'whole case' may change qualitatively if a single key part is altered or changed in some way" (Ragin, 2000, p. 70). This sometimes means modeling events, sometimes putting them into a more expansive contexts, integrating them into narratives, or making cases out of them and comparing them to other cases. The resulting models and accounts are admittedly peculiar in that the idea is not to reduce complexities but to add to them by showing how the phenomena are related to other events and situations and partly produced through these relations. The kind of work from which I take inspiration, ethnography, uses all these tactics:

> Ethnographic practice ... elicits the open-endedness of institutions and organizations as "society." What characterizes people's behaviour in society is precisely their capacity to tolerate loose ends, to deal with unpredictability and revel in the disconnections which mean that they live in multiple worlds, traverse different domains.... Ethnography throws up the unplanned, the counter-intuitive, the unpredictable. It tolerates disconnections. You don't have to tie up all the loose ends; on the contrary there may be data there that will only become resource from some vantage point in the future. But how does it create this situation? The device is that of crossing domains (and thus precipitating differences "between" domains). It refuses to be confined to a single domain or context of narrative. On the contrary, it tracks people's activities and narratives as they cross domains and thereby create heterogeneous social worlds for themselves.... Ethnography does in particular what social science does in general: it always adds a dimension to a phenomenon and thus refuses claims to self-sufficiency. It introduces, in the simplest way, numerical complexity of the most significant kind.... There is (always) more than "one" thing to consider. (Strathern, 2000a, pp. 4–5)

This, as you may be thinking by now, is as much a threat as a promise. And it provides a useful thought to end with: The picture here is intrinsically incomplete.

References

Abbott, A. (1988). *The system of professions: An essay on the division of expert labor.* Chicago: University of Chicago Press.

Abbott, A. (2001). Chaos of Disciplines. Chicago: University of Chicago Press.

Accepting Greater Responsibility for our own destiny. (1993, October 18). Virginia Tech: Blacksburg, VA.

Agre, P. (1997). Toward a critical technical practice: Lessons learned in trying to reform AI. In G. Bowker, S. Star, W. Turner, & L. Gasser (Eds.), *Social science, technical systems, and cooperative work* (pp. 131–157). Mahwah, NJ: Lawrence Erlbaum Associates.

Agre, P. (1999). The distances of education. *Academe, 85*(5), 37–41.

Allen, C. (1945). *The instructor, the man, and the job.* New York: Lippincott.

Allen, I. E., & Seaman, J. (2003). *Sizing the opportunity: The quality and extent of online education in the United States, 2002 and 2003.* Needham, MA: The Sloan Consortium.

Anderson, M. (1992). *Imposters in the temple.* New York: Simon & Schuster.

Anderson-Gough, F., Grey, C., & Robson, K. (2001). Tests of time: organizational time-reckoning and the making of accountants in two multinational accounting firms. *Accounting, Organizations, and Society, 26,* 99–122.

Apple, M. (1975). The adequacy of systems management procedures in education. In R. Smith (Ed.), *Regaining educational leadership: Critical essays on PBTE/CBTE, behavioral objectives and accountability* (pp. 104–121). New York: Wiley.

Apple, M., & Jungck, S. (1992). You don't have to be a teacher to teach this unit: Teaching, technology and control in the classroom. In A. Hargreaves & M. Fullan (Eds.), *Understanding teacher development* (pp. 20–42). New York: Teachers College Press.

Armbruster, B. (2000). Taking notes from lectures. In R. Flippo & D. Caverly (Eds.), *Handbook of college reading and study strategy research* (pp. 175–199). Mahwah, NJ: Lawrence Erlbaum Associates.

Assumptions for Phase II Action Plans. (1994). Virginia Tech: Blacksburg, VA.

Ausubel, D. (1967). *Learning Theory and Classroom Practice.* Bulletin No. 1. The Ontario Institute for studies in Education.

Ausubel, D. (1968). *Educational psychology: A cognitive view.* New York: Holt, Rinehart, and Winston.

Babbage, C. (1971). *On the economy of machinery and manufactures* (4th ed.). New York: Kelley.

Bachrach, P., & Botwinick, A. (1992). *Power and empowerment.* Philadelphia: Temple University Press.

Baldwin, R. (1998). Technology's impact on faculty life and work. In K. H. Gillespie (Ed.), *The impact of technology on faculty development, life, and work* (pp. 7–21). San Francisco: Jossey-Bass.

Ball, S. (1994). *Educational reform.* Buckingham, England Open University Press.

Barab, S., Kling, R., & Gray, J. (Eds.). (2004). *Designing for virtual communities in the service of learning.* Cambridge, England: Cambridge University Press.

Barnet, R., & Cavanagh, J. (1994). *Global dreams: Imperial corporations and the new world order.* New York: Simon & Schuster.

Barone, C. (2000, September/October). *National learning infrastructure initiative: Mission, perspective, principles.* Paper presented at Learning 2000, Roanoke, VA.

Barrow, C. (1995). Beyond the multiversity: Fiscal crisis and the changing structure of academic labour. In J. Smyth (Ed.), *Academic work* (pp. 159–178). Bristol, PA: Society for Research into Higher Education and Open University Press.

Bartlett, T. (2003, May 9). Big, but not bad: The best teaching doesn't always happen around a seminar table. *The Chronicle of Higher Education,* pp. A12–A14.

Bartlett, T. (2004, September 17). Taking control of the classroom: Faculty members devise strategies to keep rude students in order [Electronic version]. *Chronicle of Higher Education,* pp. 8–9.

Bates, T. (2001). *National strategies for e-learning in post-secondary education and training.* Paris: UNESCO.

Bates, T., & Poole, G. (2003). *Effective teaching with technology in higher education: Foundations for success.* San Francisco: Jossey-Bass.

Bauman, R. (1984). *Verbal art as performance.* Prospect Heights, IL: Waveland Press.

Becher, T. (1994). The significance of disciplinary differences. *Studies in Higher Education, 19,* 151–161.

Bechky, B. (2003). Object lessons: Workplace artifacts as representations of occupational jurisdiction. *American Journal of Sociology, 109,* 720–752.

Becker, H. (1964). Problems in the publication of field studies. In A. Vidich, J. Bensman, & M. Stein (Eds.), *Reflections on community studies* (pp. 267–284). New York: John Wiley and Sons.

Becker, H. (1982). *Art worlds.* Berkeley: University of California Press.

Becker, H. (1998). *Tricks of the trade.* Chicago: University of Chicago Press.

Becker, H., Geer, B., & Hughes, E. (1968). *Making the grade: The academic side of college life.* New York: Wiley.

Benjamin, E. (1995). A faculty response to the fiscal crisis: From defense to offense. In M. Berube & C. Nelson (Eds.), *Higher education under fire: Politics, economics, and the crisis of the humanities* (pp. 52–72). New York: Routledge.

Benjamin, W. (1978). One-way street. In P. Demetz (Ed.), *Walter Benjamin: Reflections* (pp. 61–94). New York: Schocken Books.

Benjamin, W. (1999). *The Arcades project.* Cambridge, MA: Harvard University Press.

Benner, C. (2002). *Work in the new economy: Flexible labor markets in Silicon Valley.* Malden, MA: Blackwell.

Berg, M., & Timmermans, S. (2000). Orders and their others: On the constitution of universalities in medical work. *Configurations, 8,* 31–61.

Berger, J. (1972). *Ways of seeing.* Harmondsworth, England: Penguin Books.

Berger, J. (1979). *Pig earth.* London: Readers and Writers.

Berkman, D. (1977). Instructional television: The medium whose future has passed. In J. Ackerman & L. Lipsitz (Eds.), *Instructional television: Status and directions* (pp. 95–108). Englewood Cliffs, NJ: Educational Technology.

Bess, J. (1998). Teaching well: Do you have to be schizophrenic? *Review of Higher Education, 22,* 1–15.

Bess, J. & Associates (2000). *Teaching alone, teaching together: Transforming the structure of teams for teaching.* San Francisco: Jossey-Bass.

Biglan, A. (1973). The characteristics of subject matter in different scientific areas. *Journal of Applied Psychology, 57,* 195–203.

Bigum, C. (2002). Design sensibilities, schools and the new computing and communication technologies. In I. Snyder (Ed.), *Silicon literacies: Communication, innovation and education in the electronic age* (pp. 130–140). New York: Routledge.

Biological Sciences Initiative (BSI) web page. Retrieved October 4, 1999 from http://www.bsi.vt.edu

Blake, A. (1995, May 14). Budget cuts affecting Tech's College of Engineering. *The Roanoke Times,* pp. D1, D7.

Bloom, A. (1987). *The closing of the American mind.* New York: Simon & Schuster.

Blumenstyk, G. (1999a, September 17). Colleges object as companies put class notes on web sites. *The Chronicle of Higher Education,* p. A41.

Blumenstyk, G. (1999b, July 23). Distance learning at the Open University [Electronic version]. *The Chronicle of Higher Education,* pp. 34–35.

Blumenstyk, G. (2001, February 9). Knowledge is "a form of venture capital" for a top Columbia administrator. *The Chronicle of Higher Education,* pp. A29–A31.

Boden, D., & Molotch, H. (1994). The compulsion of proximity. In R. Friedland & D. Boden (Eds.), *Now here: Space, time and modernity* (pp. 257–286). Berkeley: University of California Press.

Bonk, C., & Cummings, J. (1998). A dozen recommendations for placing the student at the center of web-based learning. *Educational Media International, 35*(2), 82–89.

Born, G. (1995). *Rationalizing culture: IRCAM, Boulez, and the institutional-ization of the avant-garde*. Berkeley: University of California Press.

Boucher, R. (1993, September 1). A science policy for the 21st Century. *The Chronicle of Higher Education*, p. B1.

Bourdieu, P. (1984). *Distinction* (R. Nice, Trans.) Cambridge, MA: Harvard University Press. (Original work published 1979)

Bowker, G., & Star, S. (1999). *Sorting things out: Classification and its conse-quences*. Cambridge, MA: MIT Press.

Brabazon, T. (2002). *Digital hemlock: Internet education and the poisoning of teaching*. Sydney, Australia: University of New South Wales Press.

Braverman, H. (1974). *Labor and monopoly capital: The degredation of work in the twentieth century*. New York: Monthly Review Press.

Brotherton, J., & Abowd, G. (2002). eClass. In R. Hazemi & S. Hailes (Eds.), *The digital university: Building a learning community* (pp. 71–93). New York City: Springer.

Brown, D. (1995). *Degrees of control: A sociology of educational expansion and occupational credentialism*. New York: Teachers College Press.

Burawoy, M. (1979). The anthropology of industrial work. *Annual Review of Anthropology 8*, 231–266.

Burton, J., Moore, M., & Magliaro, S. (1996). Behaviorism and instruc-tional technology. In D. Jonassen (Ed.), *Handbook of research for educa-tional communications and technology* (pp. 46–73). New York: Simon & Schuster.

Callahan, R. (1962). *Education and the cult of efficiency*. Chicago: University of Chicago Press.

Carlisle, E. (1991). *Blacksburg budget blues*. Blacksburg: Office of the Provost, Virginia Tech.

Carnevale, D. (1999, December 10). A distance-learning forecast called for megaclasses [Electronic version] *The Chronicle of Higher Education*, p. A47.

Carnevale, D. (2000, August 4). Turning traditional courses into distance education: Instructional designers translate professors' teaching styles into electronic content. *The Chronicle of Higher Education*, pp. A37–A38.

Carnevale, D. (2001, February 23). As online education surges, some col-leges remain untouched [Electronic version]. *The Chronicle of Higher Education*, p. A41.

Carnevale, D. (2004a, October, 15). More professors teach by using other colleges' online courses: New efforts help institutions trade curricula, but some faculty members are wary. *The Chronicle of Higher Education*, pp. A28–A29.

Carnevale, D. (2004b, August 13). Professors seek compensation for online courses: They want extra pay or time off, but financially strapped colleges are reluctant. *The Chronicle of Higher Education*, pp. A27–A28.

Carnevale, D., & Olsen, F. (2003, June 13). How to succeed in distance education: By going after the right audience, online programs build a viable industry. *The Chronicle of Higher Education*, pp. A31–A33.

Carnevale, D., & Young, J. (1999, December 17). Who owns on-line courses? Colleges and professors start to sort it out. *The Chronicle of Higher Education*, p. A45.

Carr, S. (2001, February 16). Is anyone making money on distance education? *The Chronicle of Higher Education*, pp. A41–A43.

Carruthers, B., & Espeland, W. (1991). Accounting for rationality: Double-entry bookkeeping and the rhetoric of economic rationality. *American Journal of Sociology, 97*, 31–69.

Center For Innovation in Learning (CIL) web page. Retrieved February 17, 2000 http://www.cdtech.vt.edu/cil/

Chickering, A., & Ehrmann, S. C. (1996). Implementing the seven principles: Technology as lever [Electronic version]. *AAHE Bulletin, 49*, Vol. 2, 3–6.

Chickering, A., & Gamson, Z. (Eds.). (1991). *Applying the seven principles for good practice in undergraduate education*. San Francisco: Jossey-Bass.

Clarke, A., & Fujimura, J. (1992). What tools? Which jobs? Why right? In A. Clark & J. Fujimura (Eds.), *The right tools for the job: At work in twentieth-century life sciences* (pp. 3–44). Princeton, NJ: Princeton University Press.

Clegg, S. (1990). *Frameworks of power*. London: Sage.

Cochran-Smith, M., & Lytle, S. (1999). Relationships of knowledge and practice: Teacher learning in communities. In A. Iran-Nejad & P. D. Pearson (Eds.), *Review of research in education 24* (pp. 249–305). Washington, DC: American Educational Research Association.

Commission on the Future of Higher Education in Virginia. (1996, January). *Making connections: Matching Virginia higher education's strengths with the commonwealth's needs*. Richmond, VA: Author.

Committee to Plan the Center for Excellence in Undergraduate Education (1993, May 21). *Report Submitted to E. Fred Carlisle, Senior Vice President and University Provost*. Virginia Tech: Blacksburg, VA.

Commonwealth of Virginia Commission on the University of the 21st Century. (1989). *A case for change*. Retrieved December, 17, 2005 http://minerva.acc.virginia.edu/admin/tarex/u21rpth.html

Cooper, R. (1998). Assemblage notes. In R. Chia (Ed.), *Organizational worlds: Explorations in technology and organization with Robert Cooper* (pp. 108–129). London: Routledge.

Cornford, J., & Pollock, N. (2002). Working through the work of making work mobile. In K. Robins & F. Webster (Eds.), *The virtual university: Knowledge, markets, and management* (pp. 87–104). New York: Oxford University Press.

Crook, C., & Light, P. (2002). Virtual society and the cultural practice of study. In S. Woolgar (Ed.), *Virtual society? Technology, cyberbole, reality* (pp. 153–175). Oxford, England: Oxford University Press.

Cuban, L. (1993). Computers meet classroom: Classroom wins. *Teachers College Record, 95*, 185–210.

D'Andrea, V.-M. (2003). Organizing teaching and learning: Outcomes-based planning. In H. Fry, S. Ketteridge, & S. Marshall (Eds.), *A handbook for teaching and learning in higher education: Enhancing academic practice* (2nd ed., pp. 26–41). London: Kogan Page.

David, P. (2000). *Path dependence, its critics and the quest for "historical economics".* Retrieved January 28, 2004, from http://www-econ.stanford. edu/faculty/workp/swp00011.pdf

Davies, G. (1986). The importance of being general: Philosophy, politics, and institutional mission statements. In J. Smart (Ed.), *Higher education: Handbook of theory and research* (Vol. 2, pp. 85–108). New York: Agathon Press.

Davies, G. (1997, October 3). Higher-education systems as cartels: The end is near. *The Chronicle of Higher Education,* p. A68.

Davies, G. (2004, July 2). Today, even B students are getting squeezed out. *The Chronicle of Higher Education,* p. B20.

DeLoughry, T. (1993a, June 23). A "meeting of minds" on internet's future. *The Chronicle of Higher Education,* p. A15.

DeLoughry, T. (1993b, May 19). Struggle for the future of computer networking. *The Chronicle of Higher Education,* p. A25.

Deuten, J. J., & Rip, A. (2000). Narrative infrastructure in product creation processes. *Organization, 7,* 69–93.

Dick, W. (1987). A history of instructional design and its impact on educational psychology. In J. Glover & R. Ronning (Eds.), *Historical foundations of educational psychology* (pp. 183–202). New York: Plenum Press.

Diesing, P. (1971). *Patterns of discovery in the social sciences.* Chicago: Aldine.

Diesing, P. (1991). *How does social science work? Reflections on practice.* Pittsburgh, PA: University of Pittsburgh Press.

Dimaggio, P., & Powell, W. (1983). The iron cage revisited: Institutional isomorphism and collective rationality in organizational fields. *American Sociological Review, 48,* 147–160.

Dreyfus, H. (2001). *On the internet.* London: Routledge.

Duderstadt, J. (1999). Can colleges and universities survive in the information age? R. Katz, and Associates. *Dancing with the devil: Information technology and the new competition in higher education* (pp. 1–25). San Francisco: Jossey-Bass.

Dunkel, P., & Davey, S. (1989). The heuristic of lecture notetaking: Perceptions of American and international students regarding the value and practice of notetaking. *English for Specific Purposes, 8,* 33–50.

Dutton, W., & Loader, B. (Ed.). (2002). *Digital academe: The new media and institutions of higher education and learning.* London: Routledge.

Edwards, R. (1979). *Contested terrain.* New York: Basic Books.

Entwistle, N., & Ramsden, P. (1982). *Understanding student learning.* London: Croom Helm.

Entwistle, N., McCune, V., & Hounsell, J. (2002). *Approaches to studying and perceptions of university teaching-learning environments: Concepts, measures and preliminary findings* [Occasional Report No. 1]. Edinburgh, Scotland: University of Edinburgh School of Education.

Espeland, W. N., & Stevens, M. (1998). Commensuration as a social process. *Annual Review of Sociology, 24,* 313–343.

Evans, C., Gibbons, N., Shah, K., & Griffin, D. (2004). Virtual learning in the biological sciences: Pitfalls of simply "putting notes on the web". *Computers and Education, 43,* 49–61.

Farmelo, A. (1997). *The unifying consequences of grooving: An introductory ethnographic approach to unity through music.* Retrieved December 13, 2001, from http://www.musekids.org/UCS.html

Farrell, E. (2003, February 14). Phoenix's unusual way of crafting courses: The for-profit giant uses a systematic grid and a guy named "Joe" to set curriculum. *The Chronicle of Higher Education,* p. A10.

Fenwick, R., & Tausig, M. (2004). The health and family-social consequences of shift-work and schedule control: 1977 and 1997. In C. F. Epstein & A. Kalleberg (Eds.), *Fighting for time: Shifting boundaries of work and social life* (pp. 77–110). New York: Sage.

Fligstein, N. (1990). *The transformation of the American corporation.* Cambridge, MA: Harvard University Press.

Fligstein, N., & Freeland, R. (1995). Theoretical and comparative perspectives on corporate organization. *Annual Review of Sociology, 21,* 21–43.

Forsythe, D. (1999). Ethics and politics of studying up in technoscience. *Anthropology of Work Review, 20,* 6–11.

Forsythe, D. (2001). *Studying those who study us.* Stanford, CA: Stanford University Press.

Foucault, M. (1979). *Discipline and punish.* New York: Vintage Books.

Foucault, M. (1980). Power and strategies. In C. Gordon (Ed.), *Power/knowledge: Selected interviews and other writings, 1972–1977 by Michel Foucault* (pp. 134–145). New York: Pantheon Books.

FQ (1998a). Emporium management and marketing. Retrieved December 19, 2005. http://www.math.vt.edu/people/quinn/education/emp-inc.pdf.

FQ (1998b). Remote help for computer-based math courses. Retrieved December 19, 2005. http://www.math.vt.edu/people/quinn/education/on-line.help.pdf.

Fraser, J. (2001). *White-collar sweat-shop.* New York: Norton.

Frith, S. (1996). *Performing rites: On the value of popular music.* Cambridge, MA: Harvard University Press.

Fry, H., Ketteridge, S., & S. Marshall, S. (Eds.). (2003). *A handbook for teaching and learning in higher education: Enhancing academic practice* (2nd ed.) London: Kogan Page.

Gagliardi, P. (1996). Exploring the aesthetic side of organizational life. In S. Clegg, C. Hardy, & W. Nord (Eds.), *Handbook of organization studies* (pp. 565–580). London: Sage.

Gagne, R. (1967). Curriculum research and the promotion of learning. In R. Tyler, R. Gagne, & M. Scriven (Eds.), *Perspectives of curriculum evaluation* (pp. 19–38). Chicago: Rand McNally.

Gagne, R., Briggs, L., & Wager, W. (1992). *Principles of instructional design.* Fort Worth, TX: Harcourt Brace.

Gaskell, J., & Hepburn, G. (1998). The course as token: A construction of/by networks. *Research in Science Education, 28,* 65–76.

Geiger, R. (2004). *Knowledge and money: Research universities and the paradox of the marketplace.* Stanford, CA: Stanford University Press.

Gibson, J. J. (1979). *The ecological approach to visual perception.* Boston: Houghton Mifflin.

Gillespie, F. (1998). Instructional design for the new technologies. In K. H. Gillespie (Ed.), *The impact of technology on faculty development, life, and work* (pp. 39–52). San Francisco: Jossey-Bass.

Gittell, R., & Sedgley, N. (2000). High technology and state higher education policy. *American Behavioral Scientist, 43,* 1092–1120.

Goffman, E. (1981). *Forms of talk.* Philadelphia: University of Pennsylvania Press.

Goldfarb, B. (2002). *Visual pedagogy: Media cultures in and beyond the classroom.* Durham, NC: Duke University Press.

Goodyear, P., Salmon, G., Spector, J. M., Steeples, C., & Tickner, S. (2001). Competencies for online teaching: A special report. *Educational Technology Research and Development, 49,* 65–72.

Green, C., & Dorn, D. (1999). The changing classroom: The meaning of shifts in higher education for teaching and learning. In B. Pescosolido & R. Aminzade (Eds.), *The social worlds of higher education: Handbook for teaching in a new century* (pp. 59–79). Thousand Oaks, CA: Pine Forge Press.

Hakken, D. (2003). *The knowledge landscapes of cyberspace.* New York: Routledge.

Hall, E. (1959). *The silent language.* New York: Doubleday.

Halpin, D., & Troyna, B. (1995). The politics of education policy borrowing. *Comparative Education, 31,* 303–309.

Hamilton, S., & Zimmerman, J. (2002). Breaking through zero-sum academics: Two students' perspectives on computer-mediated learning environments. In K. Rudestam & J. Schoenholtz-Read (Eds.), *Handbook of online learning: Innovations in higher education and corporate training* (pp. 257–276). Thousand Oaks, CA: Sage.

Hannsgen, K. & Bradley, K. (2001). Appendix 1. Assessment Pew Program in Course Redesign. Virginia Tech-Linear Algebra Project. Retrieved May 8, 2003 http://Filebox.vt.edu/users/hannsgen/reference/vTaccers.pdf

Hara, N., & Kling, R. (2000). *Students' distress with a web-based distance education course* (CSI Working Paper No. 00-01-A1). Bloomington: Indiana University, Center for Social Informatics. Retrieved February 21, 2001, from http://www.slis.indiana.edu/CSI/wp00-01.html

Hargreaves, A. (1992). Time and teachers' work: An analysis of the intensification thesis. *Teachers College Record, 94,* 87–108.

Hartman, J., & Truman-Davis, B. (2001). The Holy Grail: Developing scalable solutions and sustainable support solutions. In C. Barone & P. Hagner (Eds.), *Technology-enhanced teaching and learning: Leading and supporting the transformation on your campus* (pp. 45–56). San Francisco: Jossey-Bass.

Hativa, N., & Marincovich, M. (Eds.). (1995). *Disciplinary differences in teaching and learning: Implications for practice. New Directions for Teaching and Learning, 64.* San Francisco: Jossey-Bass.

Hawkins, B., Rudy, J., & Madsen, J. (2003). *Educause core data service, 2002 summary report.* Washington, DC: Educause.

Hawkins, H. (1979). University identity: The teaching and research functions. In A. Oleson & J. Voss (Eds.), *The organization of knowledge in modern America, 1860–1920* (pp. 285–312). Baltimore: Johns Hopkins University Press.

Henwood, D. (2003). *After the new economy.* New York: New Press.

Hess, D. (1999). The autonomy question and the changing conditions of social scientific work. *Anthropology of Work Review, 20*(1), 27–34.

Heterick, R. (1995). The four horsemen [Electronic version]. *Educom Review, 30*(4), 60.

Heterick, R. (1998). Educom: A retrospective [Electronic version]. *Educom Review, 33*(5) 42–47.

Heterick, R., & Twigg, C. (1997). Interpolating the future [Electronic version]. *Educom Review, 32*(1), 60.

Hopwood, A. (1987). The archeology of accounting systems. *Accounting, Organizations and Society, 12*(3), 207–234.

Hopwood, A. (1990). Accounting and organisation change. *Accounting, Auditing, and Accountability Journal, 3*(1), 7–17.

Hornborg, A. (2001). Symbolic technologies: Machines and the Marxian notion of fetishism. *Anthropological Theory, 1,* 473–496.

Hoskin, K. (1996). The awful idea of accountability: Inscribing people into the measurement of objects. In R. Munro & J. Mouritsen (Eds.), *Accountability: Power, ethos and the technologies of managing* (pp. 265–282). London: Thomson Business Press.

Hsu, S. (1995, January 13). Virginia failing in funding, colleges say. *The Washington Post,* pp. A1, A8.

Huber, R. (1992). *How professors are the cats guarding the cream: Why we're paying more and getting less in higher education.* Fairfax, VA: George Mason University Press.

Hutchins, E. (1995). *Cognition in the wild.* Cambridge, MA: MIT Press.

Information Systems. (1995). *Student scenarios.* Retrieved March 26, 2002 from http://filebox.vt.edu/is/vp/studscen.html

Ingerman, B. (2001). Form follows function: Establishing the necessary infrastructure. In C. Barone & P. Hagner (Eds.), *Technology-enhanced teaching and learning: Leading and supporting the transformation on your campus.* (pp. 79–92). San Francisco: Jossey-Bass.

Institute for Higher Education Policy. (2000). *Quality on the line.* Washington DC: Institute For Higher Education Policy.

International Labor Organization. (1991). *Teachers: Challenges of the 1990s, Second joint meeting on conditions of work of teachers.* Geneva: Author.

Intress, R. (1993, September 16). Sharing only a lack of money. *The Roanoke Times,* pp. A1, A5.

Irvine, J. (1996). Shadow conversations: The indeterminacy of participant roles. In M. Silverstein & G. Urban (Eds.), *Natural histories of discourse* (pp. 131–159). Chicago: University of Chicago Press.

JR and Barke, B. (2001, February). *Lab Exercises.* CD-ROM. Blacksburg, VA: Virginia College of Veterinary Medicine.

Jakobson, R. (1960). Concluding statement: Linguistics and poetics. In T. Sebeok (Ed.), *Style in language* (pp. 350–377). Cambridge, MA: MIT Press.

Jewitt, C., Kress, G., Ogborn, J. & Tsatsarelis. (2001). *Multimodal Teaching and learning.* London: Continuum.

Jonassen, D., Marra, R., & Palmer, B. (2004). Epistemological development: An implicit entailment of constructivist learning environments. In N. Seel & S. Dijkstra (Eds.), *Curriculum, plans, and processes in instructional design* (pp. 75–88). Mahwah, NJ: Lawrence Erlbaum Associates.

Jonassen, D., Tessmer, M., & Hannum, W. (1999). *Task analysis methods for instructional design.* Mahwah, NJ: Lawrence Erlbaum Associates.

Kane, R., Sandretto, S., & Heath, C. (2002). Telling half the story: A critical review of research on the teaching beliefs and practices of university academics. *Review of Educational Research, 72,* 177–207.

Kaplan, A. (1964). *The conduct of inquiry: Methodology for behavioral science.* San Francisco: Chandler.

Katz, R. (1999). Competitive strategies for higher education in the information age. In R. Katz and Associates. *Dancing with the devil: Information technology and the new competition in higher education* (pp. 27–49). San Francisco: Jossey-Bass.

Keil, C. (1994). Participatory discrepancies and the power of music. In C. Keil & S. Feld (Eds.), *Music grooves* (pp. 96–108). Chicago: University of Chicago Press.

Kidwell, J. (1997). *The transformation of education in the digital age: Report on the Learning Partnership Roundtable, July 1997, PricewaterhouseCoopers.* Retrieved September 25, 2000 http://www. pwcglobal. com/extweb/ indissue.nsf/DocID/FB7890836B0520518525664 E00721748

King, T., & Bannon, E. (2002). *At what cost? The price that working students pay for a college education.* Washington, DC: State PIRG's Higher Education Project.

Kitto, S., & Higgins, V. (2003). Online university education: Liberating the student? *Science as Culture, 12,* 23–58.

Kondo, D. (1996). Shades of twilight: Anna Deavere Smith and Twilight: Los Angeles 1992. In G. Marcus (Ed.), *Connected: Engagements with media* (pp. 313–346). Chicago: University of Chicago Press.

Kramarae, C. (2001). *The third shift: Women learning online.* Washington, DC: American Association of University Women.

Kuh, G., & Hu, S. (2000, April). *The effects of computer and information technology on student learning and other college experiences.* Paper presented at the annual meeting of the American Education Research Association, New Orleans, LA.

Labaree, D. (2000). Resisting educational standards [Electronic version]. *Phi Delta Kappan, 82,* 28–33.

Larner, W., & Le Heron, R. (2002). The spaces and subjects of a globalising economy: A situated exploration of method. *Environment and Planning D: Society and Space, 20,* 753–774.

Lash, S., & Urry, J. (1994). *Economies of signs and space*. Newbury Park, CA: Sage.

Lasher, W., & Sullivan, C. (2004). Follow the money: The changing world of budgeting in higher education. In J. C. Smart (Ed.), *Higher education: Handbook of theory and research* (Vol. 19, pp. 197–240). Dordrecht: Kluwer.

Latour, B. (1987). *Science in action*. Cambridge, MA: Harvard University Press.

Latour, B. (1996). *Aramis, or the love of technology*. Cambridge, MA: Harvard University Press.

Lauter, P. (1995). "Political correctness" and the attack on American colleges. In M. Berube & C. Nelson (Eds.), *Higher education under fire: Politics, economics, and the crisis of the humanities* (pp. 73–90). New York: Routledge.

Law, J. (1994). *Organizing modernity*. Oxford, England Blackwell.

Lee, A., Green, B., & Brennan, M. (2000). Organisational knowledge, professional practice and the professional doctorate at work. In J. Garrick & C. Rhodes (Eds.), *Research and knowledge at work: Perspectives, case-studies and innovative strategies* (pp. 117–136). London: Routledge.

Lemke, J. (2000). Multimedia literacy demands of the scientific curriculum. *Linguistics and Education, 10,* 247–271.

Levine, A. (2000, October 27). The Future of colleges, 9 inevitable changes. *The Chronicle of Higher Education,* B10–11.

Levine, A. (2001). Privatization in higher education. In H. Levin (Ed.), *Privatizing education* (pp. 133–148). Boulder, CO: Westview Press.

Levinson, S. (1988). Putting linguistics on a proper footing: Explorations in Goffman's concepts of participation. In P. Drew & A. Wootton (Eds.), Goffman: *An interdisciplinary appreciation* (pp. 161–227). Cambridge, England: Polity Press.

Lewis, B., Massey, C., & Smith, R. (2001). *The tower under siege: Technology, power, and education*. Montreal: McGill-Queen's University Press.

Lewis, L. (1996). *Marginal worth: Teaching and the academic labor market*. New Brunswick, NJ: Transaction.

Lowgren, J., & Lauren, U. (1993). Supporting the use of guidelines and style guides in professional user interface design. *Interacting with Computers, 5,* 385–396.

Macintyre, M. (2000). *Audit, education, and Goodhart's Law or, taking rigidity seriously*. Retrieved December 18, 2005 http://www.atm.damtp.cam.ac.uk/people/mem/papers/LHCE/dilnot-analysis.html

Mager, R. (1962). *Preparing objectives For programmed instruction*. Belmont, CA: Fearon.

Magolda, M. B. (2000). *Teaching to promote intellectual and personal maturity*. San Francisco: Jossey-Bass.

March, J., & Simon, H. (1958). *Organizations*. New York: Wiley.

Marine, R. (2002). A systems framework for evaluation of faculty web-work. In C. Colbeck (Ed.), *Evaluating faculty performance* (pp. 63–71). San Francisco: Jossey-Bass.

Marsh, H. W., & Ware, J. E. (1982). Effects of expressiveness, content coverage, and incentive on multi-dimensional student rating scales:

New interpretations of the Dr. Fox effect. *Journal of Educational Psychology, 74*, 126–134.

Martin, R. (1994). Stateless monies, global financial integration and national economic autonomy: The end of geography? In S. Corbridge, R. Martin, & N. Thrift (Eds.), *Money, power, and space* (pp. 253–278). Oxford, England: Blackwell.

McCollow, J., & Lingard, B. (1996). Changing discourses and practices of academic work. *Australian Universities Review, 39*(2), 11–19.

McCune, V., & Entwistle, N. (2000, August-September). *The deep approach to learning: Analytic abstraction and idiosyncratic development.* Paper presented at the Innovations in Higher Education Conference, Helsinki, Finland.

McKeachie, W. (1999). *Teaching tips* (10th Ed.) New York: Houghton Mifflin.

McSweeney, B. (1996). The arrival of an accountability: Explaining the imposition of management by accounting. In R. Munro & J. Mouritsen (Eds.), *Accountability: Power, ethos and the technologies of managing* (pp. 201–224). London: Thomson Business Press.

McWilliam, E., & Taylor, P. (1998). Teacher im/material: Challenging the new pedagogies of instructional design. *Educational Researcher, 27*, 8, 29–34.

Means, G. (2000). *Metacapitalism and higher education: The one percent solution.* Retrieved September 25, 2000 from http://www.pwcglobal.com/extweb/newcolth.nsf/docid/4DECD594ED980C628525692D0067B72E?OpenDocument

Mehrotra, C. M., Hollister, C. D., & McGahey, L. (2001). *Distance learning: Principles for effective design, delivery, and evaluation.* Thousand Oaks, CA: Sage.

Miller, M. (1994). Pressures to measure faculty work. In J. Wergin (Ed.), *Analyzing faculty workloads* (pp. 5–14). San Francisco: Jossey-Bass.

Miller, P., & O'Leary, T. (1987). Accounting and the construction of the governable person. *Accounting, Organizations and Society, 12*, 235–265.

Molenda, M. (1997). Historical and philosophical foundations of instructional design: A North American view. In R. Tennyson, F. Schott, N. Sel, & S. Dijkstra (Eds.), *Instructional design: International perspectives* (Vol. 1, pp. 41–53). Mahwah, NJ: Lawrence Erlbaum Associates.

Moore, R. (2003). Attendance and performance: How important is it for students to attend class? *Journal of College Science Teaching, 32*, 367–371.

MS. (1985, January) VCR and CRT: The latest media marriage. *inCider,* 32–36.

Mumper, M. (1996). *Removing college price barriers.* Albany: State University of New York Press.

Munn, N. (1992). The cultural anthropology of time: A critical essay. *Annual Review of Anthropology, 21*, 93–123.

Munro, R. (1996). Alignment and identity work: The study of accounts and accountability. In R. Munro & J. Mouritsen (Eds.), *Accountability: Power, ethos and the technologies of managing* (pp. 1–19). London: Thomson Business Press.

Naftulin, D. H., Ware, J. W., & Donnelly, F. A. (1973). The Doctor Fox lecture: A paradigm of educational seduction. *Journal of Medical Education*, 48, 630–635.

Naidu, S. (Ed.). (2003). *Learning and teaching with technology*. London: Kogan Page.

Nardi, B., & O'Day, V. (1999). *Information ecologies*. Cambridge, MA: MIT Press.

National Governors Association. (2001). *The state of e-learning in the states*. Retrieved June 16, 2001 http://www.nga.org/cda/files/060601 elearning.pdf

Nelson, C. (1999). On the persistence of unicorns: The trade-off between content and critical thinking revisited. In B. Pescosolido & R. Aminzade (Eds.), *The social worlds of higher education: Handbook for teaching in a new century* (pp. 168–184). Thousand Oaks, CA: Pine Forge Press.

Nespor, J. (1994). *Knowledge in motion*. London: Falmer.

Nespor, J. (2000). Anonymity and place in qualitative inquiry. *Qualitative Inquiry*, 6, 546–569.

Neumann, R. (2001). Disciplinary differences and university teaching. *Studies in Higher Education*, 26, 135–146.

Neumann, R., Parry, S., & Becher, T. (2002). Teaching and learning in their disciplinary contexts: A conceptual analysis. *Studies in Higher Education*, 27, 405–417.

Neumann, W. (1979). Educational responses to the concern for proficiency. In G. Grant (Ed.), *On competence: A critical analysis of competency-based reforms in higher education* (pp. 67–95). San Francisco: Jossey-Bass.

Newman, D., Griffen, P., & Cole, M. (1988). *The construction zone: Working for cognitive change in school*. Cambridge, England: Cambridge University Press.

Noble, D. (1984). *Forces of production: A social history of industrial automation*. New York: Knopf.

Noble, D. (2001). *Digital diploma mills*. New York: Monthly Review Press.

Noble, D. (1991). *The classroom arsenal*. Philadelphia: Falmer.

Norton, L., Tilley, A., Newstead, S., & A. Franklyn-Stokes, A. (2004). The pressures of assessment in undergraduate courses and their effect on student behaviours. In M. Tight (Ed.), *The RoutledgeFalmer reader in higher education* (pp. 68–84). London: RoutledgeFalmer.

Nutter, D. (2000). University dedicates high-tech Torgersen Hall. *Virginia Tech Spectrum*, 23(8), 1, 4.

Olin, R. (2001). The math emporium: Student-paced mathematics 24/7. Paper prepared for The Institute on Learning Technology of the National Institute for Science Education. Retrieved November 29, 2004 from http://www.wcer.wise.edu/nise/cl1/115/extra/downloaed/solution/olinw60

Olsen, F. (1999a, October 29). Faculty wariness of technology remains a challenge, computing survey finds. *The Chronicle of Higher Education*, p. A65.

Olsen, F. (1999b, October 8). The promise and problems of a new way of teaching math [Electronic version]. *The Chronicle of Higher Education*, p. A31.

Paulsen, M., & St. John, E. (2002). Budget incentive structures and the improvement of college teaching. In D. Priest, W. Becker, D. Hossler, & E. St. John (Eds.), *Incentive-based budgeting systems in public universities* (pp. 161–184). Cheltenham, England: Elgar.

Pelz, B. (2004). (My) three principles of effective online pedagogy [Electronic version]. *Journal of Asynchronous Learning Networks, 8*(3), 33–46.

Perley, J. (1999). Back to the future of education: Real teaching, real learning [Electronic version]. *Technology Source*, Retrieved December 18, 2005 http://horizon.unc.edu/TS/commentary/1999-09.asp

Perrow, C. (1984). *Normal accidents: Living with high-risk technologies.* New York: Basic Books.

Perry, W. (1968). *Forms of intellectual and ethical development in the college years.* New York: Holt, Rinehart, and Winston.

Pescosolido, B., & Aminzade, R. (Eds.). (1999). *The social worlds of higher education: Handbook for teaching in a new century.* Thousand Oaks, CA: Pine Forge Press.

Phillips, K. (1993). *Boiling point.* New York: Harper.

Phipps, R., & Merisotis, J. (1999). *What's the difference: A review of contemporary research on the effectiveness of distance learning in higher education.* Washington, DC: Institute for Higher Education Policy.

Pierson, P. (2003). Big, slow-moving, and ... invisible. In J. Mahoney & D. Rueschemeyer (Eds.), *Comparative historical analysis in the social sciences* (pp. 177–207). Cambridge, England: Cambridge University Press.

Pollock, N., & Cornford, J. (2003). *Putting the University online.* Philadelphia: Open University Press.

Power, M. (1994). *The audit explosion.* London: Demos.

Presser, H. (2004). Employment in a 24/7 economy: Challenges for the family. In C. F. Epstein & A. Kalleberg (Eds.), *Fighting for time: Shifting boundaries of work and social life* (pp. 46–76). New York: Russell Sage.

Pressey, S. L. (1960 [1932]). A third and fourth contribution toward the coming "industrial revolution" in education. In A. A. Lumsdaine & R. Glaser (Eds.), *Teaching machines and programmed learning: A source book* (pp. 47–51). Washington, DC: National Education Association of the United States.

Provost and the Council of Deans. (1993, February 1). *Where do we stand and what might we do?* Virginia Tech: Blacksburg, VA.

FQ. (1994, May 6). *A self-study computer version of 3034* (Memorandum). Retrieved January 24, 2003, from http://www.math.vt.edu/people/quinn/education/computer3034.pdf

FQ. (1998, April 10). *Emporium management and marketing.* (Memorandum). Retrieved January 24, from URL http://www.math.vt.edu/people/quinn/education/emp-inc.pdf

Ragin, C. (2000). *Fuzzy-set social science,* Chicago: University of Chicago Press.

Ramsden, P. (Ed.). (1988). *Improving learning: New perspectives.* London: Kogan Page.

Reed, M. (2001). Organization, trust and control: A realist analysis. *Organization Studies, 22,* 201–228.

Reed, M., & Deem, R. (2002). New managerialism: The manager-academic and technologies of management in universities—looking forward to virtuality? In K. Robins & F. Webster (Eds.), *The virtual university? Knowledge, markets, and management* (pp. 126–147). Oxford, England: Oxford University Press.

Reigeluth, C. (1999). What is instructional-design theory and how is it changing? In C. Reigeluth (Ed.), *Instructional-design theories and models: A new paradigm of instructional theory* (pp. 5–29). Mahwah, NJ: Lawrence Erlbaum Associates.

Reiser, R. (2001a). A history of instructional design and technology: Part I: A history of instructional media. *Educational Technology Research and Development, 49*(1), 53–64.

Reiser, R. (2001b). A history of instructional design and technology: Part II: A history of instructional design. *Educational Technology Research and Development, 49*(2), 57–67.

Rhoades, G., & Slaughter, S. (1997). Academic capitalism, managed professionals, and supply-side higher education. *Social Text, 15*(2), 9–38.

Rhoades, G., & Slaughter, S. (1998). Academic capitalism, managed professionals, and supply-side higher education. In R. Martin (Ed.), *Chalk lines: The politics of work in the managed university* (pp. 33–60). Durham, NC: Duke University Press.

Roemer, R., & Schnitz, J. (1982). Academic employment as day labor. *Journal of Higher Education, 53,* 514–530.

Rose, M. (2004). *The mind at work.* New York: Viking.

Rudestam, K., & Schoenholtz-Read, J. (Eds.). (2002). *Handbook of online learning: Innovations in higher education and corporate training.* Thousand Oaks, CA: Sage.

Rudolph, F. (1977). *Curriculum: A history of the American undergraduate course of study since 1636.* San Francisco: Jossey-Bass.

Ryan, S., Scott, B., Freeman, H., & Patel, D. (2000). *The virtual university: The internet and resource-based learning.* London: Kogan Page.

St. Clair, K. (1999). A case against compulsory class attendance policies in higher education. *Innovative Higher Education, 23*(3), 171–180.

St. John, E. (1994). *Prices, productivity and investment: Assessing financial strategies in higher education* (ASHE/ERIC Higher Education Report No. 3). Washington, DC: George Washington University.

Sarason, S. (1979). *Teaching as a performing art.* New York: Teachers College Press.

Schorger, J. (1997). *A qualitative study of the development and first year of implementation of the Blacksburg Electronic Village.* Unpublished doctoral dissertation, Virginia Polytechnic Institute and State University, Blacksburg.

Scott, J. (1998). *Seeing like a state.* New Haven, CT: Yale University Press.

Seel, N., & Dijkstra, S. (Eds.). (2004a). *Curriculum, plans, and processes in instructional design.* Mahwah, NJ: Lawrence Erlbaum Associates.

Seel, N., & Dijkstra, S. (2004b). Introduction: Instructional design and curriculum development. In N. Seel & S. Dijkstra (Eds.), *Curriculum, plans, and processes in instructional design* (pp. 1–24). Mahwah, NJ: Lawrence Erlbaum Associates.

Segall, A. (2004). Revisiting pedagogical content knowledge: The pedagogy of content/the content of pedagogy. *Teaching and Teacher Education, 20,* 489–504.

Selingo, J. (1999, July 14). Businesses say they turn to for-profit schools because of public colleges' inertia [Electronic version]. *The Chronicle of Higher Education,* Retrieved December 18, 2005 http://chronicle.com/daily/99/07/99071401n.htm

Shaiken, H., Herzenberg, S., & Kuhn, S. (1986). The workplace under more flexible production. *Industrial Relations, 25,* 167–183.

Shapiro, S. (1987). The social control of impersonal trust. *American Journal of Sociology, 93,* 623–658.

Shore, C., & Wright, S. (2000). Coercive accountability: The rise of audit culture in higher education. In M. Strathern (Ed.), *Audit cultures: Anthropological studies in accountability, ethics and the academy* (pp. 57–89). London: Routledge.

Silverstein, M., & Urban, G. (1996). The natural history of discourse. In M. Silverstein & G. Urban (Eds.), *Natural histories of discourse* (pp. 1–19). Chicago: University of Chicago Press.

Simonson, M. (2000). Making decisions: The use of electronic technology in online courses. In R. Weiss, D. Knowlton, & B. Speck (Eds.), *Principles of effective teaching in the online classroom* (pp. 29–34). San Francisco: Jossey-Bass.

Sizer, F., & Whitney, E. (2000). *Nutrition: Concepts and controversies.* Belmont, CA: Wadsworth.

Skinner, B. F. (1965). Reflections on a decade of teaching machines. In R. Glaser (Ed.), *Teaching machines and Programmed learning II: Data and directions* (pp. 5–20). Washington, DC: NEA-DAVI. National Education Association-Department of Audiovisual Instruction.

Skinner, B. F. (1968). *The technology of teaching.* Englewood Cliffs, NJ: Prentice Hall.

Sklar, H. (1995). *Chaos or community?* Boston: South End Press.

Slater, D. (2001). Social relationships and identity online and offline. In L. Lievrouw & S. Livingstone (Eds.), *Handbook of new media: Social shaping and consequences of ICTs* (pp. 534–546). London: Sage.

Slaughter, S. (1993). Retrenchment in the 1980s: The politics of gender and prestige. *Journal of Higher Education, 64,* 250–311.

Slaughter, S. (1998). Federal policy and supply-side institutional resource allocation at public research universities. *Review of Higher Education, 21,* 209–244.

Slaughter, S., & Leslie, L. (2001). Expanding and elaborating the concept of academic capitalism. *Organization, 8,* 154–161.

Slaughter, S., & Rhoades, G. (2004). *Academic capitalism and the new economy.* Baltimore: Johns Hopkins University Press.

Slosson, E. (1910). *Great American universities.* New York: Macmillan.

Smith, P., & Ragan, T. (1992). *Instructional design.* New York: MacMillan.

Snelbecker, G. (1999). Some thoughts about theories, perfection, and instruction. In C. Reigeluth (Ed.), *Instructional-design theories and models: A new paradigm of instructional theory* (pp. 31–47). Mahwah, NJ: Lawrence Erlbaum Associates.

Stanley, C., & Porter, E. (2002). *Engaging large classes.* Bolton, MA: Anker.

Star, S., & Griesemer, J. (1999). Institutional ecology, "translation," and boundary objects: Amateurs and professionals in Berkeley's Museum of Vertebrate Zoology, 1907–1939. In M. Biagioli (Ed.), *The science studies reader* (pp. 505–524). New York: Routledge.

Star, S. L., & Ruhleder, K. (1996). Steps toward an ecology of infrastructure: Design and access for large information spaces. *Information Systems Research, 7,* 111–134.

Stark, J. (2002). Planning introductory college courses. In N. Hativa & P. Goodyear (Eds.), *Teacher thinking, beliefs and knowledge in higher education* (pp. 127–150). Dordrecht: Kluwer.

State Council of Higher Education in Virginia. (1993). *Change and improvement in higher education: A preliminary report to the Governor and General Assembly, January 1993.* Retrieved May 14, 1999, from http://minerva.acc.virginia.edu/admin/tarex/aovrpt.html

Stepanek, M. (1999, October 4). A small town reveals America's digital divide. *Business Week Online,* Retrieved December 17, 2005. http://www.businessweek.com/1999/99_40/b3649027.htm

Stoddard, A. J. (1957). *Schools for tomorrow: An educator's blueprint.* New York: Fund for the Advancement of Education.

Strange, S. (1994). From Bretton Woods to the casino economy. In S. Corbridge, R. Martin, & N. Thrift (Eds.), *Money, power, and space* (pp. 49–62). Oxford, England: Blackwell.

Strassmann, P. (1997). *The squandered computer: Evaluating the business alignment of information technologies.* New Canaan, CT: Information Economics Press.

Strathern, M. (1992). *After nature: English kinship in the late twentieth century.* Cambridge, England: Cambridge University Press.

Strathern, M. (1997). "Improving ratings": Audit in the British University system. *European Review, 5,* 305–321.

Strathern, M. (2000a, Month). *Abstraction and decontextualization: An anthropological comment or: e for ethnography.* Retrieved June 15, 2001 http://www.brunel.ac.uk/research/virsoc/GRpapers/strathern.htm

Strathern, M. (2000b). The tyranny of transparency. *British Educational Research Journal, 26,* 309–321.

Strauss, A. (1985). Work and the division of labor. *Sociological Quarterly, 26,* 1–19.

Suchman, L. (1987). *Plans and situated actions: The problem of human-machine communication.* Cambridge, England: Cambridge University Press.

Suchman, L., Trigg, R., & Blomberg, J. (2002). Working artefacts: ethno-methods of the prototype. *British Journal of Sociology, 53*(2), 163–179.

Suter, V. (2001). Managing complexity in a transforming environment. In C. Barone & P. Hagner (Eds.), *Technology-enhanced teaching and learning: Leading and supporting the transformation on your campus* (pp. 25–34). San Francisco: Jossey-Bass.

Sutherland, R. (with the InterActive Project Team). (2004). Designs for learning: ICT and knowledge in the classroom. *Computers and Education, 43*, 5–16.

Tapscott, D., & Ticoll, D. (2003). *The naked corporation: How the age of transparency will revolutionize business.* New York: Free Press.

Taylor, D., Roy, L., & Moore, J. (1997). *ACCESS webpage.* Retrieved February 1, 2000, from http://www.edtech.vt.edu/access

Taylor, M. (2001). *The moment of complexity: Emerging network culture.* Chicago: University of Chicago Press.

Tennyson, R., & Schott, F. (1997). Instructional design theory, research, and models. In R. Tennyson, F. Schott, N. Sel, & S. Dijkstra (Eds.), *Instructional design: International perspectives* (Vol. 1, pp. 1–16). Mahwah, NJ: Lawrence Erlbaum Associates.

Thelen, K. (2003). How institutions evolve. In J. Mahoney & D. Rueschemeyer (Eds.), *Comparative historical analysis in the social sciences* (pp. 208–240). Cambridge, England: Cambridge University Press.

Thompson, D. W. (1948). *On growth and form.* New York: Macmillan.

Tierney, W., & Rhoads, R. (1995). The culture of assessment. In J. Smyth (Ed.), *Academic work* (pp. 99–111). Bristol, PA: Society for Research into Higher Education and Open University Press.

Tight, M. (Ed.). (2004). *The RoutledgeFalmer reader in higher education.* London: RoutledgeFalmer.

Tilly, C. (2001). Mechanisms in political processes. *Annual Review of Political Science, 4*, 21–41.

Tilly, C. (2002). *Stories, identities, and political change.* Lanham, MD: Roman & Littlefield.

Tirelli, V. (1998). Adjuncts and more adjuncts: Labor segmentation and the transformation of higher education. In R. Martin (Ed.), *Chalk lines: The politics of work in the managed university* (pp. 181–201). Durham, NC: Duke University Press.

Tomlinson-Keasey, C. (2002). Becoming digital: The challenge of weaving technology throughout higher education. In S. Brint (Ed.), *The future of the city of intellect* (pp. 133–158). Stanford, CA: Stanford University Press.

Tompkins, E., & Gaumnitz, W. (1954). *The Carnegie unit: Its origin, status, and trends* (U.S. Department of Health, Education, and Welfare, Bulletin 1954, No. 7). Washington, DC: U.S. Government Printing Office.

Torgersen, P. (1995, April 10). *The Virginia Tech Pledge.* Virginia Tech: Blacksburg, VA.

Trowler, P. (2001). Captured by the discourse? The socially constitutive power of new higher education discourse in the UK. *Organization, 8*, 183–201.

Tufte, E. (2003). *The cognitive style of PowerPoint.* Cheshire, CT: Graphics Press.

Twigg, C. (1992). Improving productivity in higher education: The need for a paradigm shift [Electronic version]. *Cause/Effect, 15*(2), 39–46.

Twigg, C. (1995). The one percent solution [Electronic version]. *Educom Review, 30*(6), 16–17. Retrieved September 25, 2000 http://www.edu cause.edu/pub/er/review/reviewArticles/30616.html

Twigg, C. (1996a). *Academic productivity: The case for instructional software. A report from the Broadmoor Roundtable, Colorado Springs, CO: July 1996.* Retrieved March 13, 2000, from http://www.educause.edu/nlii/key docs/broadmoor.html

Twigg, C. (1996b). *The virtual university: A Report from a Joint Educom/IBM Roundtable, Washington, DC, November 5–6.* Retrieved March 13, 2000, from http://www.educause.edu/nlii/VU.html

Twigg, C. (2002). The impact of the changing economy on four-year institutions of higher education: The importance of the internet. In P. Graham & N. Stacey (Eds.), *The knowledge economy and postsecondary education: Report of a workshop* (pp. 77–103). Washington, DC: National Academy Press.

Tyack, D., & Cuban, L. (1995). *Tinkering toward utopia.* Cambridge, MA: Harvard University Press.

University of Illinois Faculty Seminar. (1999). *Teaching at an internet distance: The pedagogy of online teaching and learning: The report of a 1998–1999 University of Illinois Faculty Seminar.* Retrieved March 27, 2000, from http://www.vpaa.uillinois. edu/tid/report/tid_ report.html

University Task Force on the Impact of Digital Technology on the Classroom Environment. (1989). *Final report.* Retrieved February 07, 2000 from http://www.cyber.vt.edu/docs/DigitalClassrooms.html

Usher, R., & Edwards, R. (2000). Virtual research in performative times. In J. Garrick & C. Rhodes (Eds.), *Research and knowledge at work: Perspectives, case-studies and innovative strategies* (pp. 250–268). London: Routledge.

Veblen, T. (1957). The higher learning in America. New York: Hill & Wang.

Vidovich, L., & Slee, R. (2001). Bringing universities to account? Exploring some global and local policy tensions. *Journal of Education Policy, 16,* 431–453.

Vice President For Information Systems (1995a). *Abstract: Course Transformation Project.* Retrieved March 26, 2002 from http://filebox.vt.edu/ 15/vp/inintro.html.

Vice President For Information Systems (1995b). *Technology Initiative: Course Transformation.* Retrieved March 23, 2002 from http://filebox. vt.edu/15/]vp/courseliens.html.

Virginia Commission on the University of the 21st Century. (1989). *The Case For Change.* Retrieved February 3, 2000 from http://minerva. acc. virginia.edu/admin/tarex/uzlrpth.html.

Virginia Tech Alumni Association. (1993). *Special report on higher education.* Blacksburg, VA: Alumni Hall.

Virginia Tech (1997). 1996–1998 University Self Study. Retrieved January 4, 1997 from http://www.vt.edu/0021/admin/provost/selfstudy/draft chap3.html.

Waks, L. (1975). Educational objectives and existential heros. In R. Smith (Ed.), *Regaining educational leadership: Critical essays on PBTE/ CBTE, behavioral objectives and accountability* (pp. 87–103). New York: Wiley.

Wallhaus, R. (2000). E-learning: From institutions to providers, from students to learners. In R. Katz & D. Oblinger (Eds.), *The "e" is for everything: e-commerce, e-Business, and e-Learning in the future of higher education* (pp. 21–52). San Francisco: Jossey-Bass.

Walzer, P. (1993, September 14). Professors not often in class. *The Roanoke Times*, pp. A1, A6.

Ward, M., & Newlands, D. (1998). Use of the web in undergraduate teaching. *Computers and Education, 31,* 171–184.

Watson, D., & Andersen, J. (Eds.). (2002). *Networking the learner: Computers in education.* Boston: Kluwer.

Weber, M. (1946). Science as a vocation. In H. Gerth & C. W. Mills (Eds.), *From Max Weber: Essays in sociology* (pp. 129–156). New York: Oxford University Press.

Webster's New World Dictionary of the American Language. (1951) Cleveland: The New World Publishing Company.

Weller, M. (2002). *Delivering learning on the net: The why, what, and how of online learning.* London: Kogan Page.

Welsch, W. (1996). Aestheticization processes: Phenomena, distinctions and prospects. *Theory, Culture and Society, 13,* 1–24.

Whitehead, A. N. (1967). *Science and the modern world.* New York: Macmillan.

Williams, M. (n.d.). *When is a new paradigm really a new paradigm?* Retrieved November 29, 2004, from http://www.math.vt.edu/people/ williams/files/webct_article.html

Wilson, R. (2001, June 1). Ohio State "Taxes" departments to make a select few top-notch: Is this how public universities can improve in a frugal era? *The Chronicle of Higher Education,* p. A8.

Woolgar, S. (2002). Five rules of virtuality. In S. Woolgar (Ed.), *Virtual society? Technology, cyberbole, reality* (pp. 1–22). Oxford, England: Oxford University Press.

Young, J. (1999, May 28). U. of Washington tries a soft sell to woo professors to technology [Electronic version]. *The Chronicle of Higher Education,* p. A23.

Young, J. (2002, March 22). Hybrid teaching seeks to end the divide between traditional and online instruction: By blending approaches, colleges hope to save money and meet students' needs. *The Chronicle of Higher Education,* p. A33.

Zack, I. (1997a, December 22). Professors: University has become "uncivil." *The Roanoke Times,* pp. A1, A2.

Zack, I. (1997b, November 17). There's no teacher to confuse me. *The Roanoke Times,* pp. A1, A4.

Zack, I. (1998, August 19). Masses in classes perplex professors. *The Roanoke Times,* pp. B1, B3.

Author Index

Subject Index